A PRACTICAL APPROACH TO BANK LENDING

A
PRACTICAL APPROACH
TO BANK LENDING

L.S. DYER

Fellow of The Chartered Institute of Bankers

Third Edition

The Chartered
Institute
of Bankers

10 Lombard Street, London EC3V 9AS

First Published 1974 by The Institute of Bankers
Reprinted with revisions 1977
Second edition 1980
Reprinted with amendments 1983
Reprinted 1983
Third edition 1987 published by Bankers Books Ltd.

Chartered Institute of Bankers (CIB) Publications are published by Bankers Books Limited under an exclusive license and royalty agreement. Bankers Books Limited is a company owned by The Chartered Institute of Bankers.

Enquiries should be sent to the publishers at the undermentioned address:

BANKERS BOOKS LIMITED
c/o The Chartered Institute of Bankers
10 Lombard Street
London EC3V 9AS

B L   British Library Cataloguing in Publication Data

Dyer, L.S.
A practical approach to bank lending
– 3rd ed.
1. Bank Loans – Great Britain
I. Title II. Institute of Bankers
332.1.'753' 0941 HG1642.G7

ISBN 0-85297-181-8

Typeset in 10 on 12pt Times by F.S. Moore Ltd.
Printed and bound by Eyre & Spottiswoode Ltd.
Text: 70gsm Cover: Invercote G 240gsm

A PRACTICAL APPROACH TO BANK LENDING
(3rd Edition)

CONTENTS   Page no.

1	General Considerations	1
2	Accounts	19
3	Overtrading	25
4	Solid and Swinging Accounts	35
5	Supervision of Lending	43
6	Management Accounts	52
7	New Ventures	87
8	Estate Development	105
9	Produce Loans	128
10	Hire-purchase and Finance Companies	146
11	Importing and Exporting	161
12	Farming	180
13	Medium-term Lending	194
14	The Effect of Inflation	213
15	Other Sources of Finance	224
16	Conclusion	234
	Index	239

1. General Considerations

There have been numerous books written about bank lending but, even so, it is difficult for the young banker to learn how much is reasonable to lend in a given set of circumstances.

This is due, in the main, to a variety of circumstances which surround each request to borrow money, and most banking books stress that no two propositions are alike and each has to be dealt with on its merits. While this is true, there must naturally be some points of similarity between propositions and I think that more emphasis should be given to the similarities than to the differences. In this way, it should be possible to establish reasoned methods which can be used as bases upon which to consider each particular problem.

A banker always has more confidence when dealing with a request which is similar in many aspects to one put to him previously. This is because the good and bad aspects are clear to him at the start of the interview. If, however, he approaches each interview on the basis that the request he is to receive is different from all other requests previously considered, he will be making life very hard for himself.

To have a balance sheet put in front of a banker with the accompanying thought that each proposition is different is to invite trouble. Let us concentrate on the similarities first of all and then, subsequently, take into account the divergencies.

These chapters, therefore, will quote methods and proportions, which I hope are backed with sound reasoning and will give the young banker a basis upon which to look at lending requests. This is not to say that I consider that the examples will fit every set of circumstances (as I too believe that each proposition should be treated on its merits), but it will give a start to the thoughts of a banker when considering lending propositions in practice.

It has been a quality of bankers through the years to leave themselves room to 'hedge' and, comforting though this always is, it seems the approach of the amateur. Competition is severe, legal requirements are subject to rapid change, and bankers must be knowledgeable in many subjects which affect their work. Banking ideas are continually changing and a professional approach is necessary.

I have tried not to 'hedge' in the ideas put forward and I have tried to justify my contentions, but my object is not to get young bankers to adhere slavishly to the proportions set out but to use these proportions as a starting point to enable them to tackle each banking request with an enquiring mind.

If a banker considers he should use a different method of assessing a lending problem, I would have no quarrel with him providing that he has sound reasons for his decisions. I would, however, quarrel with the person who judges propositions based on some imagined sixth sense.

Banking will continue to expand, and new trades, industries and ideas will mean changes in the pattern of life. Bankers will, of course, have to keep abreast of changes which affect them. The plea I make is that, if what is set out in this book is correct now, a banker will not conform to these ideas in years to come without asking himself 'Is this correct in present circumstances?' An enquiring mind will continue to be of great importance.

Appreciation of Accounts

A knowledge of accountancy is essential to a banker as also is a knowledge of security work, and I am assuming that any reader of these chapters will possess at least a modicum of knowledge of these subjects. A knowledge of book-keeping methods, however, is not to be confused with an appreciation of what the book-keeping figures reveal and I will therefore begin by dealing with a few aspects of accounts in order that my meaning will be clear.

In my view it is tedious to have balance sheets of the double sided variety when accompanied by a text, as the eyes have to be moved back and forth in order to grasp the points made. I have therefore used, in all but the simple examples, a columnar method of setting out figures. This has enabled me to write short comments against some of the figures and I hope it will help to focus on the essential points to be grasped before passing on to the text. Also, of course, the columnar method is the one most often used nowadays.

Confusion can often occur over the term 'profits'. Branch managers will be well aware of customers who have told them that they have made a good profit and who firmly believe this to be the case, whereas an analysis of the relative trading and profit and loss accounts will reveal that the profit is much different from that imagined. Part of the difficulty is, of course, that not everybody has had instruction in accountancy, and also that it is not always appreciated that there are considerable differences between trading profit, gross profit and net profit. The greatest confusion arises when considering net profit, and accountants often do not help to clarify matters by calling items net profit before all proper deductions have been made.

Net Profits

To make for good communication, we should all know what we mean by net profit. This is the figure after all income applicable to the accounting period has been included and after deduction of all revenue expenses and disbursements for the same period: it should take into account depreciation and directors' fees. If there are non-recurring items of significance, a separate note should be made of them.

The following example will illustrate that net profit is not always the figure in the accounts which is so specified:

	£	£
Net profit for year		30,000
Rents		3,000
Dividends received		5,000
Profit on sale of car		1,000
		39,000
less depreciation	3,000	
directors' fees	4,000	7,000
		32,000

The figure quoted as net profit is not correct, as it has to be adjusted for the other items shown. The correct net profit is £32,000, in which is included a non-recurring item for £1,000 being profit on sale of car.

This is a simple question of adjustment, but in practice there is more difficulty as tax items will appear. The tax regulations are now so complicated that even after accounts have been audited it is still necessary to make adjustments in tax provisions in subsequent years. It would be simple if a banker was able to say that a certain tax provision was the correct one and that therefore an occasional adjustment could be looked upon as a non-recurring item. However, adjustments are so numerous that a far better picture of profits is obtained by netting all the tax items appearing in the accounts and then looking at the net profit both before tax and after tax and keeping in mind whether it has been a heavy or a light year for tax.

A simple example would be:

	£	£
Net Profit for year		30,000
Tax refund for year B		4,000
		34,000
less tax adjustment for year A	1,000	
tax for current year	10,000	11,000
Net profit after tax		23,000

The amount of tax with which we are concerned and which in our analysis will appear as a deduction from net profit is £7,000 — ie, £1,000 plus £10,000 minus £4,000.

If we amalgamate the last two examples, we get the following appropriation account:

	£	£
Net profit		30,000
Tax refund for year B		4,000
Rents		3,000
Dividends		5,000
Profit on sale of car		1,000
		43,000
less depreciation	3,000	
directors' fees	4,000	
tax adjustment for year A	1,000	
tax adjustment for current year	10,000	18,000
carried forward to balance sheet		25,000

The calculations for a correct assessment are as already shown, with the result that our analysis of the account would be:

	£
Net profit before tax	32,000
Taxation	7,000
Net profit after tax	25,000

Comparisons

We will look now at a more complicated example, and at the same time try to show how much easier it is to understand a company's accounts when the items for each year are listed in columns for a comparison to be made. We will ignore the balance sheet items and concentrate on the revenue accounts as before.

Apart from specifying the net profit, it is also useful to have a note of the amount of non-recurring items together with the amounts of additions to or disbursements from the net profit, such as dividends paid away and transfers to or from reserves. If also directors' remuneration is noted (which is deducted before net profit is struck), a good all-round picture of the earning ability of the company can be seen.

YEAR A
Group trading position for the year

	£
Parent company	10,000
Australian company	40,000
Profit before taxation	50,000

These figures are after charging:

	£
Depreciation	5,000
Auditors	1,000
Directors	36,000
Loan stock interest	4,000

Taxation	30,000
Net profit for year	20,000
Balance from previous year	260,000
	280,000

Appropriations	£	
Dividends, net preference	8,000	
Transfers to reserves	18,000	26,000
Balance forward		254,000

YEAR B
Group trading position for the year

		£
Parent company — loss, including £70,000 written off as special obsolescence of stock		(80,000)
Australian company — profit . . .		40,000
Loss before taxation		(40,000)

These figures are after charging:

	£
Depreciation	7,000
Auditors	1,000
Directors	36,000
Loan stock interest . . .	4,000

		£
Less Taxation		3,000
Net loss for year		(43,000)
Balance from previous year .	254,000	
Taxation provisions no longer required . . .	24,000	278,000
		235,000
Appropriations	£	
Dividends, net preference . .	8,000	
Transfers to reserves . . .	7,000	15,000
Balance forward		220,000

It will be seen that it is very difficult to compare the results for the two years by looking at the figures in their present layout, and if the figures have to be consulted several times a year (if excess overdrafts arise) much time will be wasted.

If the figures are properly analysed and put in columnar form, an instant assessment can be obtained. Year A is straightforward but in Year B an amount of £24,000 is written back into the accounts for taxation provisions no longer required, while the taxation debited in the profit and loss account is shown as £3,000. The tax position in Year B following the method given above will therefore be £24,000 less £3,000 = £21,000 which is a net tax refund. The net loss given in the accounts is £43,000 but this is before taking into account the tax refund of £24,000, and the true net loss after tax is therefore £19,000.

	Year A £	Year B £
Net profit before taxation . . .	50,000	(40,000) Loss
Taxation	30,000	21,000 Refund
Net profit after taxation . . .	20,000	(19,000) Loss
Non-recurring items		(70,000) Debit
Special items		
Directors' remuneration . . .	36,000	36,000
Dividends	8,000	8,000
Appropriations to reserve . . .	18,000	7,000
Carried forward	254,000	220,000

It is now a simple matter to see that, although a profit has been turned into a loss, this is after taking into account a large debit for non-recurring items. The effect has been lessened to a large extent by a refund of tax, and the directors have continued to draw the same remuneration and pay the same amount in dividends while making a smaller transfer to reserves from an ample amount carried forward.

The 'carried forward' amount should always be checked in the analysis by adding the net profit after tax to the previous year's figure and deducting dividends and transfers to reserves or making any other additions or subtractions which have altered the resultant carried forward figure.

The calculations in the example above are:

	£
Carried forward year A . . .	254,000
Less net loss (after tax) year B . .	19,000
	235,000
Less dividends year B . . .	8,000
	227,000
Less transfers to reserves year B . .	7,000
	220,000

In short, the points to keep in mind when making an analysis of revenue accounts are:

i net the tax;

ii agree the carried forward figure from year to year.

Lending against a Balance Sheet

As all good bankers know, there is no such thing as lending a certain amount just because a balance sheet is produced, in the same way that there is no proportion that is lent just because stocks and shares are produced as security. The first consideration is the proposition and the second consideration is the security. But having said this, we still come to the point that, if a satisfactory proposition is forthcoming, a banker must assess how far he can lend to a business on his knowledge of the business and after considering the strength of the balance sheet.

Before looking at the balance sheet it will be necessary to examine the profit and loss account to be satisfied that the business has the ability to generate sufficient funds to provide the repayment terms, and at the same time the banker must keep in mind the period covered by the accounts and the date at which the balance sheet was prepared. So often accounts are well out of date when seen by a banker and provide only historical knowledge. A banker will therefore need to be aware of any trends which would have affected the business, and will also need to scrutinise the banking account and any interim figures produced to assess whether any radical change in the business has been likely since the balance sheet date.

Let us first of all keep the figures in a simple form by taking a new business for which the proprietor has £40,000 which he will use as capital. The proprietor will have to consider how much he must use for premises, plant and machinery, fixtures and fittings, initial expenses, motor vehicles and any other fixed assets, and, as fixed assets are not held primarily for sale, the proprietor will also need some funds to purchase stock and to support debtors. He will, however, also be able to take into account the credit he will be allowed by his suppliers.

In short, a proprietor will require sufficient capital to provide the fixed assets and allow for working capital.

After a period of trading the balance sheet of the business could appear as:

		£			£	
Capital		40,000	Leasehold . . .		2,000	Fixed
Creditors . . .		16,000	Plant and machinery .		26,000	assets
			Motor vehicles . .		8,000	
			Stock		10,000	Current
			Debtors		8,000	assets
			Cash		2,000	
		56,000			56,000	

We see that the £40,000 capital was used to buy fixed assets of £36,000 (leasehold, plant and machinery and motor vehicles) and to provide working capital of £4,000 (stock, debtors, and cash £20,000 less creditors £16,000).

If there is no pressure from creditors, and the business is making profits, there is no reason why the business cannot continue with the same level of activity and not have to resort to bank borrowing.

If, however, the turnover increases and more stock has to be carried, it could be that the working capital of £4,000 would be insufficient. If both creditors and debtors rose to £24,000 each and it was necessary to carry stock of £16,000, the required working capital would be:

		£
Current assets — stock	. . .	16,000
debtors	. .	24,000
		40,000
Less		
Current liabilities — creditors	. .	24,000
		16,000

Should the proprietor be unable to provide additional funds, he might well turn to his banker for help.

The banker should look at the fixed assets first of all to see what the proprietor has provided. These assets, however, are incidental to the circulating assets from which the profit is generated and, if we are considering unsecured lending, can only be kept in mind as evidence of means. If the business should fail, the fixed assets might fetch little. In the present example the leasehold on a forced sale would probably be valueless and the plant and machinery could well be difficult to sell. The motor vehicles might provide some funds on sale but a knowledge of the type and age of the vehicles would be essential in order to gauge this. If a business should fail and the bank be lending unsecured, it would stand on the same basis as other creditors in the final accounting and a proportion only of the amount owing would normally be recovered.

A proprietor should in any event provide sufficient funds to purchase the fixed assets, and, although a banker could well take them into account if they are substantial and would realise good sums on a break-up, unsecured lending is more in the province of lending which is repaid rapidly from normal trading. The funds which will provide such repayment, maybe several times a year, will come from the circulating assets of work in progress, stock, debtors and cash.

The Bank's Stake

In the present example we have seen that the revised working capital requirements are £16,000 and, as we are expecting a proprietor to purchase the fixed assets and also provide some funds for working capital, we must consider what proportion of working capital can be provided as an overdraft by a banker.

If a banker provided as overdraft an amount equivalent to one-third of the working capital, the proprietor would have to provide two-thirds. This might not be considered unreasonable as the proprietor has control of the business, is more able to tell whether profits or losses are being made and the bank is having faith in the ability of the proprietor to use its money well. Additionally the proprietor will know whether or not the current assets are quoted at correct values. There may well be doubtful debts or unsaleable stock. A banker should enquire about these matters when considering lending propositions.

Could the banker go further than one-third of the working capital? If he went as high as one-half, he would be matching the proprietor's stake in providing the necessary funds towards the circulating assets from which profits should be generated, and this on an unsecured basis is faith indeed in a proprietor's ability. Any further facilities would be in the nature of providing part of the capital required by the business and, bank finance being the cheapest normal form of finance, would hardly be appropriate.

We are now left with our example to solve. Formula lending is never very satisfactory, as there are many other considerations which have to be taken into account, such as the experience, ability and integrity of the proprietor, and the profitability of the business. If these are satisfactory, then we might go as far as one-half of the working capital requirements − say £8,000. The proprietor has already provided £4,000 and he will therefore be £4,000 short of his requirements. The banker will have to decide whether to produce the additional £4,000 required − which, on an unsecured basis, and taking into account the possible negligible value on break-up of the fixed assets, would look distinctly over-generous − or whether he should call for security. The proprietor will have to decide whether to infuse more funds by means of capital or loans, whether he can get through by taking longer credit and giving less, or whether he will have to curtail his activities to within his resources.

Debenture as Security

We can now take the example further by considering how much could be lent if the business was a limited company and a debenture was taken by the bank as security. Again we must first look at the fixed assets to see if there is anything of value which can be considered suitable as security. In the present instance, we have already considered this and have decided that on a forced sale very little might be realised from the fixed assets. We can now turn to the current assets, and, whereas when considering unsecured lending we said that the provision of half of the amount of the working capital could well be generous, we need not now consider the creditors. The debenture will stand in front of the creditors apart from preferential creditors and, if these preferential creditors are not large, then a banker might well lend up to half of the current assets.

In the present case, with stock at £16,000 and debtors at £24,000, the current assets should be sufficient to support bank borrowing of £20,000. The company would have to run through a bad patch to lose half of its liquid resources and thereby jeopardise the bank lending but, even so, a banker will call for the regular submission of figures for liquid assets and liabilities in order to see that his lending continues to be on a satisfactory basis. Naturally debtors are worth more than stock, and a good spread of debtors is much more satisfactory than if they are in a few hands. The company's record of losses through bad debts should be considered, as well as the type of stock and whether it is easily saleable to a wide market. It is also important to be sure that the stock is free from any lien imposed by the suppliers. There may well be special considerations with the business which must be taken into account and the banker will have to watch the liquid figures produced to see, among other requirements, that stock does not build up while debtors decrease. It is useless working to a set formula without using commonsense and an intelligent appreciation of the facts.

Our problem now is to see how far a bank may lend to a company against a debenture. At the moment, the capital in our example is £40,000 and, with a debenture over the assets, the bank is prepared to lend £20,000. The turnover of the business can rise and this is generally accompanied by increased current assets which can provide additional security behind the debenture.

Proprietor and Banker

We should now consider the respective interests of proprietor and banker. The proprietor is in business for profits that can be made and, being the entrepreneur, is the risk-taker in the hope of big profits. The banker is lending money at the cheapest market rate and is therefore concerned with safety and a sure return of interest on the money lent. The banker with a debenture will stand before the proprietors in a liquidation, but the proprietors have the use of the banker's money and, being closer to the day-to-day running of the business, are much better placed to see that their own capital is not in jeopardy. If therefore a banker more than matches a proprietor's stake (and by this I mean capital and any other amounts left in the company reserves and profit and loss balance), the banker will probably be providing capital which it is not his normal function to supply. Therefore for the bulk of businesses a proprietor's stake should be more than that of a banker.

Naturally, when banking has taken on wide and varied aspects of lending which are in no way stereotyped, there are exceptions to this.

The banker is interested in providing money which can be put to good use, is safely lent, and which in a widely swinging account provides frequent repayment by a swing into credit. There are some businesses which from the very nature of their activities provide a rapid turnover of money and which give and receive only a relatively small amount of credit for short periods. If such businesses are well run by people with a specialist knowledge of the trade and the bank can be secured, it can well form part of the bank's function to supplement the working capital of these businesses in excess of the proprietor's stake.

Businesses which fall into this category are those for which a well developed market has evolved and in which goods can pass easily by reason of description or classification. In lending above the proprietor's stake the banker must, of course, take stringent precautions to protect his advance and must keep additional control over the day-to-day position.

Produce loans are one of the types of lending which fall within this category and we will coonsider separately a banker's requirements for advances of this nature.

Although I have expressed proportions which can be used for deciding how much a banker can lend, there are very many cases which do not fit the proportions mentioned. If they do fit, care must always be taken to see that there is nothing in the surrounding circumstances which would warrant further enquiry and, if they do not fit, then an adequate reason should be available to justify the arrangement proposed.

The world does not stay still and variations in practice and custom will continue to evolve. The banker must move with changing circumstances and not be inflexible in his approach. He should, however, have a reason for his lending methods and be able to justify them.

Let us now look at some more complicated figures:

CASE 1

Years	A £	B £	C £	
Current liabilities				
Bank		1,000	5,000	Relatively small
Creditors	64,700	78,700	72,400	Not rising greatly
Current taxation . .	2,000	2,600	5,600	
Total current liabilities . .	66,700	82,300	83,000	Rising
Future taxation . . .	1,500	6,500	10,000	Rising
	68,200	88,800	93,000	
Capital	5,000	5,000	5,000	Same
P & L account . .	8,000	20,600	37,000	Good plough back
Totals	81,200	114,400	135,000	
Current assets				
Cash	750		350	
Debtors	65,000	88,000	94,000	Rising
Stock	8,000	12,000	23,000	Rising
Total current assets . .	73,750	100,000	117,350	Rising
Leaseholds		8,000	8,000	A short leasehold
Plant and machinery . .	4,500	3,800	7,500	Small
Fixtures and fittings . .	2,950	2,600	2,150	
Totals	81,200	114,400	135,000	
Turnover	150,000	220,000	285,000	Rising
Net profit before tax . .	4,800	22,770	27,500	
Tax	4,100	10,170	11,100	
Net profit after tax . .	700	12,600	16,400	Sharp increase
Directors' fees . . .	34,000	34,000	37,000	
Carried forward . . .	8,000	20,600	37,000	Rising
Net current assets . .	7,050	17,700	34,350	Rising
Net worth	13,000	25,600	42,000	Rising

The figures for this business show that excellent progress has been made in a few years, with good profits which have been retained in the business. Obviously, if such a profit performance was continued, the company would have little difficulty in dealing with a bank overdraft considerably in excess of the £5,000 shown as owing to the bank in the Year C figures. We will assume that the leasehold has only a few years to run and for security purposes is of little value. Also we will assume that there are no adverse factors to take into account and that the company's trading future looks good.

If we now apply our principles to the consideration of unsecured lending, a bank could well lend half of the net current assets to this successful company, which would mean, say, £17,000. If a debenture was given to the bank as security, it could lend half of the current assets, say £60,000, with a limitation of matching the amount of the customer's stake of £42,000. In fact, for such a successful company, it would be reasonable to exceed the customer's stake for a short while if the knowledge of the customer's business was sufficient to indicate that profits were continuing at a high rate and were being left in the business, as the net worth would continue to increase rapidly.

It will be seen that the ratio of debtors to turnover is approximately one to three, which indicates that an average of four months' credit is being granted. Although the figure for purchases is not given, the ratio of creditors to purchases cannot be much different.

If the managing director should then approach the bank and say that subsequent to the Year C balance sheet the creditors and debtors have increased to £90,000 and £125,000 respectively and that, although he is unable to shorten the period of credit given, his creditors have asked him to pay within one month, the result will be that he has to find approximately £60,000. Additionally he says that the company has to renew machinery and has placed an order which will cost £25,000; their total borrowing requirements are £90,000 (including the £5,000 limit already available at the bank), but they have already arranged to factor their debtors to raise £70,000 and they require to borrow from the bank £20,000.

The banker is certainly faced with a problem as, on the one hand, he has a very good customer while, on the other, the best asset in the balance sheet, namely debtors, is to be sold to a factoring company. The debtors sold will be turned into cash which will be used to satisfy creditors. The remaining assets in the balance sheet will hardly be sufficient to support a loan of £20,000, even allowing for the new machinery to be purchased, and the banker will therefore have to make further enquiries.

First of all he will want to know the details concerning the factoring of the debtors, particularly as regards the cost and the timing of payments. The cost is important as the banker will have to see how this will affect the profit which is expected to be earned. If it is not excessive and will be covered by the profit on the increased business being transacted, a good profit level can still be anticipated. As for the terms, these might be immediate payment of 75 per cent of debtors with the remaining 25 per cent at the end of three months.

If this is so and the limit of the factoring is £70,000, then the debtors which will have to be sold to produce this amount immediately will be £97,000 approximately.

At this stage the banker will be able to see that there will be some debtors still remaining which could be picked up by a debenture. If £28,000 of debtors remained together with £23,000 of stock, a slender case could be made out for lending £20,000 with the security of a debenture and an agreement with the company that up to £97,000 of the debtors could be factored. The debenture could stipulate that debtors were to be at least equal to the bank debt, with total current assets covering the bank debt with a margin of 100 per cent.

In such a situation as this, an academic exercise by itself is insufficient as much will depend upon the banker's knowledge of the business and of the directors. However, if lending on these lines were agreed, care would be necessary subsequently to see that liquid asset and liability figures were submitted promptly and regularly and were scrutinised with care.

CASE 2

A company which manufactures metal fittings has had an overdraft limit of £10,000, £15,000 and £20,000 respectively for each of the last three years. The account has been swinging fairly well, although in the past year a hard core of borrowing of around £7,000 appeared. As security the bank held a guarantee of a relation of one of the directors, and the guarantee was adequately supported with collateral security.

Recently the company has been taking advantage of an export scheme for the smaller exporters promoted by the bank, by which it has been able to have advances of up to 85% of its invoices to approved overseas customers with the remaining 15% drawn on settlement of the accounts; all such invoices are fully covered by ECGD insurance. The amount agreed with the bank on this Smaller Exports Scheme is £30,000. Nevertheless, the company has not lessened its demands upon the bank for its normal overdraft requirements and still wishes to have £20,000 available. The directors say that turnover is increasing, and that as the company has an extensive overseas business they should not be restricted in their requirements. Furthermore, the guarantor wishes now to be released from his liability and the directors insist that their record with the bank has been good and that their balance sheet results justify unsecured facilities.

Up to date figures are available and those for the last two years are as follows:

	Year A £	Year B £	
Current liabilities			
Bank	16,000	22,000	Increasing
Creditors	44,000	50,000	In excess of debtors
Current taxation	3,000	6,000	
Directors' loans	13,000	13,000	Same
Temporary loan	—	15,000	To be repaid from investment
Total current liabilities	76,000	106,000	
Mortgage	—	47,000	On freeholds
	76,000	153,000	
Capital	35,000	35,000	
Reserves	9,000	9,000	
Profit and loss account	9,000	15,000	Profits ploughed back
Totals	129,000	212,000	
Current assets			
Cash	1,000	1,000	
Debtors	35,000	42,000	Less than creditors
Stock	27,000	34,000	
Short-term investment	15,000	15,000	Will repay temporary loan
Total current assets	78,000	92,000	
Freeholds	—	58,000	Morgaged
Leaseholds	19,000	18,000	Term unexpired is 18 years
Plant and machinery	14,000	24,000	Large increase
Fixtures and fittings	7,000	6,000	
Motor cars	8,000	10,000	
	126,000	208,000	

Intangibles:			
Goodwill	3,000	4,000	Has additional business been purchased?
Totals	129,000	212,000	
Turnover	160,000	225,000	Increasing
Net profit before tax	6,000	14,000	Increasing
Tax	3,000	8,000	
Net profit after tax	3,000	6,000	Increasing
Directors' fees	9,000	20,000	Increasing
Carried forward	9,000	15,000	Increasing
Net worth	50,000	55,000	Increasing

We can now get a picture of the company. It is slightly illiquid and in the past year has purchased on mortgage a freehold property. It has also made a large purchase of additional plant and machinery. The company is profitable and the profits are ploughed back into the company. The profits in the coming year may not be so good if large interest has to be paid on the mortgage. Income from the short-term investment will also not be available, as the realisation of this asset is to be used to repay the temporary loan. Turnover is increasing well and so is net worth.

There are a number of questions which will need to be asked to obtain a full impression of the company's plans for the coming year, but we will concern ourselves here with the problem of whether unsecured accommodation of £20,000 for the next 12 months is justified on the figures produced. The company is certainly successful and some support by the bank is warranted, but should this be granted on an unsecured basis?

Normally, when examining a balance sheet for unsecured facilities, we would expect to find a net current liquidity, and that if all else was favourable then an advance of up to one-half of the net current assets could be considered. In the present case there is a net deficit which has increased during the last year. Even if the directors' loans of £13,000 were postponed to the bank as regards repayment, there would still be a small net current deficit.

Upon what else could we base justification for unsecured facilities? Let us look at the other assets. There is a small freehold which is mortgaged and the equity of £11,000 in this property is hardly sufficient to justify any lending without a second mortgage being taken, and, if a factory is involved, sufficient margin would not be available even then. The leasehold is relatively short, and even if charged to the bank an advance of £9,000 against it might be considered quite sufficient if it is factory property. The remaining assets of plant and machinery, fixtures and fittings, motor cars and goodwill are not items upon which much can be lent, even if a debenture was given in favour of the bank. Certainly they hardly justify unsecured facilities.

Let us give further consideration now to the debtors. We know that there is an arrangement to borrow on the bank Smaller Exports Scheme up to £30,000. As advances may be taken against overseas debtors the result will be that there will be less in the way of debtors remaining free for consideration for normal bank overdraft purposes. Even if there happened to be a net current liquid situation it would be necessary to take into account the Smaller Exports Scheme facility. The result, although it does not lessen the net liquidity as cash is received in lieu of debtors, is that any unsecured lending then relies predominantly upon stock instead of debtors, which is unsatisfactory. The company should not, in fact, be able to borrow twice in respect of the same debtors.

In the present case the company is borrowing £47,000 and has given a charge over its freeholds; it will be able to borrow up to £30,000 on the Smaller Exports Scheme and will assign debtors to cover; it wishes to borrow £20,000 unsecured on the evidence of its remaining position when the choicest assets have been removed.

Unsecured facilities in these circumstances are unjustified.

If the directors then suggest giving the bank a debenture and it is decided that the valuation of the leasehold is sufficient to support lending of £10,000, we should have to consider if the remaining assets are good for a further £10,000 in an emergency. There would perhaps be little to be salvaged from the fixed assets and, if the stock was specialised and not easily saleable, we would again come back to the debtors. If the bad debts record was good it would be reasonable (after taking the other assets into consideration) to ask for a margin of, say, 100 per cent of current assets in excess of the bank debt over £10,000 and for the current assets to include debtors with a margin of 25 per cent over and above the amount by which the bank debt exceeded £10,000. This would allow the Smaller Exports Scheme to be relied upon fairly fully.

In view of the shortness of the lease, however, a fresh look at the arrangements would be particularly necessary every year.

2. Accounts for Tax Purposes

There are three aspects to be considered for every lending proposition — character, capability and capital (the three Cs). It has long been thought that the most important of these is character, and many eminent bankers have laid great stress on this. I do not wish to deride such an assumption, as character is very important, but I cannot go as far as some authorities in saying that, if there is a blemish on the character of a person, a banker should proceed no further and refuse to lend. If bankers were now to adopt this attitude they would be blind to the world about them. The world is far from a perfect place, and we have to live in the world as it is and not as we should like it to be.

If we should find, as bankers, that we are dealing with rogues or unscrupulous people, I would say undoubtedly that we should be well advised to close their acccounts or a loss will probably be made. There is, however, a very large body of people who are dishonest in what they consider to be a minor way — eg, those who consider themselves justified in declaring a false figure on their income tax returns.

All bank managers will know people who, when producing their audited accounts, say that the accounts are not accurate as they have been prepared for tax purposes. The inference is that the business is much better than would appear from the accounts. It would therefore be useful if we looked at a simple set of accounts to see what variations are possible and how they affect a banker.

A not uncommon situation is for a customer running a small company to have lodged as security for the company's overdraft limit of £20,000 the deeds of his dwelling house worth £75,000. He then approaches his bank manager with the request for an increased limit of another £40,000 (£60,000 in all), in order that the company may purchase for £80,000 the freehold of the factory it is at present renting. The customer, seeing an opportunity of providing continuity for his company's business, and being anxious to borrow the necessary funds, will quite probably be optimistic in his view of the company's ability to repay the additional funds in five or seven years. When asked for his audited accounts, he produces the following, and at the same time stresses that the business is much better than it appears to be on paper:

Trading and Profit and Loss Account

(Period of one year)

		£	£	
	Sales		236,000	
Less	Purchases . . .	140,000		
Plus	Opening Stock . .	20,000		
		160,000		
Less	Final stock . . .	16,000	144,000	
	Gross profit . . .		92,000	38% of sales
Less	Rent	1,600		
	Rates	3,200		
	Salaries . . .	41,200		
	Advertising . . .	2,800		
	Bank charges . . .	4,200		
	Telephone . . .	1,200		
	Stationery . . .	1,400		
	Bad debts . . .	1,200		
	Depreciation . . .	4,000		
	Directors' fees . .	26,000	86,800	
	Net profits . . .		5,200	2.2% of sales
Less	Dividends . . .		2,600	
	Transferred to balance sheet .		2,600	

Balance Sheet

	£	£
Leasehold		16,000
Plant and machinery . . .		40,000
Fixtures and fittings		4,000
Stock		32,000
Debtors		28,400
Cash		400
		120,800

Less Creditors.	.	.	.	40,800	
Bank	.	.	.	20,000	
Dividends	.	.	.	2,600	
Directors' loans	.	.	21,400	84,800
Proprietor's stake	.	.	.	.	36,000
Capital	.	.	.	24,000	
P & L account	.	.	.	12,000	
				36,000	

The money retained in the business and therefore available for repayment, if there are no other calls upon it, consists of the net profit, less dividends (£2,600), plus the amount in the accounts for depreciation (£4,000), a total of £6,600. I am considering that the directors' loans to the company have been at the same figure of £21,400 for several years and the directors have therefore not left money in the business out of the fees of £26,000.

A much greater generation of money than this will be necessary to provide the promised repayment, as there will be, for a start, additional interest on the extra £80,000 required, less the rent which will be saved.

Let us now consider the individual items.

Sales

These can, of course, be understated but, as cheques received will have been paid into the company's account, this will occur only when there is a cash element in the sales and the cash is taken straight out of the business without going through the books. Whether this is being done or not can quite often be seen by examining the percentage of gross profit to sales. If this is consistently below the average for similar businesses, then understating of sales could be occurring regularly. If the gross profit percentage dropped abruptly in one year without an adequate explanation, this too would lead one to think that money had been extracted from the takings.

Let us assume that, in the present instance, £40 per week is being taken out of the till by the proprietors. If we adjust the figures, the only difference would be that the gross profit would be increased by £2,000 and, likewise, the directors' fees would be increased by £2,000. The funds left in the business would be unchanged and the additional £2,000 of gross profit would be of no use at all in helping to prove the potential repayment ability of the business. If the directors have spent all the money that has been drawn from the business in normal living expenses, all that has been proved is that the business provides a better living than is apparent from the accounts. If the directors have had the ability to save over the years, then this can of course be taken into account, and not only can such past savings provide a stake towards the additional contemplated expenditure, but an amount equivalent to the annual savings can in future be left in the business to help with repayments. A person in this position will have to consider whether or not such an alteration in his finances is going to draw the attention of his tax inspector. Such avoidance of tax is hardly worth sleepless nights.

Purchases

These can be overstated with a similar effect to that caused by an understatement of sales but the result could be a build up of stock instead of extraction of cash, and, if accounts are audited by qualified accountants, forged invoices would have to be produced. If there are such blatant frauds, then the banker would be well advised to close the account.

Stock

Apart from taking money out of the till, valuations of stock provide the most common form of deception. Stock is generally valued at cost or market value, whichever is the lower, as otherwise profit is shown which may never materialise. It is no more than prudent to err on the side of caution, as some stock may deteriorate or, in the course of time, become unsaleable, and care should be taken to see that in no event must there be an overvaluation. Naturally an under-valuation of closing stock keeps down the profit and, of course, the tax payable of such profit. The closing stock of the first year becomes the opening stock of the second year, and, if the stock has been greatly undervalued, then the closing stock of the second year will have to be very greatly undervalued if a similar gross profit ratio is to be shown for both years. For example, if stock at the close of the first year is undervalued by £1,000, the profit will likewise be kept down by £1,000. In the second year, if both the opening and closing stock are undervalued by £1,000, the profit will be unaffected and will be the actual profit earned. If it is desired to make the profit £1,000 less than actual, in line with the first year, then the closing stock will have to be undervalued by another

£1,000, making the stock evaluation £2,000 less than it actually is. The proprietor's problems are only just beginning, because, to keep the same ratio of gross profit to sales, the stock will have to be undervalued more and more each year and the build-up will mean that in the course of time too much stock will be held in the business and the proprietor will not know what to do with it. If the excess is sold against cheques, the cheques will show in a banking account; it is not easy to sell bulk stock for cash at its full market value. As so many people have found, undervaluation of stock causes a great deal of difficulty.

In the present instance, it is not any help for the customer to say that his stock is worth £42,000 unless it is his intention to restrict purchases and bring the excess stock back into the account and therefore increase his profit and his tax. By comparing the gross profit ratio over a few years and by careful questioning, it should be fairly straightforward for a banker to judge the true position about a customer's stock valuation methods, and to consider if they alter in substance the trading figures produced.

Profit and Loss Account Entries

Debits to the profits and loss account can be made to include the personal expenditure of the proprietors, but this will only have the same effect as taking money out of the till, in that it will mean that the business provides a better living than is apparent. It will not, however, mean that there is any additional money available for the repayment of a loan.

Repairs and Renewals

Sometimes these appear as a large figure in a profit and loss account, and it can occur that some capital expenditure has been included in this figure. The point to establish is whether capital expenditure will still be necessary in future years, and the same consideration apply as to other debits in the profit and loss account. What are the figures for the individual items estimated to be in future years?

Depreciation

This item is a debit in the accounts, but no money passes out of the business. There are various methods for estimating the correct amount to be written off assets according to accounting principles, but in practice the amount allowed by the Finance Acts has an important bearing. It may be necessary to ask a customer or his accountant how the depreciation has been calculated and what effect on future accounts the following years' depreciation will have. As mentioned above, the sum charged for depreciation is retained in the business and is therefore available for loan repayments. We must, however, keep in mind that the true amount for depreciation is much more than a book entry. If an asset has to be replaced — the amounts written off as depreciation having been used for loan repayments — the business may need to borrow more money to replace the asset.

Balance Sheet Items

Alterations in these figures will not affect the ability of a business to repay a loan, and we have already considered the items for stock and plant and machinery (which is affected by depreciation). Debtors could be undervalued by an excessive write-off of bad debts but the net result of any undervaluation of assets only means that there is a secret reserve — ie, an undervaluation of assets by £3,000 would be offset, if written up to true value, by a capital reserve of the same amount as a contra entry on the other side of the balance sheet.

It will by now be apparent that a set of audited accounts, far from being no guide to a business, is a very good guide indeed from a banker's point of view. A customer who says that his business is much better than the audited accounts indicate should be asked to point out which figures are incorrect. Intelligent probing by a banker will soon establish the true position and in very many cases will demonstrate to the customer that his assumption that his business is so good does not stand up to a detailed enquiry.

In the present instance, we have seen that the cash generated in the business is £6,600. The stock held in the business is between one and two months' supply and we have already seen how little an incorrect stock valuation can affect a business's ability to service a loan. Without a knowledge of the kind of business, we cannot say if the gross profit ratio is high or low, but the individual items for expenses might appear to leave little room for pruning, but this will have to be discussed with the directors. At all events, it looks as if the directors will have to produce other evidence, and be very persuasive, if they are to convince a banker of their ability to repay an additional £40,000 over five or seven years.

3. Overtrading

There is a great deal of confusion about the term 'overtrading', perhaps in part because the term is not expressive enough. If trade engenders profits, and more trade more profits, why then should even more trade lead to the dangerous situation of 'overtrading'?

It would be easier for those not well versed in accountancy to use the word 'over-extended', as this would more easily enable them to envisage the cause of difficulties encountered by too large a turnover on too small a capital.

A simple way of understanding overtrading is to consider firstly the weekly budget of a wage earner earning, say, £150 per week after tax, which is expended as follows:

	£
Rent and rates	37
Food, etc	50
Fuel and light	17
Clothing	13
Travelling	12
	129
For extras	21
	£150

His position is solvent, but he may subsequently decide to buy a motor car which he estimates will cost him £10 per week to run. At the same time he has some money to put down on buying the car and can take the remainder on hire-purchase at £14 per week. If he then has no further capital, he will be unable to meet his outgoings unless he economises on some of his expenditure or increases his income by, say, overtime working. If he finds that he can manage by these means, he is able still to keep solvent; but if he has stretched his resources in labour and finance to the full, he would be most unwise then to enter into further hire-purchase to buy furniture at £6 a week, a television set at £5 per week, and a garden shed at £4 per week.

He would at this stage have over-extended himself, with the result that, after payment of a number of instalments, he might find that the goods have to be returned and he will, of course, be worse off than when he started his hire-purchase commitments. Money paid in instalments will have been lost, and possibly loans taken to try to keep up the instalments will still remain to be repaid.

If instead of furniture, etc, he purchased an article — say, a printing machine — which could be put to use to earn sufficient money to keep up the instalments on the printing machine, then an over-extended position would not arise.

He would have extended his position, but prudently he would have arranged for sufficient income to meet outgoings and no financial difficulties need occur.

If we now move into the realms of business, similar situations will be seen. Should a trading concern have sufficient receipts to enable it to meet its expenditure as payments become due, no financial trouble is met. Should, however, receipts be delayed, it may be necessary for the proprietor to arrange to put in more capital or to borrow.

If borrowing is resorted to and the business continues to expand, if more fixed assets are necessary, and if extended credit has to be given, the business may well reach the limit of the borrowing it is able to arrange. Should, however, at this point, the business still find that sufficient receipts are not obtained to meet expenditure as it becomes due, then the business will have over-extended itself and the situation known as overtrading will have arisen.

Many people who get into this position cannot understand why their bankers will not advance them further funds. They can show that they have good orders and seem surprised that no extra finance is forthcoming. They are unable to see that, with over-extended finances, any further funds provided will incur greater risk; and that they themselves are of such a nature that they will then wish to expand even further and thereby require still more funds. Such funds may then have to be provided to protect the original stake of the lender.

Profitability of the business may well be possible at increased levels of turnover but, if more risk is entailed, any additional funds provided should receive interest at a rate sufficient to compensate for the risk taken. Such additional risk interest will of course cut into the profit being made and the proper course is for more capital to be provided.

In simple terms, therefore, overtrading occurs when a profitable business has so extended itself that it has used all its available cash resources both in capital and borrowed funds but is not able to meet its expenditure as it becomes due. I have specified a profitable business: if it is unprofitable, its troubles stem from other causes. A profitable business beset by overtrading difficulties can soon become unprofitable as large interest is paid on borrowed funds, discounts are lost, opportunities for purchases at favourable rates cannot be taken and stock has to be sold at cut prices to meet pressing payments.

As will be seen, it is not possible to say that a certain turnover can be maintained on a certain capital. There can be no ratio which will automatically indicate when a business becomes over-extended, as much will depend upon the terms of the trade in which the business operates. When money is slow in circulating through the business only a relatively small turnover can be maintained on a given amount of capital but, when it is usual for money to turn over quickly, a much larger turnover can be supported.

Generally, when a well-organised market is in being, the businesses closely connected with the market are able to sustain a large turnover on a small capital. This is because active sellers and buyers are in touch with each other, goods can be sold by description and settlement is for cash or on very short terms. This can be easily seen if we consider the Stock Exchange, where purchases and sales of shares are arranged in large amounts by member firms whose turnover can be astronomical when compared with their capital. Commodity markets likewise are able to sustain trading in large amounts when compared with the capital resources employed.

Having said this, we cannot just dismiss the problem of overtrading when dealing with businesses with close connections to markets. Exactly the same considerations apply. Are the businesses able to meet their expenditures as they become due, after using their resources in capital and borrowed money? If not, even though settlement terms in the market are quick, trouble through an over-extended position will occur.

Moreover, greater care will be necessary with such businesses, as the quick receipt of funds which are used to meet creditors can often cloak a situation which needs careful watching.

Let us look at a few examples:

CASE 1

T Company Limited has several retail shops where most of the trade is for cash. The trading and profit and loss account for Year B shows:

		£	£	
Sales			423,000	
Less Purchases		366,000		
Opening stock		48,000		
		414,000		
Closing stock		81,000	333,000	
Gross profit			90,000	21.3%
Less Sundry expenses		39,800		
Depreciation		4,200		
Directors' fees		37,000	81,000	
Net profit			9,000	2.1% A small margin
	Less tax		3,600	
			5,400	
Add balance brought forward			8,100	
Balance brought forward			13,500	

The balance sheet and summary figures for two years are:

	Year	A	B	
		£	£	
Current liabilities				
Bank		13,500	36,000	Sharp increase
Creditors		63,000	132,000	Sharp increase
Current taxation		4,200	4,800	
Directors' loans		7,500	10,500	Increased by £3,000
Total current liabilities		88,200	183,300	
Future taxation		3,900	7,500	
Hire purchase			4,800	Appears Year B
		92,100	195,600	
Capital		1,500	1,500	
Profit and loss account		8,100	13,500	Good increase
Total liabilities		101,700	210,600	

Current assets

Debtors	18,00	9,000	Decreasing
Stock	48,000	81,000	Up
Total current assets	**66,000**	**90,000**	

Fixed assets

Freeholds		69,000	Appears Year B
Plant and machinery . . .	7,500	21,000	Big increase
Fixtures and fittings . . .	1,800	1,800	
Motor cars	4,200	8,400	More vehicles
	79,500	190,200	
Goodwill	22,200	20,400	£1,800 writtenoff
Total assets	**101,700**	**210,600**	

Summary

Trading turnover	270,000	423,000	Big increase
Net profit before taxation . .	7,500	9,000	Up
Less Taxation	3,900	3,600	
Net profit after taxation . .	3,600	5,400	Up
Directors' remuneration . .	30,000	37,000	Up
Carried forward	7,100	13,500	
Net current deficit . . .	22,200	93,300	Deficiency increasing
Net total deficit	12,600	5,400	Deficiency decreasing

The salient points revealed by these figures are:

1. A profit of £5,400 has been made in Year B and this has been retained in the business.

2. Out of the directors' remuneration, an additional £3,000 has been retained in the business by means of an increase in directors' loans.

3. The bank overdraft is up; presumably for part payment for the freeholds which have appeared for the first time in Year B.

4. Hire-purchase is probably taken on the increased plant and machinery.

5. Turnover is increasing rapidly.

6. The company is insolvent when goodwill is deducted, but the directors' loans cover the insolvency. The capital (£1,500) plus the profit and loss account (£13,500) plus the directors loans (£10,500) give a total of

£25,500 and this only exceeds the goodwill of £20,400 by £5,100. This does not even cover the cost of the motor vehicles and leaves nothing towards the remainder of the fixed assets or towards the working capital to support a turnover of £423,000.

7. The amount written off goodwill must be queried as goodwill has to be written off over its useful economic life.

8. There is a large net current deficiency and, as creditors are sharply up at £132,000, it is difficult to know how the company is able to manage. If receipts are regular, approximately £35,000 per month is being received; this, together with debtors of £9,000, will go only a third of the way in one month towards meeting the outstanding creditors. Perhaps the creditors are prepared to give more than three months' credit. This is a question which must be asked. The amount going out monthly on hire-purchase will also cause a drain on the liquid resources of the company.

9. It certainly looks as if the company will be under strain in meeting its day-to-day commitments; and, if the directors are of a mind to expand further, the company could come crashing down.

Let us now suppose that the directors call at the bank and say that, since the accounts were produced, turnover has continued to rise and is now running at the rate of £480,000 per annum. The company is so impressed with its progress and the profits made that it wishes to buy another leasehold retail shop for £51,000. The directors are able to raise £21,000 and wish the bank to advance £30,000 on top of the £36,000 they have already borrowed. They offer repayments at the rate of £18,000 per annum. When questioned about the repayments, they state that they anticipate a profit after tax of £9,000; the directors will plough back £4,500 from their fees; and depreciation of £4,200 is also retained in the business. They state that the £21,000 they can raise is the full amount of their assets outside the business, that their record with the bank has been good, and that, as they have built up a successful business and are prepared to put in their entire assets, they feel entitled to expect the bank to help.

The bank is offered as security the leasehold deeds of the property to be purchased at £51,000 plus the deeds already held (purchase price £69,000) against the overdraft of £66,000.

A bank manager faced with this situation will find very little use in telling the directors that they are overtrading, in the hope that this bare fact will be sufficient to satisfy the company and that the directors will meekly accept that the bank will not lend.

It will be necessary for the bank manager to use his full persuasive powers and convince the directors that he wishes to help the company to the fullest extent, and then proceed to ferret out all the facts relating to the credit the company obtains. He will also need to remind the directors that they have forgotten the hire-purchase payments and the increased interest on the larger overdraft, together with such items as fitting out the new premises, extra staff, and additional stock which will mean more creditors.

Although the company is making profits, these profits will not help to solve any creditor pressure if they are to be used to enable further expansion to take place and neither will they be available to reduce the bank borrowing.

The bank manager, if he wishes to retain his customer's goodwill, will have to try, on the basis of the accounts for Year B, to build up a cash projection and a creditor projection to show how creditor pressure will be unbearable. If he is able to convince his customers of this, he may also be able to get them to put in the £21,000 they have, in order to help the present situation, and at the same time get the customers to forget about expanding their business further until their present liquidity problems are eased. He may also be able to bring in the company's accountant, whose views could well give weight to the bank manager's points.

If the bank manager is successful in putting across his views, he will have done much to save his customers misfortune, but experience shows that people intent on expansion at all costs take more than a little convincing that their financial acumen is wrong. In these circumstances, all the bank will be able to do will be to see that it is adequately secured, so that there will be no difficulty in recouping the overdraft when the crash occurs. A debenture in the present situation might well cause additional creditor pressure almost immediately the registration of the debenture is noted in trade journals.

CASE 2

A further illustration with some variations will, I think, be sufficient to bring home the difficulties which a company can get into by overextending itself.

The company is engaged in light engineering work and there is a steady demand for its products. Borrowing from the bank is arranged for £20,000 with the security of a debenture, and a second debenture has been given to a friend of the managing director. It has been agreed that the hire purchase company can stand before both debenture holders in respect of the machinery and vehicles being purchased.

ANALYSIS OF ACCOUNTS OF 'A' COMPANY LIMITED

	Years	X £	Y £	
Current liabilities				
Bank	. . . .	11,400	17,250	Increase
Creditors	. . .	47,400	58,500	Increase of £11,000
Taxation	. . .	6,000	8,000	
Total current liabilities	. .	64,800	83,750	
Hire purchase	. . .	24,000	23,000	Why so little reduced?
2nd debenture	. . .	10,000	15,000	Increased borrowing
		98,800	121,750	
Capital .	. . . .	10,000	10,000	
Reserves	. . . .	2,000	2,000	
Profit and loss account.	.	9,000	15,000	A good increase
Total liabilities	. . .	119,800	148,750	
Current assets				
Debtors	. . . .	14,000	22,000	Increase of £8,000
Stock .	. . . .	32,000	26,000	Decrease of £6,000
Work in progress	. .	21,000	28,000	Increase of £7,000
Total current assets.	. .	67,000	76,000	
Fixed assets				
Plant and machinery	. .	44,000	55,000	Increase
Fixtures and fittings	. .	1,000	1,000	
Motor vehicles	. .	7,800	16,750	Increase
Total assets	. . .	119,800	148,750	
Summary				
Trading turnover	. .	250,000	325,000	Increasing
Net profit before taxation	. .	10,350	13,700	Increasing
Less Taxation .	. . .	2,350	4,300	Relatively low
Net profit after taxation .	.	8,000	9,400	Increasing
Directors' remuneration .	.	20,000	23,000	Increasing
Dividends	. . .		3,400	
Carried forward	. .	9,000	15,000	
Net worth	. . .	21,000	27,000	Increasing

The salient points of the balance sheet are:

1. In Year Y the net current asset position has been turned into a net current deficit.

2. Hire-purchase appears to be large and has not decreased much in the year, indicating that probably more hire purchase has been taken during the year. This would seem to be borne out by the increases seen in plant and machinery and motor vehicles.

3. The company's borrowing commitments are large – bank £17,250, second debenture £15,000, and hire purchase £23,000 – whereas the proprietor's stake is only £27,000.

4. A good profit has been made and £6,000 was retained in the business during Year Y.

The question that begs to be answered is 'Can the company manage to meet its day-to-day commitments when its liabilities are so large?

Enquiry reveals that retentions in the business, apart from the retained £6,000, were £5,000 written off for depreciation and that hire-purchase instalments are £1,500 per month. There is therefore a drain on the business through hire-purchase payments of more than the cash generated by the business, with the result that the net current deficit will become worse. This in itself might not be too serious as, if the deficit increases by £7,000 in the year and creditors increase by the same amount to £65,000, the company may still be able, by reason of its turnover and quick collection of debtors, to meet its liabilities without causing its creditors to press unduly. However, with the proprietors' stake of £27,000 being only one-half the amount of the plant and machinery and therefore providing nothing towards the other fixed assets or working capital, the company seems certainly to be well-extended.

Detailed questioning will be necessary to obtain all the information needed to come to a conclusive opinion, and the continued prosperity of the business will be essential for the company to be able to meet the large liabilities.

If now the managing director were to approach his bank with a further request for £25,000 in order to repay his friend's second debenture of £15,000 and to provide £10,000 for a lease for additional premises (which are to be stocked with more machinery to be taken on hire-purchase), the bank manager should be aware of all the risks he is being asked to take.

While the company may have been able to meet its commitments with a great deal of effort while a loan of £15,000 was provided, a far different situation would arise if this were to be replaced by short-term borrowing from a bank.

The solution for the company is to obtain a replacement of the loan by another long-term loan or, better still, to arrange for more capital to be provided. Another loan might only be obtained at a very high rate of interest to compensate for the risk taken and this might cut into profits. The company is very short of capital and this should be rectified as the risk involved is a large one and rightly belongs to the proprietors.

4. Solid and Swinging Accounts

One of the main objects of bankers is to enable the 'raw material' of credit balances which depositors are not immediately requiring to be used by other customers who need loans. Money left with banks on deposit or savings bank accounts is repayable at short notice, and money on current account is repayable on demand. It is therefore important that the lending that banks arrange is to a large extent on a short-term basis also, as there is no quicker way of getting into difficulties than to borrow short and lend long.

Attractive borrowing propositions are therefore those which involve short-term finance with a certain source of repayment or borrowing from time to time for short-term needs. This latter type of borrowing is often required by businesses which need help pending the receipt of income from sales. The banking account is an important step in the cycle of events reflected in the changing flow of current assets and liabilities, and finance for normal trading purposes is a natural feature of numerous bank lending agreements.

Normal Trading Finance

This is quite often incorrectly referred to as finance for working capital, but a knowledge of the term 'working capital' shows that this cannot be so. Working capital is the excess of current assets over current liabilities. Bank overdraft finance is repayable on demand, and therefore any overdraft taken by a business is reflected in the current liabilities and so cannot increase working capital. (Long-term finance such as debenture borrowing, or loans which are not repayable on demand, increase working capital, as also do profits left in a business or additional finance provided by the proprietors.) The correct way to describe this type of finance is 'normal trading finance'.

With lending of this nature, the result of purchases of stock and subsequent payment of creditors is reflected by a large overdraft in the banking account: conversely receipt of money from debtors for sales made will reduce the overdraft, or convert the overdraft into a credit balance. The pattern of the banking account should therefore be one showing a swing from small debit or credit figures to larger debit figures as money flows in and out of the account, and this can be looked upon as a normal consequence of trade for a flourishing business. If the account frequently returns to a credit position, the borrowing previously taken is of course repaid: such accounts fit naturally into the banking structure as they provide a means for short-term advances which are ideal for the use of funds which are subject to withdrawal on demand.

There is at times confusion in the minds of some people in thinking that overdraft facilities granted on swinging accounts which frequently revert to credit should be subject to a reduction programme each year. This is based on the view that, as profits are made, so should it be possible to rely less upon a bank overdraft. There is no valid reason why this should be the case. Why should profits be used to reduce a bank overdraft if they can be used to better effect in the purchase of fixed assets or, in fact, in distribution to shareholders? If the banking account has a regular swing into credit from normal trading and the business is prospering, overdraft facilities for the normal trading of the business can be renewed without reduction in the overdraft limit.

Solid Borrowing

For the reasons previously stated, solid borrowing is not suitable for much bank lending and neither is long-term borrowing. Numerous requests for facilities over a term of 20 years are not welcome but there are many occasions when a certain amount of term lending is granted by banks — particularly if there are associated accounts which are profitable to the bank. Some concession to rich customers is a matter of good business sense.

Let us consider, for example, the case of a thriving business with a turnover of £200,000 per annum making good profits, and keeping a satisfactory account with adequate security for modest normal trading requirements. If the managing director then calls on the bank and says that he personally wishes to buy a car costing £30,000 and he can produce £15,000 and can repay the remainder at £3,000 per annum, it would obviously be good business sense for the banker to agree to help the managing director if the repayments envisaged were feasible.

Where solid borrowing is evident, annual reductions are normally necessary to provide repayments over a short term but, where the borrowing is not solid and swings frequently into credit, reductions in the overdraft limits are unnecessary.

Lending to some businesses becomes solid even though originally a good swing into credit was anticipated, while in other instances it is expected that part of the lending will be solid for a short while. In both cases, it should be the object of the banker to cut the solid element of the lending.

If, for example, a company has an overdraft limit of £30,000 and the swing in the account is frequently within the range of £12,000 debit to £30,000 debit, this part of the overdraft should be acceptable to the banker (it being assumed that the company is trading profitably and there are no untoward aspects). The first £12,000 of the overdraft is, however, solid and reductions annually should be looked for in this part of the overdraft. If the banker is prepared to accept a clearance of solidity over a period of four years, then reductions in the overdraft should be, say, £3,000 per annum to bring the overdraft limit down eventually to £18,000.

Term Lending

This type of lending has been developed to provide much needed funds for industry and for those purposes for which on-demand overdrafts are unsuitable. For example, if a large engineering company wishes to re-tool extensively for a new production line it could well take, say, two years to complete the re-tooling and, perhaps, a further year or so to reach breakeven point. It would, therefore, not be possible to start repayment from the cash flow of this particular part of the enterprise until after three years had elapsed. If a credit squeeze or some other cut back in lending occurred during that period, the company could well find itself in severe difficulties if it had not arranged for finance for this project to be available for a period long enough for its purpose. An overdraft would therefore be an unsuitable form of finance for such a project. The needs of the project should be assessed and finance for an appropriate length of time arranged.

To cover these circumstances, which by their nature involve large amounts, the banks provide medium-term facilities, normally for periods of up to five years, but sometimes stretched to seven years or longer. It would be dangerous for the banks to provide these term facilities out of their on-demand or short-term deposits other than for a relatively small proportion and they therefore obtain deposits on longer terms from the wholesale funds available on the London money market.

On occasions, it is possible for the bank to match the term of its lending with the term of its borrowing but it is more usual for these not to coincide. A five year term may be required by a customer, but the bank may find that the longest term it is able to arrange at the appropriate time is, say, one year. The loan could still be made, however, by agreeing to lend over a five year period but with the loan being taken for an initial interest period of one year with an annual roll-over. In this way the change in the interest rate which may occur on the roll-over date becomes the responsibility of the borrower. Detailed conditions covering all aspects of the loan must be agreed at the outset. Term loans, unlike overdrafts are evidenced by documentation as it must be made clear to both parties the obligations and liabilities to which each has agreed. This type of lending is dealt with in more detail in Chapter 13.

Remoulding a Proposition

The considerations of swinging accounts and solid lending are important to bankers and it can sometimes be arranged for lending propositions to be adapted to make them suitable for bank lending even though the original proposition may have been unsuitable. I give below one example where a remoulding of an unsatisfactory proposition is possible. Many other instances could be given, but a study of the following example should be sufficient to understand the principle involved and to enable other unsatisfactory propositions to be remoulded into a better state.

A bank is approached by the manager of a light engineering company which has been a customer for a considerable number of years. He says that he has the opportunity of buying all the shares of the company from the present directors (man and wife) as they have decided to retire from business. Owing to his long service with the company, he is being offered the shares cheaply. He wishes to borrow £27,000 (being the full cost of £30,000, less £3,000 he is able to provide himself) and he can promise repayment of £1,500 per annum. As security, apart from the value of the private company's shares, he offers a charge over a share in a trust which will come to him in 25 years time and which is valued at £30,000.

On the face of it, this does not look an attractive proposition, as the repayment term is long at 18 years, there is little margin in the value of the reversionary interest over the amount of the requested loan and private company shares are not attractive as security. Nevertheless no propositoin should be brushed aside without full scrutiny, and audited accounts should be requested.

When the audited accounts are produced, it is seen that a steady business has existed for the past three years and that results each year have been similar. I am therefore showing the figures for only one year.

£

Liabilities

Creditors	. . .	27,000	
Corporation tax	. .	4,500	
Directors' undrawn remuneration	.	18,000	Is this to remain in the business?
Total current liabilities	. .	49,500	
Future corporation tax	. . .	1,500	
		51,000	
Capital	. . .	9,000	}
Reserves	. . .	1,500	} Net worth £33,000
Profit and loss account	. .	22,500	}
		84,000	

Assets

Cash	. . .	750	
Debtors	. . .	53,250	Almost twice the amount of creditors
Stock	. . .	10,500	Not large in relation to turnover
Work in progress	. .	10,500	Not large in relation to turnover
Total current assets	. .	75,000	Strong liquid position and exceeds current liabilities by £25,500
Leasehold	. . .	1,500	
Plant and machinery	. .	6,000	
Fixtures and fittings	. .	750	
Motor car	. .	750	
		84,000	
Trading turnover	. . .	240,000	
Net profit before taxation	. .	2,850	
Taxation	. . .	1,500	
Net profit after taxation	. .	1,350	
Directors' fees	. .	12,000	
Dividends	. . .	Nil	

To get a full picture it is necessary also to see how the banking account has been working and figures for the last three years show:

Year	Total of Debits	Highest Credit	Lowest Credit	Av. Cr. Bal.
A	217,000	20,000	700	6,200
B	239,000	17,000	1,400	5,100
C	280,000	19,000	600	5,200

It is obvious now that the business is a good one, and a banker would be anxious to help if at all possible. We have been told that the shares are to be purchased for £30,000 and the net worth is £33,000: this figure does not include goodwill which, for a successful business such as this, could be valuable. The shares are indeed worth purchasing. However, as £18,000 is included in the liabilities of the company as directors' undrawn remuneration, we shall wish to know what is to happen to this money, as complete withdrawal will be an embarrassment for the company and will necessitate borrowing on its own behalf. It will also be necessary to know the expected income of the new proprietors.

We are told that the present proprietors have no near relatives and have no desire to withdraw the directors' undrawn remuneration from the company. They want it to be converted into a loan and require to be paid 6 per cent interest on this money until the death of both husband and wife. On the death of them both, the loan is to be cancelled. The manager of the engineering company has been a faithful and hardworking servant of the company for many years; he has been in sole charge of the company for long stretches of time during illnesses of the managing director and, in consequence, the present offer of shares and the eventual cancellation of the loan are by way of a well deserved reward.

This makes the purchase of shares even more attractive. The banker's first thought will be to try and see if the proposed repayment programme can be increased to make the term reasonable.

It is explained, however, that, although the present salary of the manager is £10,000 and this could be increased in a few years' time by part of the £12,000 directors' fees there are plans for buying more machinery and replacing the old motor car which will, in effect, mean that the past level of directors' fees will have to be cut. There will also, of course, be the interest of £1,080 to be paid in future to the present directors, but this can be paid out of what was previously retained profits.

It is obvious that careful calculations have been made and that £1,500 as reduction is the top figure which can be managed.

An Alternative Approach

We are therefore back to the original proposition whereby £27,000 has been requested, with repayment at £1,500 per annum and not very satisfactory security. The reduction has to be made out of earned income which will have borne full tax, with the result that undue effort will have to be made for several years before this particular millstone will be able to be removed from the neck of the purchaser of the shares. The bank will be faced with solid borrowing over a long term and this is unsatisfactory for banking finance for what is a commercial proposition.

However, the company's account is an excellent one with a good swing and surely some satisfactory arrangement can be devised.

We know that the present proprietors wish to receive £30,000 plus £1,080 per annum. These are the basic facts and there seems no reason why the £1,080 per annum should be related to loans. Why cannot the company pay the directors a pension of this amount? This can be arranged in a legal way to the satisfaction of all parties.

If arrangements can now be made with the bank for overdraft facilities for the company, then the £18,000 of directors' undrawn remuneration can be drawn out, leaving the present manager of the company to produce £12,000, out of which he already has £3,000. Naturally, if £18,000 is drawn from the company, the sale price of the shares can be reduced to £12,000.

We now have a revised proposition:

1. the company borrows £18,000;
2. the new proprietor borrows £9,000.

We have seen from the figures for past years that the company keeps an average of approximately £5,000 on its account and that its account swings annually by about £18,000. An overdraft limit of £18,000 should therefore be satisfactory to the bank (subject to security) and it should not be necessary to seek annual reductions.

As for security, there is a strong liquid position but this is hardly sufficient for unsecured facilities of £18,000. A debenture, however, would give adequate cover.

The new proprietor would only have to borrow £9,000, and reductions of £1,500 per annum would see him clear in six years. Security over the reversionary interest (subject to the normal banking requirements for this type of security) should be sufficient.

A proposition for solid borrowing over an extended term has now been turned into one for a much smaller amount over a satisfactory length of time, allied to one for an overdraft on a business account for normal trading purposes and subject to a good swing.

5. Supervision of Lending

Once a lending proposition has been agreed, one might assume that it is only necessary to review the facility annually. Unfortunately a variety of unexpected events can combine to modify the hoped-for trend of borrowing and it may be necessary for a branch manager to have frequent discussions with customers when their overdraft limits have been exceeded, when trading conditions have changed, or because the original arrangements specified that certain trading figures should be produced at regular intervals.

One of the most effective ways of studying the health of a business is by examining regular balance sheets and profit and loss accounts, but today, with the complexity of the taxation laws and the consequent overburdening of accountants, balance sheets when produced are very often well out of date.

In order to overcome this disadvantage, bankers frequently ask for figures of current assets and current liabilities to be produced at regular intervals (monthly, quarterly, or half-yearly). In many cases bank debentures call for regular figures and lay down the margin of cover (as related to the bank debt) which must be kept in current assets. Naturally, when dealing with businesses which are not incorporated companies, debentures cannot be taken, but there is nothing to prevent a banker from making the submission of regular figures a condition of an advance.

Current Assets and Current Liabilities

We must now consider how figures for current assets and current liabilities are able to assist a banker.

First of all let us look at a simple profit and loss account and balance sheet:

ARTHUR COMPANY LIMITED
Profit and Loss Account for the year to 31 March

	£	£	
Sales		120,000	
Closing stock		30,000	
		150,000	
Less Purchases	90,000		
Opening stock	24,000	114,000	
Gross profit		36,000	Being 30% of sales
Less Trading expenses	6,000		
Administration expenses	6,000		
Taxation	3,000		
Depreciation	3,000	18,000	
Net profit		18,000	Being 15% of sales

Balance Sheet as at 31 March

	£	£	
Current liabilities			
Bank	18,000		
Creditors	18,000		
Taxation	3,000		
Loans	3,000	42,000	
Provisions		3,000	
Profit and loss account		18,000 }	In excess of fixed assets
Capital		15,000 }	
		78,000	
Current assets			
Cash	600		
Debtors	21,000		More than cover creditors
Stock	30,000	51,600	In excess of current liabilities
Fixed assets			
Plant and machinery	18,000		
Fixtures and fittings	3,000		
Motor car	5,400		
		78,000	

When stock is purchased, a creditor is made; and when a creditor is paid, cash is reduced or a bank overdraft increased. When stock is sold, a debtor appears; and when the debtor pays, cash is increased or a bank overdraft appears; and when the debtor pays, cash is increased or a bank overdraft reduced. In the trading operations, therefore, only the current assets and current liabilities need be considered, as the fixed assets are much more static.

It follows that, where a business is profitable, the ratio of current assets to current liabilities should change, with the current assets increasing when compared with the current liabilities. The converse would be the case when a business is losing money.

However, we must also take into account items in the profit and loss account which are charged or received at irregular intervals, or which occur with long intervals between payment or receipt, or which involve no actual cash disbursement or receipt during the current trading year. If we are considering monthly figures, then, in the example above, the following items would call for special consideration:

i rates and rent	if paid other than monthly.
ii other expenses	if paid other than monthly.
iii taxation	for the current year.
iv depreciation	
v taxation	paid for a previous year.

As will be seen, the company at the balance sheet date has current assets of £51,600 and current liabilities of £42,000,, giving net current assets of £9,600. If the business is to continue to be profitable, we should expect monthly figures to show an increase of net current assets, as, for example:

	April £	May £	June £	July £	Aug £	Sept £
Current assets	52,400	55,800	55,800	60,000	61,800	63,600
Current liabilities	43,200	43,800	42,600	42,000	43,200	43,200
Net current assets	10,200	12,000	13,200	18,000	18,600	20,400

Although the rise in net current assets has not been of a regular pattern each month — which we might put down to irregular payments or seasonal considerations — the rise in six months from £9,600 to £20,400 — ie, £10,800 (or, say, £21,600 for a full year), is sufficient for us to see that the company is trading profitably and that a similar profit after depreciation could be shown for the current year as that shown in the last profit and loss account.

This example does, of course, simplify the problem, but it serves to illustrate the general principle. In practice, many other factors will have to be taken into account, such as the type of business and the nature of its operations. Also the constituent parts of the current assets and current liabilities will have to be examined. When accountants prepare these figures for customers they quite often apportion irregular payments on a monthly basis, which naturally helps a banker to see the trend of the trading.

Variations

It is as well to keep in mind that alterations in these liquid figures can only be caused by profits or losses, or by funds injected into or drawn out of the company, or by the sale or purchase of fixed assets. An increase in the net current assets is normally a welcome sign to a banker, but a decrease might well mean that enquiry is necessary. As will be readily appreciated, one set of monthly figures would normally be insufficient for satisfactory conclusions to be reached and only in extreme cases would it be necessary to make enquiries based on such meagre information.

Let us consider now the following monthly figures produced by a company which has given a debenture to the bank, which calls for current assets to be maintained at a figure twice that of the bank debt. The bank debt must be that shown in the company's books and not the bank's books, as considerable variation can occur between these figures and we can only get a proper comparison if all figures are extracted on the same basis.

	Jan £	Feb £	March £	April £	May £	June £
Current assets						
Good book debts . .	82,649	87,609	86,518	76,925	77,393	78,354
Stock (free of lien) .	40,000	43,000	42,000	42,000	43,000	42,000
Total	122,649	130,609	128,518	118,925	120,393	120,354

	Jan £	Feb £	March £	April £	May £	June £
Current liabilities						
Preferential liabilities .	1,200	2,000	1,000	2,000	3,000	2,000
Other creditors .	50,000	53,000	53,000	50,000	48,000	49,000
Bank debt . .	3,765	4,702	5,825	18,312	15,393	21,786
Total . .	54,965	59,702	59,825	70,312	66,393	72,786
Liquid assets are called for under debenture (twice bank debt)	7,530	9,404	11,650	36,624	30,786	43,572

If we look first of all at the bottom line of figures (which shows the amount of liquid assets which must be kept to satisfy the terms of the debenture) and then compare these figures with those shown for the total current assets, it will be seen that much more than sufficient cover is kept in every month. However, to dismiss the figures without further examination might well lead one to overlook what might be an important point.

It will be seen that stock is fairly constant over the period but that debtors, although increased in the February/March months, dropped towards the end of the period. The resulting drop in the total current assets in the six months' period should be reflected in a drop in the current liabilities, especially if we are also looking for a profit being earned during the period.

In fact the reverse is true and total current liabilities have increased by about £18,000. This is shown by an increase in the bank debt.

If we now extract the next current assets (current assets less current liabilities) we get:

Jan £	Feb £	March £	April £	May £	June £
67,784	70,907	68,693	48,613	54,000	47,568

It is now easy to see that the figures for the first three months are fairly constant and that those for the last three months are also fairly constant. Between the March and April figures, however, there occurred either:

    i an exceptionally large loss;

    ii a purchase of fixed assets to the extent of approximately £20,000;

    iii a withdrawal of approximately £20,000 from the business;

or iv a mistake in the preparation of the figures.

The Need for Enquiry

A knowledge of the business might enable a banker to say which alternative is probable and, dependent upon the arrangements with the customer and all other circumstances concerning the account, the banker will have to decide whether he should make specific enquiries of the customer.

It will have been seen that in this example stock and creditors have been quoted as round amounts to the nearest thousand pounds. It is of course no more difficult to obtain a figure for creditors than it is for debtors and, in order for the figures to be a proper guide, greater accuracy should be achieved. As for stock, this does cause more difficulty as stock-taking is a lengthy procedure and it is not generally expected that a full stock check should be made monthly. However, fairly accurate figures can be obtained for many businesses by adding to the existing figure for stock the purchases in the month and deducting the figure for sales less the average gross mark up.

Surrounding circumstances will always have to be considered before the banker decides what degree of accuracy he must insist upon. A check on the accuracy of the figures should be made when balance sheets are produced, by comparing the balance sheet figures with the liquid figures produced at the same date.

Let us look at another example:

	July £	Aug £	Sept £
Current assets			
Good book debts	40,618	41,684	33,206
Stock (free of lien)	10,918	14,752	10,652
Total	51,536	56,436	43,858
Current liabilities			
Preferential liabilities	4,310	8,619	8,687
Other creditors and bills payable	35,211	40,219	73,492
Bank debt	15,594	15,999	16,513
Total	55,115	64,837	98,692
Liquid assets as called for under debenture (twice bank debt)	31,188	31,998	33,026

Again we see that the current assets are in every month more than twice the bank debt, but the total current assets have fallen away considerably while the current liabilities have increased very rapidly. Enquiry seems to be imperative, especially as the creditor figure indicates that a large change may have taken place in the company's affairs.

A few moments' thought will bring one to the conclusion that there is probably something wrong with the figures produced, as such a large increase in the creditors in one month (to make them twice the debtors, whereas previously creditors were less than debtors) should be reflected in a similar increase in either stock or debtors if the goods had been subsequently sold. Fixed assets could have been purchased but, on the slim evidence we are considering, the resultant increase in creditors for such a purpose might have been very unwise.

Let us suppose that enquiry was made and it was found that the company was now acting as a central purchasing agency for a group of companies and that amounts due from associated companies had been omitted. The revised figures produced are:

	September
	£
Current assets	
Good book debts.	33,206
Associated companies	49,204
Stock (free of lien)	10,652
Total	93,062
Current liabilities	
Preferential creditors	8,687
Other creditors and bills payable . .	73,492
Bank debt	16,513
Total	98,692
Liquid assetes as called for under debenture (twice bank debt)	33,026

All now seems in order, and the figures produced are more or less in line with those seen for previous months except that debtors and creditors have risen sharply. However, this too may call for further enquiry. It is probable over the next month or so that all book debts will disappear, apart from the sums due from associated companies, which will likewise rise.

Then the debtors to which the bank will look for cover will be concentrated in a few hands only, and it may be imperative to see the balance sheets of the associated companies to establish that they are perfectly solvent and well able to meet their creditors.

Analysing the Figures

A further example will, I think, suffice to illustrate the importance of examining in detail the periodical figures produced:

	Sept £	Oct £	Nov £
Current assets			
Debtors	78,792	58,156	28,581
Stock (free of lien)	72,226	67,718	90,267
Work in progress	53,333	90,791	86,824
Totals	204,351	216,665	205,672
Current liabilities			
Preferential liabilities	26,150	22,036	36,424
Other creditors	94,573	90,451	54,387
Bills payable	30,000	30,769	41,026
Bank	37,076	55,961	54,839
Totals	187,799	199,217	186,676
Current assets as called for by debenture (bank debt plus 50%)	55,614	83,941	82,258

A quick look at these figures will show that, apart from the bank debt being well covered, the excess of current assets over current liabilities is approximately £17,000, £17,000 and £19,000 in the three consecutive months. How dangerous such a quick look can be is soon seen by a closer examination of the figures. In September the figure for debtors (£78,792) was more than twice the bank debt (£37,076), but the debtors have dropped so quickly and the bank debt has risen so much that the bank debt in November was not covered by the debtors to the extent of £26,000. For cover for this part of the bank debt, we must now look to stock and work in progress and, as this has been increasing rapidly, it could be that the company has a large amount of unsaleable stock on its hands.

A look at the liabilities will show that preferential liabilities are at a high level and that, if the company went into liquidation in November, there would be insufficient debtors to settle the preferential claim and the bank would be looking entirely to the stock and work in progress to cover its lending (I am assuming that there is little in the way of fixed assets). Clearly in this instance some detailed enquiries will be necessary.

I should like to add that, in order to make a proper assessment of a company's figures, a knowledge of the company's business is essential and this is one of a bank manager's duties. With this knowledge and an intelligent look at the figures produced, a banker should be able to gauge with reasonable accuracy the health of the business.

In the examples given, any fixed assets which would have strengthened a company's position and any possible additional security have been ignored.

I should like to make the point, however, that, when there is little to fall back upon of any real value in the fixed assets, great care should be taken, as in adverse conditions current assets can be rapidly lost, especially when a company is over-extended.

6. Management Accounts

Although the method of supervision of lending explained in the last chapter will be the method which will have to be used for numerous businesses it should, in some cases, be possible to use the customer's own accounting system for the same purpose.

Unfortunately, many businesses are not using management accountancy methods of forward planning and monitoring of actual results regardless of the benefit that can ensue. In a nation where individual freedom is prized this is not be wondered at as it would be unusual to find everyone conforming to a single management system. However, the force of competition will gradually compel businesses to use more efficient methods. As management accounting systems are introduced, bankers will have available, with the customer's co-operation, a tool which can be used to look ahead to the probable trend of the bank balance and to monitor the performance of the company.

Management accounting is a subject which needs separate study and is outside the subject matter of this book. In essence it involves examining the capability of the business, its costs and probable sales and with this knowledge evolving a forward plan. Also any capital investments will be costed and the return on the investment assessed. A full management accounting system will look at every item in a balance sheet and subject each one to the overall plan.

Such systems provide the information to enable directors and executives to run their businesses efficiently. Naturally, any input of information must be of a high standard and the forward assessments dealt with carefully or the final plan will be unreliable.

Certain aspects of the overall plan and the on-going monitoring are of use to banks when considering initial lending requests and for subsequent supervision of the lending. These are:

　i Estimated profit and loss account;
　ii Estimated balance sheet;
　iii Appraisals of capital projects;
　iv Cash projection;
　v Comparisons of actual results against estimates;
　vi Debtors and creditors lists.

All these items are important, but the first three are mainly required to assist with the initial consideration of a borrowing proposal. In practice many businesses do not prepare detailed appraisals of capital projects and this is unfortunate as capital investment then becomes an investment made only on instinct or hope or because of any tax allowances obtained. Also some businesses stop short at the estimated profit and loss account stage and do not progress to the preparation of an estimated balance sheet. This need not concern the banker provided he knows how the profit will be used – ie, will it be retained in the business as working capital or in fixed assets or will it be withdrawn? This information can also generally be obtained from the cash projection.

After the initial consideration of the proposal the important documents required for on-going monitoring are the cash projection and the comparison of actual results against estimates. Debtors and creditors lists are a useful addition when the actual cash position shows a wide variation from the projection.

Traditionally, bankers have looked at past results as a guide to the ability of the customer and to give them confidence or otherwise in deciding whether to back fresh requests for more borrowing. Management accounting looks forward and this in itself, without some proven track record of ability, is insufficient to use as a basis for deciding whether or not to lend. An instance can be quoted of a large and adequately financed new project which came too grief within 18 months although full and detailed management accounts were in use. Very capable accountants were used in the business who, from the information fed to them, produced cash projections and estimated profit and loss accounts showing satisfactory cash liquidity and profitable trading. In fact, the accountants were so good and numerous that they were able to revise quickly their forecasts and cover any new fact which came to light. Nevertheless, the business lost money from its first day and continued to do so until its eventual collapse. For the initial 12 months the forward plans continued to show that profitable trading would soon be achieved but this was not to be. The fault did not lie with the accountants who were good at their job, but with the proprietors who proved to be incapable of running the business successfully. The accountants were only able to produce figures upon the assumptions given to them by the people running the business and there can be a wide gulf between hope and ability.

Forward planning must, therefore, be subject to detailed scrutiny and the projections viewed critically. If a record of achievement in meeting targets can be shown with cash projections and profit estimates proving to be reasonably accurate when compared with actual results, the track record for which bankers look will have been established; this will be of additional help to both banker and customer and will supplement a past record of profitable trading and a satisfactory borrowing record.

The intelligent use of accounting ratios should also not be overlooked. Numerous ratios of the figures in balance sheets and profit and loss accounts can be calculated but bankers should beware of reading too much into ratios calculated on the bare figures given in published accounts. Detailed breakdowns of the individual figures are often required if wrong conclusions are not to be drawn. A thorough knowledge of the use of ratios is important for lending bankers and a study should be made of these from accountancy textbooks.

When a banker calculates ratios he should keep in mind that the trends of such ratios year by year are important and can often indicate changes in the nature of the business.

The most important ratios from the point of view of the lending banker are as follows:

Rate of gross profit. This shows the percentage of profit on sales and is the starting point in trading as all expenses and the remuneration for the proprietor have to come out of the gross profit.

Rate of net profit. This will help to indicate whether expenses are fully under control.

Current ratio. The relationship of current assets to current liabilities is of vital importance as sufficient working capital is essential for all businesses; also as trading expands more working capital is needed.

Rate of stock turnover. This indicates whether the business is one of rapid turnover or not. Note that a reduction in the rate of turnover can sometimes show that some unsaleable stock is being held.

Length of credit given (debtor ratio). This can be allied to ageing lists for debtors to show the efficiency of the business in collecting its debts.

Length of credit taken (creditor ratio). Long average credit taken is always a danger sign. This ratio, too, can indicate the need for obtaining ageing lists of creditors.

Debtors to creditors. This can indicate a shift in the terms of trade. Sufficient funds must be generated from debtors and cash sales to pay creditors as they become due.

Return on net assets (i.e. on capital employed). This indicates the efficiency or otherwise of the business.

Gearing. The amount of borrowing in relation to the net worth of the business is of great importance and is a pointer to the amount of risk involved. Additionally, a banker should consider the amount of interest being paid on borrowed money and relate this to the profitability of the business and the cover which is thereby provided.

For all ratios the validity of them should be understood in the context of each particular business being examined. All ratios need not be calculated for every set of accounts. Only those appropriate to the situation need be used.

Any other accountancy aids to understanding accounts should also be used when the position requires it. Funds flow statements come into this category. In simple accounts it is easy to see how funds have been generated and how they have been used but in more complicated accounts the drawing up of a statement of source and application of funds can readily show if sufficient funds are being retained in the business and whether they are going into fixed or floating assets.

Of course, it is not necessary in all cases for a banker to see management accounts. There is a limit of time available and a bank manager must judge which accounts he wishes to monitor by this means. Obviously, when dealing with a successful business with a good track record which is borrowing a relatively small amount, the examination of management accounts will be superfluous.

CASE 1

Henry James is a man in his early 40s with many years of engineering experience. A few years ago he started a company in which he and his wife are the sole shareholders. The company manufactures ironmongers' sundries such as nuts, bolts, screws and washers and then packages them for displays and sale. The account has been trouble-free with a limit of £6,000 for which the bank holds as security the guarantee of Mr James supported by stocks and shares worth £9,000. It is aware that the bulk of the company's borrowing is taken from a finance company.

Mr James now tells the bank that he wishes to expand the turnover of the company and to do this will require a larger overdraft facility. He explains that the finance company is lending his company £35,000 with the security of a debenture and that he would like the bank to take over from the finance company. Additionally, more finance will be required and the bank is asked to increase its lending from £6,000 to £55,000.

Mr James produces accounts for the last three years and also a profit forecast and a cash projection for the coming 12 months. He explains that the small leasehold factory which is in the balance sheet at £30,000 is now worth £40,000 and he expects no difficulty in reducing the £55,000 overdraft to £45,000 after 12 months. The bank manager's knowledge of the industrial estate on which the factory is situated and the terms of the lease is sufficient for him to estimate the value as being at least £40,000 and to be suitable as security for an advance of £20,000.

In answer to further questions Mr James says that he is very satisfied with the way the business is progressing and that it is going according to plans and objectives he has set himself. He has a good accouuntant helping him and the company has met its forecasts in the three years since it was incorporated.

The documents produced by Mr James can be summarised as follows:

HENRY JAMES LTD
Balance Sheets

	£000			
	Year A	Year B	Year C	
Capital	11	17	17	£6,000 introduced Year B
Reserves	4	7	10	Increasing
Profit and loss account. .	2	3	6	Increasing
	17	27	33	
Creditors	20	20	32	In excess of debtors
Bank		6	4	Small
Finance company . . .	35	35	35	
	72	88	104	

Leaseholds	30	30	30	
Plant and machinery . .	5	7	12	
Fixtures and fittings . .	4	3	3	
Vehicles	10	12	9	
Stock	10	18	27	Well covers creditors
Debtors. . . .	12	17	23	and bank borrowing
Cash	1	1	—	
	72	88	104	
Turnover	100	170	240	
Directors' fees . . .	10	12	15	
Profit after tax . . .	2	4	6	Ploughed back
Net current assets. . .	(32)	(25)	(21)	Finance Company borrowing assumed short-term
Net worth	17	27	33	

ESTIMATED PROFIT AND LOSS ACCOUNT STATISTICS FOR COMING 12 MONTHS

Turnover, £370,000 (an increase from £240,000)
Directors' fees, £15,000 (as previous year)
Profit after tax, £15,000
No capital expenditure

ESTIMATED CASH PROJECTION FOR COMING 12 MONTHS

£000s

Month	1	2	3	4	5	6	7	8	9	10	11	12
Bank overdraft at start of month .	41	43	45	47	50	50	55	53	51	49	47	45
Payments . .	22	22	24	29	30	38	32	33	35	36	36	38
	63	65	69	76	80	88	87	86	86	85	83	83
Receipts . .	20	20	22	26	30	33	34	35	37	38	38	38
Bank overdraft at end of month .	43	45	47	50	50	55	53	51	49	47	45	45

From the banking account the following figures are available:

	Swing in account		
Year A	from Cr £8,000	to	Cr £2,000
Year B	from Cr £4,000	to	Dr £6,000
Year C	from Cr £8,000	to	Dr £6,000

It will be seen from the balance sheet that the proprietor's stake has increased from £17,000 to £33,000 in three years although £6,000 of this was an injection of additional capital. The remainder was achieved from profits left in the business. There is a deficit on net current assets but the finance company has not been pressing for reductions and there are adequate liquid assets to cover the amounts due to the creditors and the bank. From a security point of view and using the criteria already mentioned in Chapter 1, a satisfactory amount to lend against a debenture would be:

Against	£		£
Factory	20,000		20,000
Half of liquid assets . . .	25,000	or half of debtors . . .	13,000
		quarter of stock . . .	5,000
Stocks and shares . . .	6,000		6,000
	51,000		44,000

The net worth, however, is only £33,000. It seems, therefore, that the request for £55,000 is somewhat high.

However, we must look further at the estimated profit and loss account, the cash projection and the experience on the banking account. The banking account is swinging by £14,000 on a turnover of £240,000 and it would be reasonable to expect a larger swing on the projected increased turnover of £370,000. A good proportion of the borrowing (say, £20,000) will, therefore, be the swinging element and £35,000 the loan element for which reductions will be required.

The profit projection on the increased turnover is £15,000 but Mr James intends to keep his fees at £15,000. No capital expenditure is envisaged and a good plough back of profits into the business can be expected. The cash projection shows a satisfactory trend.

If the lending is agreed the position in 12 months' time would be lending of £45,000 to a stronger company with both liquid asets and net worth increased by £15,000. The lending could then be looked upon as very satisfactory.

The point to be decided is whether to expect the customer's projected results to be converted into reality. From the record of achievement in meeting past targets and from the conduct of the company's affairs, the bank should be quite satisifed with Mr James and his ability and could take a justifiable risk in lending the full amount. However, in view of the additional risk, the bank should make it a condition that the company submits actual results monthly for comparison against the forecast. The bank will, therefore, be warned at an early stage if anything is amiss.

CASE 2

John French has been running the Esplanade Hotel for several years but it has never been a complete success. He has taken a good living out of the business but the results have shown the business to be struggling. His hotel company has been borrowing increasing amounts from the bank which has a mortgage over the hotel. The bank has not been too happy with the account and has been pressing Mr French to try and arrange a long-term mortgage over the hotel and lift the borrowing from the bank.

The last balance sheet of the company is as follows:

	£	
Hotel freehold	175,000	This is the present value
Fixtures and fittings	35,000	
Vehicles.	20,000	
Stock	15,000	
Debtors .	9,000	
	254,000	
Creditors	45,000	High in relation to turnover
Bank	85,000	
Capital .	120,000	
Profit and loss account .	4,000	
	254,000	
Turnover	180,000	
Loss	2,000	Previous year profit £2,000
Directors' fees	15,000	

This shows the bank borrowing to be well secured and much lower than the net worth of £124,000. The statistics from the banking account show solid borrowing of around £75,000 three years ago to £85,000 now and the bank has lost confidence in Mr French's ability.

However, Mr French calls at the bank and says that he thinks he can arrange a long-term mortgage but the interest rate is too high. He has, therefore, had another idea and that is to change the trading pattern of the hotel. Previously the hotel catered for the seasonal holiday trade but he has now decided to make the bar more attractive and encourage this side of the business and to welcome coach parties which previously have not been welcome. His estimate is that this will double the turnover and produce results both in profits and cash flow which will please the bank. However, for the bar alterations and to meet some pressing creditors he will need to borrow an additional £30,000 making the overdraft £115,000. For this he offers the bank a debenture over the company. To back up his asertions, he produces an estimated profit and loss account and cash projection as follows:

FROM THE ESTIMATED PROFIT AND LOSS ACCOUNT

Turnover, £350,000
Profit, £30,000
Directors' fees, £15,000 (as previous year)

CASH PROJECTION
£000s

Month	1	2	3	4	5	6	7	8	9	10	11	12
Bank balance at start of month .	85	90	105	115	110	105	100	95	90	90	85	85
Payments . .	20	30	30	30	30	30	30	30	30	30	30	30
	105	120	135	145	140	135	130	125	120	120	115	115
Receipts . .	15	15	20	35	35	35	35	35	30	35	30	30
Bank balance at end of month .	90	105	115	110	105	100	95	90	90	85	85	85

Mr French says that this shows what the business is capable of producing and although the bank will have to put up more money at the outset this additional £30,000 will be repaid in the year and thereafter rapid reductions can be expected. He emphasises that the bank will be adequately secured.

The bank could well be satisfied with the security offered, but it is the proposition which is important.

Mr French has not been successful in his business and has therefore not built up a record which would allow the bank to give much credence to his optimistic views on the success of future trading. The balance sheet shows a large creditor position and the expenses on the bar might leave little from the increased overdraft to reduce the creditor figure. The cash projection may, of course, work out in practice but the bank would be taking a considerable risk in supporting Mr French further. The cry 'I was wrong before — believe me now'' is not a justification for a bank to increase its commitments.

CASE 3

William Harvey is a bachelor who owns Harvey Engineering Ltd, which account operates satisfactorily.

Four years ago a new machine at a cost of £20,000 was required and the bank lent the company the full amount. The bank was already lending £10,000 for normal trading and the overdraft agreed was therefore £30,000. Reduction of £6/7,000 per annum were agreed on the basis that the new machine would eable this amount of extra profit to be earned. Accountants' figures were produced to substantiate this and the bank was told that the life of the machine would be a minimum of seven years. As security, the bank has a guarantee from Mr Harvey supported by a second charge on his house which is worth £55,000 with a first charge of £20,000 outstanding.

Now, two years later, the overdraft has dropped from £30,000 to £17,000 but Mr Harvey asks if his company can have a temporary excess of £15,000 to £32,000 pending receipt of monthly accounts. He explains that he does not like to keep creditors waiting as he is conscious of his good name in the trade. However, as the request is repeated in two subsequent months it becomes obvious to the bank that something is amiss and Mr Harvey is asked for an explanation. He says that some debts are proving difficult to collect and the bank therefore asks him to produce his latest set of accounts together with up to date lists of both debtors and creditors and to classify them according to the time outstanding.

Summaries of the accounts and debtors and creditors lists are as follows:

Balance Sheet (dated five months previously)

	£	
Plant and machinery	25,000	
Fixtures and fittings	2,000	
Stock	30,000	
Debtors	35,000	Equal to creditors
	92,000	

Capital	30,000	
Profit and loss account	11,000	
Creditors	35,000	
Bank	16,000	In accordance with arrangements
	92,000	

Turnover	400,000	
Profit after tax	6,000	Good plough back of profits
Directors' fees	10,000	
Dividends	Nil	

List of Debtors (as at end of last month)

Length outstanding.	1 month	2 months	3 months	over 3 months
Number and amount	75 £7,000	35 £3,000	7 £2,000	2 £25,000

Total debtors . . .	£37,000

List of Creditors (as at end of last month)

Length outstanding.	1 month	2 months	3 months	over 3 months
Number and amount	7 £30,000	6 £5,000		

Total creditors . .	£35,000

The balance sheet shows a satisfactory position with creditors and debtors being equal to each other and approximately equivalent to one month's turnover. The business is successful and £6,000 of profit was retained in the year.

The creditors list bears out Mr Harvey's statement that he likes to keep his accounts up to date but the list of debtors shows that £25,000 on two accounts has been outstanding for more than three months and this is obviously the difficulty. It shows that apart from causing the company trouble in being outstanding for so long, too much of the company's trade is with two sources. This makes the company very dependent upon two customers.

Further enquiries reveal that Mr Harvey has been aware for some months that the £25,000 outstanding for so long may, in fact, become bad debts and this will be a severe blow to the company. He has, however, had no difficulty in replacing the lost turnover but this time has spread the additional business over many customers. He explained to the bank that he was somewhat ashamed of getting himself into this difficulty and was trying to sort himself out without asking the bank for more support. This had not proved possible and he therefore requests an increased overdraft facility of £25,000 making £42,000 in all. To support his request he produced a profit and cash forecast as follows:

Profit forecast, £8,000 before tax for six months
Directors' fees, £4,000
Turnover in six months, £220,000

CASH FORECAST

£000s Month	1	2	3	4	5	6
Bank overdraft at start of month . .	17	42	40	38	36	34
Payments . .	50	35	30	35	30	35
	67	77	70	73	66	69
Receipts . .	25	37	32	37	32	32
Sale of surplus equiment . . .						7
	42	40	38	36	34	30

From the profit forecast it can be seen that the profit shown is before deduction of tax but in view of the probable losses on bad debts there should be no tax to pay. Mr Harvey has also cut his directors' fees. The cash projection looks satisfactory if it works as planned with the overdraft reducing from £42,000 to £30,000 in six months. The point is now whether to accept the forecast and lend the company the money it requires.

Mr Harvey's track record has been good and it is obvious that he has taken the right steps to rectify his error of placing too large a part of his business in few hands. He is also prepared to make a personal sacrifice in cutting his fees from the company. In view of these facts, he deserves a chance to regain his position and subject to satisfactory enquiries about the detail in the cash projection the bank should assist.

CASE 4

George Belmont started a furniture upholstery business a year ago when it was agreed that he could have an overdraft limit of £15,000 for twelve months against the good guarantee of his uncle. During this period he would be injecting £10,000 and he expected profit of more than £5,000 to put his account in credit.

However, although the £10,000 had been injected the account was still overdrawn by £7,000.

He was asked for an explanation and he wrote saying that teething troubles were now over and the overdraft would be cleared in the next six months. He said that income would be £48,000 in this period (spread evenly) and purchases would be about £5,000 per month, wages would be £2,000 per month, rent of £400 would be payable in 3 months' time and quarterly thereafter, rates would be £300 payable in 3 months' time and a further £300 payable 6 months later and VAT payable would be £2,000 in 4 months' time and £3,000 in the following quarter.

From this information a cash projection could be prepared as follows:

			Months			
	1	2	3	4	5	6
Receipts . . .	8,000	8,000	8,000	8,000	8,000	8,000
Payments						
Purchases . . .	5,000	5,000	5,000	5,000	5,000	5,000
Wages . . .	2,000	2,000	2,000	2,000	2,000	2,000
Rent . . .			400			400
Rates . . .			300			
VAT . . .				2,000		
	7,000	7,000	7,700	9,000	7,000	7,400
Net cash in . . .	1,000	1,000	300		1,000	600
Net cash out .				1,000		
Bank overdraft . .	6,000	5,000	4,700	5,700	4,700	4,100
(£7,000 at start)						

These figures show that the overdraft will not be cleared as anticipated and George Belmont will have to be tackled again.

This may seem to be a simple matter but there is an important point to be made. Although it is sometimes necessary for a banker to construct cash projections on these lines they should only be used as a check on other information. The customer should prepare the cash projection and not the banker. The customer is in a far better position to prepare such a projection as he has all the information concerning his business and should be able to ensure that all relevant information is included. The preparation of projected figures often provides salutary lessons for businessmen who are not used to preparing these figures and enables them to think more deeply about their future trading prospects. Also if the actual figures do not match up with the estimated ones the customer can be questioned about his own projections and not be confronted with ones prepared by the banker from incomplete information.

CASE 5

A customer, a director of Lex Limited has told the branch manager that he will be calling upon him tomorrow to discuss overdraft facilities. Small temporary overdrafts have occurred in the past but these have been quickly repaid and no security is held although up to date audited accounts have been submitted to the branch. Lex Limited is a retailer of ironmongery.

The manager requires the balance sheets to be examined and comments made which might help him in the interview.

The balance sheets for the last two years are as follows:

	Year A £	Year B £
Current liabilities		
Bank .	2,000	
Creditors .	28,000	30,000
Current taxation .	4,000	
Total current liabilities .	34,000	30,000
Loans .	4,000	8,000
	38,000	38,000
Capital .	50,000	50,000
Profit and loss account .	10,000	2,000
	98,000	90,000
Current assets		
Cash .		3,000
Debtors .	20,000	18,000
Stock .	24,000	30,000
Marketable investments	2,000	
Total current assets .	46,000	51,000
Freeholds .	40,000	30,000
Plant and machinery .	10,000	8,000
Fixtures, fittings, tools and equipment .	2,000	1,000
	98,000	90,000

Other items which have been extracted from the accounts are:

	Year A	Year B
	£	£
Turnover	300,000	250,000
Shareholders' funds at beginning of		
year A	57,000	
Stock at beginning of year A . .	20,000	
Purchases	279,000	239,000
Depreciation of plant and machinery .	4,000	3,000
Depreciation of fixtures etc.. . .	2,000	2,000
Gross profit	25,000	17,000
Net profit	7,000	(8,000)
before tax of	4,000	Nil

A quick look at the balance sheet will tell us that, although a loss of £8,000 has occurred in year B, the shareholders' funds are £52,000 there is only borrowing of £8,000 (none of it from the bank) and the freeholds are probably undervalued. An experienced and skilful manager could go into an interview with this scant information and be able to ask all the relevant questions but it would make life much easier for him if an analysis of the figures was made beforehand.

Let us start with the ratios and see what they reveal:

	Year A	Year B
Rate of gross profit	$\dfrac{25 \times 100}{300}$	$\dfrac{17 \times 100}{250}$
	$= 8.3\%$	$= 6.8\%$

These are low gross profit percentages and perhaps prices are being kept down to compete with the multiple D.I.Y. stores. The actual gross profit is down from £25,000 to £17,000, a difference of £8,000 but the total difference in profit for the two years is a drop of £15,000 (from a profit of £7,000 to a loss of £8,000). The drop in the gross profit percentage together with the drop in turnover is therefore not the full answer for the cause of the loss in year B.

Rate of net profit
$$\frac{7 \times 100}{300} \qquad \text{nil}$$
$$= 2.3\%$$
(very small)

This would lead to an examination of the individual figures in the profit and loss account. Let us assume that the main changes are wages up by £4,000 and administration expenses up by £1,000.

	Year A	Year B
Current ratio		
$\dfrac{\text{current assets}}{\text{current liabilities}}$	$\dfrac{46}{34}$	$\dfrac{51}{30}$
	= 1.4	= 1.7

This is improving. Losses are being made and yet the working capital situation is better. Funds must therefore have been injected into the current assets and we must find out from where they came.

Rate of stock turnover
$$\frac{\text{average stock}}{\text{cost of sales}} \qquad \frac{22 \times 365}{275} \qquad \frac{27 \times 365}{233}$$
$$= 29.2 \text{ days} \qquad = 42.3 \text{ days}$$

The cost of sales has been obtained by deducting the gross profit from the turnover. The position has deteriorated considerably in the year.

Debtor ratio
$$\frac{\text{trade debtors}}{\text{sales}} \qquad \frac{20 \times 365}{300} \qquad \frac{18 \times 365}{250}$$
$$= 24.3 \text{ days} \qquad = 26.3 \text{ days}$$

All the debtors have been assumed to be trade debtors. The ratio seems satisfactory but the figures are false as a retailer will have many cash receipts.

Creditor ratio

$$\frac{\text{trade creditors}}{\text{purchases}} \qquad \frac{28 \times 365}{279} \qquad \frac{30 \times 365}{239}$$

$$= 36.6 \text{ days} \quad = 45.8 \text{ days}$$

All creditors have been assumed to be trade creditors which is probably incorrect, but we have no detailed information. The length of credit taken in year B would certainly seem to be appreciably longer than in year A and if there is no creditor pressure at the moment a continuance of the trend will bring this about.

$$\text{Debtors to creditors} \qquad \frac{20}{28} \qquad \frac{18}{30}$$

$$= 0.7 \qquad = 0.6$$

A slight worsening of the position but in a retail business one would not expect debtors to be large.

	Year A	Year B
Return on capital employed		
$\dfrac{\text{net profit before tax}}{\text{average of shareholder's funds}}$	$\dfrac{7 \times 100}{58.5}$	nil
	$= 11.9\%$	
Gearing		
$\dfrac{\text{loans}}{\text{net worth}}$	$\dfrac{6}{60}$	$\dfrac{8}{52}$
	$= 0.1$	$= 0.15$

Both figures show an insignificant amount of borrowing in relation to the net worth.

We are still left with some queries and the next stage is to make out a statement of sources and application of funds for year B. This is obtained by comparing the balance sheet figures for year A with those for year B, listing the differences and adjusting for items which do not necessitate the use of funds. The resultant statement will be as follows:

Sources		£
Profit (loss) in year		(8,000)
Adjustment for items not requiring the use of funds		
Depreciation . . . . ., .		5,000
Funds generated from operations . . .		(3,000)
Sale of marketable investments . . .		2,000
Sale of freeholds		10,000
Increase in loans		4,000
Increase in creditors		2,000
Reduction in debtors		2,000
		17,000

Application			
Tax paid		4,000	
Bank overdraft repaid		2,000	
Net purchase of plant and machinery .		1,000	(i.e. net with)
Net purchase of fixtures etc. . . .		1,000	(depreciation)
Increase of stock		6,000	
Increase of cash		3,000	
		17,000	

This analysis shows that although the company made a loss in the year, it sold freeholds and investments, reduced its debtors and increased its creditors. From these sources it produced £17,000. The funds were used to pay tax, to buy some additional plant and fixtures and to increase its working capital. An additional £6,000 has been put into stock and the bank overdraft has been repaid and £3,000 put into a credit account.

If we now relate these conclusions to the ratios we have calculated we see that the good liquid position has only been obtained from the sale of fixed assets. This obviously cannot continue. We are left to wonder why the amount of stock has increased when turnover is falling and the rate of turnover of stock is deteriorating. Is it possible to increase the gross profit percentage? Without an increase in the gross profit the amount of expenditure in the profit and loss account cannot be covered.

With this information a short report could be made with an indication of the questions to be asked. This will make the manager's job in the interview much easier and far more comprehensive than would otherwise be the case. On the face of it the account has been a good one, causing no trouble, and there seem to be plenty of assets with little borrowing. It

A Practical Approach to Bank Lending

might be that the customer would try to brush aside the loss in year B as being exceptional and non recurring but our analysis shows that there are deeper problems and tackling them now will be to the advantage of both the bank and the customer.

CASE 6

A problem which confronts branch bank managers when they have taken up a new appointment is whether to pay cheques on accounts which are in excess of their overdraft limits. At that time recourse has to be made to files, managers' notes, customer records, audited accounts, the banking account and any other information in the branch.

Let us consider what should be done in the following instance.

Nata Engineering Ltd has been a customer for two years having previously banked with a competitor. It has an overdraft limit of £70,000 and the account is overdrawn £78,000. The bank has a mortgage over a freehold factory valued at £80,000 two years ago, plus a guarantee of £30,000 from Mr and Mrs Pearce, the sole shareholders. The guarantee is supported by a second mortgage over the Pearce's house valued at £70,000 with a first mortgage outstanding of £24,000. Your assessment is that the forced sale value of the factory is around £40,000 to £50,000 and with the security of the guarantee you feel that the overdraft is just about covered by the security.

The balance sheets for the last two years are as follows:

as at 31st December	£	year A £	£	year B £	
Freehold factory		45,000		45,000	worth £80,000
Plant and machinery		18,000		17,000	
Motor Vehicles		22.000		19,000	
Debtors.		184,000		178,000	down in year
Stock		40,000		36,000	
Work in progress		34,000		30,000	down in year
		343,000		325,000	
less bank	81,000		73,000		
creditors	154,000		152,000		covered by debtors
directors' loans	12,000	247,000	12,000	237,000	
		96,000		88,000	

Capital	50,000		50,000	
Profit and loss account. .	46,000	96,000	38,000	88,000
Sales		560,000		500,000
Net profit (after tax) . .		18,000		(8,000) loss in year B
Directors' remuneration .		23,000		20,000

These figures show that sales fell in the year and a profit was turned into a loss. As far as liquidity is concerned the debtors cover the creditors and the net current assets are as follows:

		year A		year B
	£	£	£	£
Debtors.		184,000		178,000
Stock		40,000		36,000
Work in progress. . .		34,000		30,000
		258,000		244,000
less bank	81,000		73,000	
creditors . .	154,000		152,000	
directors' loans . .	12,000	247,000	12,000	237,000
		11,000		7,000

This amount of net current assets is small for a business of this size and even if the directors' loans were capitalised the amount would still be small. Normally one sees net current assets diminishing as losses are made and in this instance the loss has been absorbed partly by a drop in net current assets and partly by the reduced values of the fixed assets.

The proprietors' stake has dropped by £8,000, the amount of the loss, but it could be increased by £12,000 if the directors' loans were capitalised; also it is intrinsically more as the freeholds are undervalued by £35,000.

In all, the figures show that the business has had a drop in its turnover causing a loss and it has little in the way of net current assets. It is not 'down and out' by any means but a continuance of the trend could cause severe difficulties. Further analysis could be done by examining the profit and loss accounts with the balance sheets and working out the ratios of gross profit, net profit, length of credit given, length of credit taken, and expenditure to sales etc. This would enable one to pinpoint the weaknesses in the business from the financial point of view.

Let us also consider that in this case some management figures were submitted monthly to the bank and they are as follows:

	year B			year C		
	Dec	Jan	Feb	Mar	Apr	May
Debtors	180,000	179,000	177,500	177,500	178,000	179,000
Stock	38,000	38,000	38,000	37,000	37,000	37,000
Work in progress . .	30,000	31,000	30,000	29,500	29,300	28,700
	248,000	248,000	245,500	244,000	244,300	244,700
Directors' loans . .	12,000	12,000	12,000	12,000	12,000	12,000
P.A.Y.E. . . .	5,000	3,000	3,500	3,000	3,000	3,300
V.A.T.		7,000	3,000	3,500	3,000	3,700
Creditors. . .	144,000	137,500	142,000	137,000	137,800	137,000
Bank	73,000	77,500	75,000	78,000	79,000	80,000
	234,000	237,000	235,500	233,500	234,800	236,000
Net current assets . .	14,000	11,000	10,000	10,500	9,500	8,700

From the management figures we see that the net current assets are still dropping and this seems to indicate that losses are still continuing. The amount of the net current assets for December year B at £14,000 is above the £7,000 shown in the audited accounts for the same date and a comparison of the figures shows that the debtors in the management account are £2,000 above those shown in the audited accounts and the creditors plus the P.A.Y.E. in the management accounts are £3,000 less than shown in the audited accounts. The figures for work in progress and bank overdraft are the same in both sets of figures but the stock differs by £2,000. Some explanation is necessary.

Could it be that when it came to the audit that some debtors were considered bad or doubtful and were written off or a provision was made against them? Did some stock also have to be written off? How are the creditors less in the management accounts? Have some been omitted? The figures for V.A.T. seem odd. Why was it missed out in December year B? It should be accounted for monthly. It also looks as if the stock is only valued quarterly and an estimated figure is used.

The net current assets have dropped during the last six months and altogether it looks as if the business is still having its problems. The only action now to take is to have an urgent talk with the proprietors (and their accountants) in order to obtain the explanations required on the management accounts and to plan for the future. Obviously more accuracy is needed with the management account figures and some additional figures are required. What we have in this example are figures which throw up queries but not the answers. The answers would be more likely to be obtained if projected trading figures had been produced and then the actual figures compared with them. In the present instance these estimates are lacking but a start should be made now. Additionally it would be as well to ask for details of the debtors and creditors showing how much has been outstanding for one month, two months, three months etc.

Naturally a banker has to do his best with the figures he obtains and these are often less than he would wish. Apart from audited accounts he should aim, in appropriate cases, for a cash projection, estimated profit and loss figures and regular submission of actual figures for comparison. More detailed figures will be called for when the bank is concerned for its safety over its advance.

Figures received from customers should not be given a hasty glance and then filed away but should be given proper scrutiny. The normal procedure is:

1. Analyse balance sheets and profit and loss accounts and calculate any ratios and fund flow statements which will help to give an understanding of the accounts.
2. Compare the estimated figures with past results to see if they are feasible.
3. When actual trading figures are received compare them with the audited acccounts for accuracy and with the estimated figures for the trading trend.
4. Query any aspect which requires explanation.

CASE 7

In this case we will consider how to use the various systems for analysing and monitoring accounts. All the methods shown need not be used in all situations. Just use what is appropriate to the circumstances. However it is necessary to have a routine for examining balance sheets and management accounts or some vital information may be overlooked.

D.E.C. Limited is a wholesaler of domestic electrical components and appliances and has 4 working directors.

The account has worked satisfactorily for many years being a good swinging account with a limit of £175,000. The bank has a mortgage over the company's freeholds worth £250,000. A typical year's results is shown in the following balance sheet (year A).

In the following year the account exceeded the limit on several occasions and some solid borrowing developed. Excesses were allowed on production of evidence of funds shortly to be received but the account did not revert to the old pattern and the peak overdraft exceeded £225,000 on occasions. The directors asked for some tolerance until the audited accounts were ready.

Five months after the year end the accounts for year B were forwarded to the bank. The accounts for the two years were as follows:

D.E.C. Limited
year to 31st December

	Year A		Year B	
	£	£	£	£
Freehold factory . . .		250,000		250,000
Plant and machinery . .		220,000		180,000 ⎫
Motor vehicles . . .		110,000		82,000 ⎬ reduced
Fixtures, fittings, etc. . .		22,000		20,000 ⎭
		602,000		532,000
Debtors.	552,000		560,000	
Stock	200,000		215,000	
Work in progress. . .	108,000		97,000	
	860,000		872,000	slight increase
Creditors	406,000		588,000	
Tax	30,000			
Bank	160,000		250,000	
	596,000		838,000	large increase
Net current assets. . .		264,000		34,000 substantial
				reduction
Net tangible assets . .		£866,000		£566,000
Financed by Hire purchase .		160,000		90,000 large reduction
Directors' loans . . .		100,000		60,000 partly repaid
Share capital. . . .		100,000		100,000
Reserves		506,000		316,000 considerable
				reduction
		£866,000		£566,000
		£		£
Sales		2,800,000		2,400,000 big drop
Purchases		2,100,000		2,000,000
Gross profit		718,000		364,000 ditto
Net profit (loss) . . .		55,000		(190,000) loss year B
before tax . . .		30,000		nil

Directors' remuneration .	150,000	120,000 reduced
Depreciation of plant . .	50,000	70,000
ditto motors . . .	20,000	30,000
ditto fixtures etc. . .	4,000	4,000
Stock at beginning of year A	190,000	
Work in progress ditto. .	100,000	
Shareholders' funds ditto .	566,000	
Trade debtors . . .	540,000	545,000
Trade creditors . . .	370,000	570,000 large increase

It can be seen from the comments made that the items for which there are the biggest differences and require further examination, from a banker's point of view, are:

1.   the large increase in creditors and reduction of current assets
2.   the repayment of part of the directors' loans
3.   the considerable fall in turnover and the consequent change from a profitable year A to a loss in year B.

Let us see if further analysis by way of calculation of ratios and preparation of a statement of source and application of funds can help us further to understand what has gone wrong.

The ratios can be calculated in the same way as shown in case 5. They are as follows:

Ratios

	Year A	Year B
Rate of gross profit	$\dfrac{718 \times 100}{2,,800} = 25.6\%$	$\dfrac{364 \times 100}{2,400} = 15.2\%$
Rate of net profit	$\dfrac{55 \times 100}{2,800} = 19.6\%$	$\dfrac{(190) \times 100}{2,400} = (7.9\%)$
Current ratio	$\dfrac{860}{596} = 1.4$	$\dfrac{872}{838} = 1.0$
Rate of stock turnover	$\dfrac{299 \times 365}{2,082} = 52.4 \text{ days}$	$\dfrac{310 \times 365}{2,036} = 55.6 \text{ days}$

Debtor ratio	$\dfrac{540 \times 365}{2,800}$ = 70.4 days	$\dfrac{545 \times 365}{2,400}$ = 82.9 days
Creditor ratio	$\dfrac{370 \times 365}{2,100}$ = 64.3 days	$\dfrac{570 \times 365}{2,000}$ = 104 days
Debtors to creditors	$\dfrac{540}{370}$ = 1.5	$\dfrac{545}{570}$ = 0.96
Return on capital employed	$\dfrac{55 \times 100}{586}$ = 9.4%	$\dfrac{(190) \times 100}{511}$ = (37.2%)
Gearing	$\dfrac{420}{606}$ = 0.7	$\dfrac{400}{416}$ = 0.96

The rate of gross profit has fallen considerably and, not surprisingly, the net profit has also suffered. However, from the actual figures, we see that the gross profit has fallen by £354,000 (from £718,000 to £364,000) whereas the net profit has fallen by less than this figure i.e. £245,000 (from a profit of £55,000 to a loss of £190,000). An effort seems, therefore, to have been made to cut expenses and the reduction in the directors' fees seems to bear this out. The current ratio is just still in balance and the stock turnover has lengthened only slightly. Debtors have not been collected so quickly and creditors are now averaging more than three months. Borrowing is almost 1 for 1 with proprietors' funds.

Let us now turn to a statement of source and application of funds which can be produced from the figures given. It is as follows:

Statement of Source and Application of Funds
Year B

Sources

Profit (loss) in year	(190,000)
Adjustment for items not requiring the use of funds	
Depreciation	104,000
Funds generated from operations . . .	(86,000)
Decrease in work in progress . . .	11,000
Increase in creditors	182,000
Increase in bank overdraft	90,000
	£197,000

Application
Net purchase of plant and machinery	.	.	30,000	net with
ditto motor vehicles	.	.	2,000	depreciation
ditto fixtures etc.	.	.	2,000	
Payment of tax	.	.	30,000	
Increase in debtors	.	.	8,000	
Increase in stock	.	.	15,000	
Decrease in hire purchase	.	.	70,000	
Repayment of directors' loans	.	.	40,000	
			£197,000	

This shows, as the main feature, the large increases in creditors and bank overdraft offset in some way by a decrease in the H.P. debt, repayment of directors' loans and some purchase of fixed assets.

With these analyses we are now fully equipped to interview the directors about their trading experience in year B, their plans for the coming year and their requirements for bank facilities.

Let us consider that we are told:

1. Considerable price cutting took place in the trade in the past year because of cheap foreign imports. The importers causing the trouble have now got into financial difficulties and have ceased trading. Profit margins have therefore reverted to their normal previous level and for the first six months of the current year the company is breaking even.

2. A director withdrew temporarily £40,000 of his loan to cover a shortage of bridging finance for a house purchase pending the sale of his present house. The sale is due for completion in a few weeks' time and the £40,000 will be reinjected. An apology was made for not informing the bank and a promise made that such a withdrawal would not be made again without the bank's consent.

3. Creditor pressure has built up and the directors are anxious to reduce the level considerably. They are devoting more effort to methods of reducing their debtors and estimate that they can soon generate £40,000 by better collection systems.

4. From the above two sources £80,000 can be produced for reducing the creditors and the directors also said that they would like to have an additional £100,000 from the bank. This would also be used to bring the creditors down to a more reasonable level. As the bank

overdraft was standing at around £250,000 this would mean having a limit of £350,000.

5. The directors stress that they have been good customers of the bank for many years and they say that they are confident of making £40,000 in the second half of the year and, because of past losses, this will be tax free. In the coming twelve months they consider that a reduction in the bank overdraft of £60,000 to £70,000 will be achieved.

After detailed discussions and considerable pressure from the directors we will assume that it was agreed to give them the help they required but on the following terms:

1. A profit forecast to be produced.
2. A cash projection to be produced.
3. Actual cash figures for comparison with the forecast to be produced monthly.
4. A debenture to be given to the bank with the stipulation that the current assets should be maintained at at least twice the amount of the bank debt.
5. Figures for current assets and current liabilities to be produced quarterly.

The profit forecast was as follows:

Profit forecast year C

1st half of year   break even

2nd half of year	£	£
Turnover		1,500,000
Gross profit (margin 25%)		375,000
Less Rates	25,000	
Electricity	3,000	
Oil	5,000	
Salaries	120,000	
Directors' fees	60,000	
Depreciation	55,000	
Office expenses	27,000	
Travelling expenses	7,000	
Entertainment expenses	3,000	
Interest	20,000	
Sundries	10,000	
Net profit	40,000	
	£375,000	£375,000

The procedure with such a forecast is to check it with past results and with the statements made by the directors.

The turnover is shown as being recovered from the previous fall and the gross margin has improved. The figures for the expenses can be checked with the past profit and loss accounts; from the skeleton figures we have been given it looks as if aprropriate allowance has been made for depreciation and for interest charges.

The cash projection was as follows:

Cash Projection

					year C			year D		
	July	August	September	October	November	December	January	February	March
RECEIPTS									
Debtors	250,000	285,000	285,000	250,000	250,000	220,000	230,000	245,000	250,000
Director	40,000								
Total receipts	290,000	285,000	285,000	250,000	250,000	220,000	230,000	245,000	250,000
PAYMENTS									
Creditors	280,000	280,000	250,000	280,000	218,000	190,000	200,000	200,000	190,000
Rates				12,500					
Electricity	1,000		600			1,000			1,000
Oil						2,500			1,500
Salaries	8,000	8,000	8,000	8,000	8,000	8,000	8,000	8,000	8,000
Directors' fees	3,000	3,000	3,000	3,000	3,000	3,000	3,000	3,000	3,000
Office expenses	1,000	1,500	3,000	3,000	2,500	2,500	2,500	2,000	2,000
Travelling	500	500	500	500	600	600	600	600	600
Entertainment	200	200	200	250	250	350	250	250	250
Interest			8,000			12,000			12,000
P.A.Y.E.	4,000	4,000	4,000	4,000	4,000	4,000	4,000	4,000	4,000
VAT			15,000			15,000			15,000
Sundries	800	800	800	800	800	800	800	800	800
	298,500	298,000	293,100	312,050	237,150	239,750	219,150	218,650	238,150
Net cash in	18,500	13,000			12,850		10,850	26,350	11,850
Net cash out			8,100	62,050		19,750			
Bank overdraft (30th June £250,000)	268,500	281,500	289,600	351,650	338,800	358,550	347,700	321,350	309,500

This also must be checked as to feasibility.

There are larger sums being collected from debtors in the early months and similarly larger payments from creditors. This bears out the statements of the directors. Also we see the £40,000 loan reinjected. The cash projection must, of course correlate with the estimated profit and loss account and we can see that the figures shown are similar and that the amounts for salaries, directors' fees plus P.A.Y.E. are near in total.

There are some small excesses above the £350,000 limit in October and December and this is not good enough. On being tackled about this the directors say that they have been cautious in preparing the figures and that they will ensure that the account does not exceed the limit and that they will personally inject further money if necessary in order to avoid excesses.

With this assurance the company was allowed to proceed to use the new limit.

The next stage, in chronological order, is the production of the actual monthly cash figures to compare with the projection. We will assume that these have been produced for the months up to November and they agree reasonably well with the projection and that also the bank overdraft did not exceed the limit.

The current assets and liabilities figures for September and December were as follows:

Current assets and current liabilities

	September £	December £
Debtors	500,000	480,000
Stock	210,000	220,000
Work in progress	100,000	110,000
	810,000	810,000
Preferential Creditors	4,000	21,000
Other creditors	506,400	469,000
Bank	289,600	350,000
	800,000	840,000
Level of current assets required 2 x bank debt	579,200	700,000

Apart from checking these figures to see that sufficient current assets are held to cover the requirements of the maintenance clause in the debenture the figures should also be compared with those in the last balance sheet.

It will be seen that the net current assets on 31st December year B were £34,000 and they dropped to £10,000 by September and to minus £30,000 by December. The reason will either be a reduction of current assets because losses have been made or a withdrawal from the current assets for payment of a dividend or purchase of fixed assets. On being tackled about this the directors were evasive but they promised that the new balance sheet would be available shortly and they would then call for a full discussion.

Before the balance sheet figures were produced the monthly cash actual figures were due. They were late in coming and pressure had to be exerted. Eventually the December figures were produced and were followed soon afterwards by the figures for January and February. The figures were as follows:

Cash actual figures

	December £	January £	February £
RECEIPTS			
Debtors	215,000	220,000	200,000
PAYMENTS			
Creditors	188,000	176,000	191,000
Electricity		1,000	
Oil		3,000	
Salaries and directors' fees	11,000	11,000	11,000
Office expenses	2,000	2,000	2,000
Travelling	1,000	1,000	1,000
Entertainment	300	400	400
Interest	12,000		
P.A.Y.E.		8,000	4,000
VAT		15,000	
Sundries	700	600	600
	215,000	218,000	210,000
Net cash in		2,000	
Net cash out			2,000
Bank overdraft	339,000	337,000	339,000
(30th November £339,000)			

One point which must be kept in mind is that the bank balance must be taken from the company's books as this will include cheques issued but not yet presented and possibly credits not yet banked.

An examination of the figures shows that the bank overdraft is almost exactly the same as in the original cash projection for November but it has not been reduced in January and February in line with the projection. There are other points, too, which call for enquiry. The P.A.Y.E. payment was not made in December and it looks as if a double payment was made in January. Also VAT has been paid later than forecast and delays of payments in both P.A.Y.E. and VAT are danger signals. If they had been paid at the correct time the overdraft limit would have been exceeded.

Before a satisfactory explanation could be obtained the balance sheet for year C was produced. It was as follows:

Balance Sheet 31st December year C

	£	£
Freeholds		250,000
Plant and machinery . . .		150,000
Motor vehicles		70,000
Fixtures, fittings, tools and equipment .		15,000
		485,000
Debtors	450,000	
Stock	220,000	
Work in progress	100,000	
	770,000	
Creditors	490,000	
Bank	350,000	
	840,000	
Net current assets . . .		(70,000)
		415,000
Hire purchase		30,000
Directors' loans		120,000
Share capital		100,000
Reserves		165,000
		415,000

Sales	2,500,000
Purchases	2,200,000
Gross profit	308,000
Net profit	(151,000)
Directors' remuneration . . .	120,000
Depreciation of plant and machinery .	30,000
Depreciation of motor vehicles . .	12,000
Depreciation of fixtures etc. . . .	5,000
Trade debtors	434,000
Trade creditors	440,000

Here again, we must have a routine for examining the figures. A preliminary look must be backed up by detailed analysis.

The procedure in a case such as this could be:

1.   Analyse balance sheets and profit and loss accounts and calculate any ratios and fund flow statements which will help to give an understanding of the accounts.
2.   If estimated figures are produced for future trading such figures should be compared with past results to see if the estimates are reasonable.
3.   Trading figures should be compared with any other figures previously submitted.
4.   Query any aspect which requires explanation.

We can see that the outcome for the year was quite different from the forecast and it seems that the directors had to inject more money (their loans are now £120,000) in order to keep within the overdraft limit. A comparison must be made with the management figures for December as previously submitted. It will be seen that the debtors in the balance sheet were £30,000 less than in the management figures. Does this mean that bad debts had to be written off? Also why was work in progress valued at £10,000 more in the management figures than in the balance sheet? These points require explanation.

To continue with our analysis we will calculate the ratios and prepare a statement for sources and application of funds.

The ratios can be worked as previously and they are set out below together with those for years A and B.

	year A	year B	year C
Rate of gross profit	25.6%	15.2%	12.3%
Rate of net profit	19.6%	(7.9%)	(6%)
Current ratio	1.4	1.0	0.9
Rate of stock turnover	52.4 days	55.6 days	52.6 days
Debtor ratio	70.4 days	82.9 days	63.3 days
Creditor ratio	64.3 days	104 days	73 days
Debtors to creditors	1.5	0.96	0.98
Return on capital employed	9.4%	(37.2%)	(44.3%)
Gearing	0.7	0.96	1.9

The main features revealed for year C are:

1. the rate of gross profit has not improved as expected
2. the debtor ratio shows the improved collection of debts
3. the creditor ratio shows that the additional funds were used to reduce the creditors.
4. the gearing is now high at almost 2 to 1.

Statement of Source and Application of Funds
Year C

£

Sources

Profit (loss) in year	(151,000)
Adjustment for items not requiring the use of funds	
Depreciation	47,000
Funds generated from operations	(104,000)
Decrease in debtors	110,000
Increase in bank overdraft	100,000
Increase in directors' loans	60,000
	166,000

Application

Decrease in creditors	98,000
Increase in stock	5,000
Increase in work in progress	3,000
Decrease in H.P.	60,000
	166,000

This statement shows that the funds produced from the increased bank overdraft, directors' loans and pressure on debtors were used, in the main to cover the loss, the decrease in debtors and the reduction in the H.P. debt. Not a happy outcome.

This full analysis has given us a good insight into the affairs of the company. The bank is safe with its security but the trading situation will have to be improved if disaster is not to fall upon the company and also cause trouble for the bank. It is fairly obvious that no competitor would be likely to take on this account and the bank is stuck with it. Efforts must be made to turn the business round. Detailed discussions will have to take place with the directors and their accountants and stricter control will have to be exercised over the timing of submission of figures. With the help of the accountants it might be possible to include monthly profit figures in the submissions to the bank. A loan account with regular reductions might be set up but the reductions will not be available if profits are not made or more money injected.

We need not take this example any further. The principle of analysis and comparison of submitted figures has been explained and similar procedures will have to be carried out during the future control of the account.

Not every account will need to be given this full treatment of analysis. There is no need to be slavish in making all the calculations on every occasion. Just be quite sure that nothing is being missed when the evidence is available.

7. New Ventures

The lending banker is regularly asked in the course of his work to supply money for new ventures. These may take the form of an extension to an existing business or of an entirely new undertaking, but in either case the proposition must be subjected to all the banker's routine but indispensable questions.

The following cases are intended to indicate the scope these questoins ought to have. The banker's role is not merely one of acceptance or rejection, and in many cases he is concerned to see what can be done to overcome weaknesses in the proposition before him and remould it into an acceptable form.

CASE 1

New Engineers Limited have kept an account for ten years and their present overdraft limit is £24,000, against which the bank holds as security a full guarantee of the directors supported by a life policy with a surrender value of £10,000, together with a debenture from the company.

The managing director approaches the bank to say that he has developed a new product about which he is very enthusiastic. Initial enquiries have been good and it is thought that the company will make very good profits in the years to come. He is anxious to explain all the details of the new product and invites the manager to the company's premises to show him what is involved in its manufacture.

Machinery costing £20,000 is required to make the new product in sufficient numbers for the expected market and the bank is asked to put up the whole of the money. There will be no additional security.

Naturally, in order to consider this proposition, it will be necessary to examine the company's audited accounts and banking account. Before we do this, however, it is worth commenting on the invitation to visit the factory and see the new process. It is always helpful to visit a customer's premises and see what he is doing. Apart from giving the bank manager a good inkling as to whether the business is organised efficiently or not, a visit is appreciated by the customer and helps to cement friendship. However, there are many thousand different occupations and industries, and a bank manager cannot be a specialist in the technical side of a customer's business, although he may well form an idea as to the quality and saleability of a product. The bank manager specialises in bank finance for individuals and businesses and he is not expected to be a specialist in other trades and professions. He naturally gains knowledge about the trades and industries carried on in the vicinity of his branch, but he remains a bank manager and not the ultimate authority on the advisability of putting a new product on the market.

I am stressing this point because it is quite usual for customers to press their bank managers (as in the present instance) to see what they are doing, in the belief that the manager will immediately become as enthusiastic as they are.

The point to bear in mind is that, if the customer is successful in his trade and his financial position warrants further bank assistance, his view on the probable success of a new project should be respected and he should be given the opportunity of justifying his belief. He should, however, shoulder the risk as the entrepreneur. If the customer has not been successful previously and his financial position does not justify further bank finance, then the fact that the bank manager sees the new product and thinks well of it will not enable the bank to put forward additional overdraft facilities by way of risk capital. This is not the function of the bank.

The details of New Engineers Limited are these:

Customer for 10 years
Overdraft limit £24,000
Security: debenture plus guarantee £24,000 (supported by
life policy value £10,000)
Requirements: additional £20,000 for new machinery
The audited accounts for the past two years show:

					Year A	Year B	
					£	£	
Current liabilities							
Bank	.	.	.	.	10,000	15,600	
Creditors.	.	.	.		14,000	19,200	
Directors' loans	.	.	.		12,000	12,000	
Total current liabilities	.	.			36,000	46,800	Similar increase to that
							for current assets

Hire-purchase	6,000	12,000	Large increase
	42,000	58,800	
Capital	2,400	2,400	
Total	44,400	61,200	
Current assets			
Debtors	12,000	16,000	
Stock	20,000	26,000	
Total current assets . . .	32,000	42,000	Not as much as current liabilities
Plant and machinery . . .	8,000	14,000	Increased, presumably by hire-purchase
Fixtures and fittings . . .	400	400	
	40,400	56,400	
Adverse profit and loss . .	4,000	4,800	
Total	44,400	61,200	
Trading turnover . . .	80,000	120,000	Up 50%
Net loss after tax . . .	4,000	800	
Directors' fees	30,000	30,000	
Net deficit	1,600	2,400	Increasing

The banking account shows that the account has been swinging between overdraft £8,000 and overdraft £26,000 (ie, in excess of the limit).

The picture we now have of the company's affairs is that current assets are insufficient to cover current liabilities; an additional commitment has been entered into for hire-purchase; losses have been made in both years and the company is insolvent.

However, if it is the intention of the directors to leave their loans in the company, we could consider the net worth as being £9,600. We also see that the loss in the second year has been considerably reduced, although trading turnover was increased by 50 per cent to bring this about. The capital element of the hire-purchase commitment has to be found from profits unless more capital is to be introduced; the solid bank borrowing will also have to be reduced from profits. As profits have not been made, we must know what the directors estimate will be the trading result for the present year. In answer to this query, they tell us that they consider they will keep the present turnover and through economies will just about break even on their present products. This is why they wish to develop the new line. This is a satisfactory reason and shows that the directors are aware that they cannot carry on without some change in their profit-making ability.

The directors (husband and wife) have drawn out £30,000 in each year, although this involved the company in a loss: if we combine the net losses with the directors' fees, we can see that the company and directors made £26,000 and £29,200 in the respective years. This could be considered as a very good return on the turnover and capital employed and would completely alter the picture of the company if we could have seen a substantial plough-back of directors' fees. This has not taken place, although of course it is still possible that the directors have saved more than the net losses shown in the accounts and will have the funds available to inject into the company now. This is a matter for inquiry but, if the directors say that their fees have been spent on their normal expenses, we are left with taking the audited figures at their face value as regards the company's losses.

If we now turn to the security aspect and we consider that the director's assets consist in the main of the life policy lodged as security and valued at £10,000, we could lend this amount in safety.

The debenture picks up current assets of £42,000 and practically nothing else, as the plant and machinery are on hire-purchase. Out of the current assets, stock takes up a large proportion and would fetch little in a liquidation. To lend up to half the current assets to this loss-making company with a large liability for hire-purchase would be taking a risk, but what proportion would be reasonable to lend would depend on the spread of the debtors, the length of outstanding accounts, and the type and saleability of stock. However, as we are looking to the life policy for £10,000, we must look to the debenture for the other £14,000, and, in the surrounding circumstances, the overdraft limit is certainly a full one. The company has in fact been exceeding its limit by £2,000 in the past and this is hardly justifiable.

The additional £20,000 required would increase the plant and machinery only, and, without going into any further details of whether any more working capital will be required for the new product, the bank's answer will have to be a refusal. Already the bank is providing more in the way of finance and support than the proprietors (bank, £24,000; proprietors, £9,600, plus security £10,000) and, although the new product may well be the salvation of the company, there is no certainty of success. The risk involved must be shouldered by the proprietors, who hope to make good profits, and not by the bank, which charges the lowest rate of interest normally obtainable, and thus receives no compensation for such risk-taking.

If we now try to suggest a method by which the bank could assist, we must put the onus and responsibility firmly on the proprietors, but at the same time provide the money to give the company a chance to make good. First of all, a cash projection should be requested. Then, if this stands up to scrutiny, an increased overdraft could be provided but only against readily realisable security, which the proprietors must understand would be sold if the substantial profits they anticipate do not come to fruition. If this is not understood at the outset, the bank could well be faced with seeing, in a year or two, a much larger solid overdraft which could not be eliminated without incurring the displeasure of the customer.

CASE 2

A customer aged 29 called John Stamp started a small company, Plastics Limited, four years ago with very little capital and has done well, with the result that on a realisation of its assets the company could produce £18,000. Mr Stamp has now been offered a very big contract which would provide him with a large amount of work for several years but for which he would have to obtain much bigger premises and new machinery.

He has examined several alternatives and wants to take advantage of the assistance granted in development areas. This is the proposition he puts to the bank:

1. He will wind down the activities of his present company over the following six months and realise its assets to produce £18,000.
2. He will purchase for £6,000 sufficient land in the development area to build a new factory, and will receive from the local council a grant of 75 per cent towards the cost of the land.
3. The factory premises will cost £48,000 and, of this, £36,000 will be lent by the local council and £12,000 will be obtained as a grant from the Government.
4. The new machinery will cost £105,000 and, in this case, a loan of £45,000 will be obtained from the Government with repayment over four years.
5. Expenses and working capital requirements will amount to £13,000.
6. He wishes to borrow £57,000 from the bank, made up as follows:

		£
Contribution towards land . . .		1,500
Contribution towards factory .		Nil
Contribution towards machinery . .		60,000
Expenses and working capital . .		13,000
		74,500
Less Cash available		18,000
		£56,500 say £57,000

7. He has no assets outside the company but offers the bank a debenture and his own guarantee for the full amount.

8. He stresses that his company is successful and that he has thereby proved his ability, and that the very lucrative contract, offered by a well-known company, will bring good profits for several years. In view of this contract, he sees no risk whatever.

To consider this proposition, we must make a few calculations. Although the capital of the company will start at £18,000, there will, after a time, be grants of £4,500 and £12,000 which we could class as a reserve. Out of the £18,000, £1,500 will be used towards the purchase of land. We therefore come to this position:

Current liabilities	£	
Bank	57,000	Large interest will be due
	57,000	Well in excess of current assets
Council loan	36,000 }	Large commitments for
Government loan	45,000 }	interest
	138,000	
Capital	18,000	
Reserves	16,500	
	172,500	
Current assets		
Cash	13,500	
	13,500	
Land and factory	54,000	Mortgaged to local council for £36,000
Plant and machinery	105,000	
	172,500	
Net worth	34,500	

It will be seen that the contract the company has obtained will have to be very lucrative to service the heavy liabilities. Also, the company will be very illiquid, and a debenture will only pick up the equity in the land and factory plus the plant and machinery, subject to any rights which the Government department may have. If the venture fails, the factory will, on sale, probably produce little if anything for the bank, and the plant and machinery only a fraction of the cost price. The bank could, of course, take a charge over the contract but this would be of little value in the event of a failure.

The company seems to be taking on liabilities which are too large for it. Despite Mr Stamp's enthusiasm at obtaining a contract which he considers to be a veritable goldmine, the risks involved are great. The only point in favour of the proposition is Mr Stamp's ability, but this cannot outweigh the other drawbacks. He should be protected from himself, and the dangers of trying to run too quickly should be explained to him.

In a proposition such as this it would be usual to expect a profit estimate and a cash projection to be produced even though such documents could hardly outweigh the drawbacks already apparent. The provision of estimates does, however, highlight for the banker the problems with which he would be faced if he agreed to the advance.

ESTIMATED PROFIT AND LOSS ACCOUNT FOR FIRST YEAR IN NEW FACTORY

Turnover, £220,000
Net profit before tax, £30,000 after interest payment of:
Council loan, £4,000
Government loan, £5,000
Bank overdraft, £6,000

Cash Projection (£000s)

Month	1	2	3	4	5	6	7	8	9	10	11	12
Opening overdraft	.	(4)	8	57	57	57	57	52	47	42	37	32
Payments out												
Land purchase . .	6											
Premises . . .	12	12	12	12								
Machinery . .			37	45	15							
Interest . . .						7.5						7.5
Loan repayments .												11
Trading payments .	0.5				15	25.5	30	30	30	30	30	30.5
	18.5	8	57	114	87	90	87	82	77	72	67	81

Receipts

	1	2	3	4	5	6	7	8	9	10	11	12
Grants	4.5			57								
Cash injected . .	18											
Trading receipts . .					30	33	35	35	35	35	35	35
	22.5	—	—	57	30	33	35	35	35	35	35	35
Closing overdraft .	(4)	8	57	57	57	57	52	47	42	37	32	46

A quick look at these figures brings out the salient points that a net profit before tax will be made of £30,000 and that the overdraft of £57,000 will be reduced to £46,000 by the end of the year. However, a more detailed look at the cash projections show that the premises are to be paid for over four months and that grants of £12,000 re the premises and £45,000 re the machinery are expected to be received in month four. It is unusual for grants to be paid quickly as the necessary documentation, inspections, and committee procedures have to be observed. It is, therefore, optimistic to expect the £12,000 grant on the premises to be received in the same month as the final payment made to the builder. It is also optimistic to expect the grant of £45,000 on the machinery to be paid before the final payment (see month five) is made for the machinery. Any delays will put the cash projection woefully adrift and it can easily be imagined that the bank overdraft could exceed £100,000 if Mr Stamp's pleas for accommodation pending receipt of grants were heeded.

This is not the end of the trouble, because trading receipts at a high level have to be obtained in months five, six and seven in order to keep within the overdraft figure of £57,000. This is too much to expect in the initial months of trading when settling into new premises and using new machinery. Teething difficulties are inevitable. The cash projection is therefore far too optimistic.

The contract may well be an outstandingly good one, but there is still a risk until the expected receipts accrue. This risk belongs to the proprietor, not the bank. Therefore, should Mr Stamp be adamant for action, come what may, the only way the bank could help would be if readily realisable security were produced and the owner of the security were aware that, if Stamp's dreams did not come to fruition, the security would be realised to repay the bank borrowing.

This type of arrangement is frequently the only way to help when new ventures are being considered. It is natural to stress the favourable aspects of a proposition when fortune seems only around the corner, and to think that disaster will be avoided. It is also much easier to do this when someone else is putting up the capital or shouldering risk without the expectation of reaping the rewards of risk-taking. In such circumstances, a bank will be acting as a real friend by making the customer realise that he takes the risk alone and that security will be forfeited without qualms if expectactions are not justified. This gives the customer a further chance to consider fully the risks involved and in many cases saves a great deal of suffering.

In the present instance, Mr Stamp might well consider the advisability of sharing his expected reward with another entrepreneur and selling some of his shares to someone with funds to support him in this enterprise. This he might not find too easy a task.

CASE 3

Bulk Stores Ltd is a grocery wholesale company which keeps its accounts at a competitor bank. Its directors come to us unexpectedly, proposing that our bank should handle the account of a new company they are intending to start. The details are promising: the new company, Mail Order Ltd, will have the sole selling rights for a range of specialised hardware items, and a turnover of £60,000 is expected in the first year of operation, rising to £120,000 thereafter. With turnover at this level, net profits should run at £14,000 per annum.

The new company will require £40,000 for the freehold of a small warehouse, £8,000 for initial stock, and £2,000 for expenses: a total of £50,000. Bulk Stores Ltd, which is a substantial local company employing a staff of 50, say that if we provide all the money they will guarantee the new company's account.

It might well strike a bank manager that this proposition presents a splendid opportunity for new business, and he will be strongly tempted to settle formalities as soon as possible to prevent Bulk Stores having second thoughts and offering the new account to their present bankers. This consideration will not help him when he begins to think about making enquiries. He cannot ask Bulk Stores' present bankers much about the firm's financial position withing giving the game away and if, on the other hand, he makes a cautious and generalised enquiry (like, for example, whether Bulk Stores are good for £50,000 over a period, and whether they are financially sound) he is not likely to get more than a guarded reply.

The banker who commits himself to lend at this point is simply leaping in the dark. The proprietors of the new company are not proposing to put a financial stake into it; it is a new venture, and it can only be surmised that Bulk Stores are financially sound. Stated in this way, it appears obvious that we have insufficient information, but propositions of this nature are often put to banks. It is essential for the banker to have an enquiring mind and remain unsatisfied with answers that do not make complete sense.

In this case it must be asked why Bulk Stores are coming to another bank; who will run the new company; and whether he has experience in the trade. We must also ask why the parent company intends to provide no stake apart from its guarantee, and it must be required to produce its audited accounts together with a detailed forecast and cash projection for the coming year. If the parent company is successful and substantial, and has obtained the services of someone well experienced in the trade, it would be as well to overlook the more unfavourable aspects of the proposition to get a share of the group's banking business: but this cannot be assumed. Full enquiries must be made and satisfactory answers obtained.

The audited accounts, when produced, reveal that the net worth of the company is £200,000 (which includes the introduction of £40,000 cash during the past year). There have been losses in the last three years of £14,000, £18,000 and £8,000 and the company is borrowing £80,000 from its bankers, who have the security of deeds quoted as £130,000. This puts an entirely different aspect on the proposition and emphasises the great value of making thorough enquiries at the outset.

It is plain to see that, as losses have been made for three consecutive years, Bulk Stores Ltd are apprehensive about approaching their present bankers for a larger overdraft for the new company's business. The £40,000 put in during the year has just covered the three years' losses and yet the company is still borrowing heavily against its property. If the value of the property is around the balance sheet figure of £130,000, it is difficult to see how the present bankers will be relieved of their lending, as it would be difficult to find another lender prepared to lift the borrowing in view of the losses made and the uncertainty of obtaining due interest and repayment instalments.

This case now cries out for a refusal to lend, but let us struggle with it further.

The parent company, although in difficulties at the moment, may in the course of time get out of them and might well then look favourably upon a banker who had tried to be helpful. It would be up to the banker to discuss the parent company's affairs thoroughly to find the reason for the losses and the possibility of profits in the future. There seems, from the figures, to be a weekness in management, and the company's ability to bring a new subsidiary immediately on to a profit-making basis must be suspect. However, if the banker feels satisfied after enquiries that a recovery in the parent company's fortune is possible and that the subsidiary company has a good chance of success, a modified scheme could be formulated. In this case the profit forecast and cash projection will have to be examined in detail.

As always, there are two possibilities. First of all, if the new company achieves success, there will be no worries and any help given could well be repaid by the receipt of good business. Secondly, if it is unsuccessful, it will be necessary to obtain repayment of the advance, and consideration must be given as to how this will be achieved. The parent company's guarantee will be difficult to turn into cash, as its bankers will hardly agree to an increased overdraft of £50,000 to relieve a competitor of its troubles. The directors should therefore be asked if there is any other readily realisable security available, and be made to understand that if trading is not successful it will be sold. It is wrong in the banking sense to look to security for repayment of an advance rather than to the proposition but, where we are trying to mould a request into some sort of acceptable form, perfection is impossible.

Failing such security, all that is now left is the warehouse which the company is expecting to purchase for £40,000. If it is freehold in a sought-after position, and a forced sale would produce say £28,000, a banker might well think it worthwhile to lend £24,000 (leaving a good margin for expenses and a drop in price) in order to get the new business. The customers would then have to find £26,000, and, if they are optimistic about the future of the new company, they might be able to find it for, after all, they found £40,000 to inject into the parent company the previous year.

If this suggestion does not meet with approval, there is nothing further that can be done.

CASE 4

A small private company, Makers Ltd, produces pre-fabricated items for the building industry and has had an account with you for a few years. The managing director and principal shareholder is well known locally and a good opinion is held of him and his company. The company has an overdraft limit of £12,000 which is used properly, and the freehold deeds of the company's premises (valued at £80,000) are legally charged as security. In other words, there is ample security for a good account.

The audited accounts for the last three years are as follows:

	Year A	Year B	Year C	
Current liabilities	£	£	£	
Bank	8,000	10,000	12,000	Small
Creditors . . .	14,800	25,000	26,000	Similar to debtors
Taxation . . .	400	3,000	8,000	
Total current liabilities	23,200	38,000	46,000	Slightly exceeds current assets
Capital	6,000	6,000	6,000	
Reserves . . .	18,000	28,000	42,000	Large increases
Total	47,200	72,000	94,000	
Current assets	£	£	£	
Cash	400			
Debtors . . .	12,000	20,000	22,000	
Stock	13,600	16,000	18,000	Small in relation to turnover
Total current assets	26,000	36,000	40,000	
Freeholds . . .	10,000	20,600	35,200	Annual increases
Plant and machinery .	10,000	14,000	18,000	
Fixtures and fittings .	1,200	1,400	800	
Total	47,200	72,000	94,000	
Turnover . . .	142,000	202,000	260,000	Annual increases
Net profit before tax .	2,800	13,000	22,000	
Tax	400	3,000	8,000	
Net profit after tax .	2,400	10,000	14,000	Good annual increases
Directors' fees . .	18,000	24,000	32,000	
Dividends . . .	Nil	Nil	Nil	No distribution of profits
Net worth . . .	24,000	34,000	48,000	Increasing rapidly

It can be seen that this company is doing very well and is making good profits which are ploughed back to support the increasing turnover and to allow for increased expenditure on property. There is a slight illiquidity but this should cause no concern, as debtors are not far short of creditors, and in view of the profit record and the adequate security held by the bank more overdraft accommodation could undoubtedly be obtained.

The managing director now comes to the bank and says that the company needs bigger premises, and suggests a bank loan of £180,000 to build a new factory on some unused land on the firm's existing site. A banker's initial reaction might well be that the company has an excellent record, is making good profits, and that the request should be granted. But if he goes no further than this, he has failed to analyse the problem and may well be doing his customer a disservice. A proposition which a customer has perhaps been considering for weeks cannot be thoroughly assessed in two minutes. The enquiring mind of the banker should come into play, because there are still many answers to be sought:

   i Will there be other expenses apart from the basic building costs — such as site roads? Has an estimate been obtained? How long will the construction take before it is completed?

   ii Will new machinery be required? Will new fixtures be required? Will more staff be employed?

   iii Will sufficient work be available to justify the new factory? Will more stock be necessary?

There will be other questions, depending on the particular circumstances disclosed. It will suffice to say that the banker should try to get a thorough understanding of the whole position.

Let us suppose that the general trend of the answers is that sufficient money will be available from profits to provide for all additional stock and machinery and that so many orders are now being turned away because of lack of space that there will assuredly be no lack of work in the future.

In other words, £180,000 only will be required.

The interest on a sum of this nature will be large and, although it will depend on current interest rates, let us suppose for the sake of this example that it will be approximately £18,000 per annum. This payment of interest would of course make a big dent in the profit figures and would have reduced the net profit before tax from £22,000 to £4,000 in the final year for which audited accounts have been produced. From where, therefore, will the annual repayments come? Are there forward projections of turnover, profits and cash? Optimism about future results is one thing, but realising them is not always easy. Regardless of the company's record it is difficult to see such a large increase in profits being obtained to enable the company to repay the bank over a relatively short number of years.

The company's stake is £48,000, or £92,800 if we add the equity in the property of £44,800 (difference between value £80,000 and £35,200 quoted in accounts), but it is asking the bank to put up twice this amount. A factory is not an easily saleable building, and adequate security for the advance would be a problem. If, after the factory was completed, orders did not flow in as anticipated, a substantial loss would quickly be made and a banker who lent on such a proposition might well be helping a progressive little company into eventual liquidation by overstretching its resources.

A refusal should be given, but this should be tempered by an explanation of the facts as seen through banking eyes. If the customer is still determined to build the new factory, then the proper financial requirements should be indicated.

Since a considerable risk is being taken, the correct method is for more risk capital to be introduced. If this cannot be done, the alternative is to obtain long-term finance with annual repayments of small amounts. The whole of the site could be used as security for long-term finance (after clearing the small banking overdraft) and not just the new factory, and if a sufficiently firm offer were available to produce adequate funds on completion of the factory the bank could help with bridging finance. This offer would have to be from a reputable source, like an insurance company, and there would have to be no clauses enabling the long-term lender to opt out of the contract. This, I would stress, should be an important point of the bridging agreement, as the bank would be in a most unfortunate position if it were left with the lending at the end of the construction.

However, depending upon the amount of advance orders and future profitability, the most satisfactory solution would probably be for the company to forgo its large-scale plans and perhaps think of development on less ambitious lines.

CASE 5

A customer aged 27 who has kept a satisfactory account for several years calls to say that he wishes to buy a business. He has been trained as a ladies' hairdresser, has been in the trade for 10 years, and for some time has been looking for a business to buy.

He has now found one which suits him, at an asking price of £18,000. He can produce £8,000, this being £4,000 he and his wife have saved and

£4,000 which his father will lend him at 6 per cent per annum. He wishes to have £1,000 leeway in his calculations for emergencies and trading expenses and he therefore asks for £11,000, which will be secured by his father-in-law's guarantee supported by a second mortgage on the father-in-law's dwelling house, which has an equity of £28,000. He promises repayment at a minimum of £2,200 per annum to clear the borrowing in five years or less.

When questioned about the repayment, he says that his wife earns £80 per week and they intend to live on this in a flat above the business premises. The business is producing £5,500 per annum and the bank repayments will come out of this. He also expects to increase the turnover and the net profit. It seems fairly obvious that this customer has thought out his requirements well and has put forward a good case. He has proved his ability to save and he has the backing of both his own and his wife's father.

The Customer's Interest

Should a bank manager make any further enquiries? Yes, he should, both in the interests of the bank and the customer. People wishing to start in business on their own account are often so anxious to be rid of the status of employee that they overlook any snags that there may be in changing it. This, of course, is very often the case with young people who wish to travel quickly and are liable to run into trouble, and a bank manager should therefore try to help his customer to see propositions in their correct light.

He will want to check that the business is producing £5,500 per annum, and in the present instance the following figures are produced:

CONTINENTAL SALONS LIMITED

	Years	A	B	C	D	
Current liabilities		£	£	£	£	
Creditors . . .		200	400	600	400	Small
Loans . . .		12,000	12,000	12,000	12,000	Constant
Total current liabilities	.	12,200	12,400	12,600	12,400	
Hire-purchase . .					2,000	First time in year D
		12,200	12,400	12,600	14,400	
Capital		200	200	200	200	No reserves
		12,400	12,600	12,800	14,600	

				A	B	C	D	
Current assets				£	£	£	£	
Cash .	.	.	.	600	800	600	400	Small
Debtors	.	.	.	400	300	200	200	Small
Stock.	.	.	.	200	400	600	200	Small
Total current assets	.	.		1,200	1,500	1,400	800	
Leasehold	.	.	.	8,000	8,000	8,000	8,000	Constant
Plant and machinery	.	.		1,500	1,400	1,700	4,100	Large increase
				10,700	10,900	11,100	12,900	
Goodwill .	.	.	.	1,700	1,700	1,700	1,700	Constant
				12,400	12,600	12,800	14,600	
Turnover	.	.	.	11,000	12,600	15,200	18,000	Rising
Net profit after tax	.	.		Nil	Nil	Nil	Nil	
Directors' fees	.	.		2,000	2,200	2,800	3,500	
Net deficit	.	.	.	1,500	1,500	1,500	1,500	

From the profit and loss account we see that all expenses are fairly constant and that there are no unduly large amounts. The annual rent is £1,000 per annum, with rates approximately £400 per annum. the accounts show us therefore that this business is improving annually with a rising turnover generating increased directors fees which, nevertheless, are small. There is no profit left in the business as this is all drawn as fees. Although there is a net deficit of £1,500 it is probable that the loan of £12,000 has been provided by the directors, which would make the directors' stake £10,500. During Year D more equipment was obtained on hire-purchase terms. We see also that there is a lease which has not been depreciated. Goodwill also is a constant figure.

On enquiry we find that the lease will expire in nine years' time.

What Kind of Bargain?

What therefore is the customer purchasing for his £18,000? No doubt the loans will be withdrawn, but what is to happen to the hire-purchase liability? Is it a condition that this will be paid by the present proprietors or will it be a liability of the new owner? Enquiry is necessary. Apart from this there is little in the balance sheet but the lease and the goodwill, and the point to consider is whether these two items are worth £18,000 less the value of the plant and machinery (£4,000 or £2,000 dependent upon the hire purchase position).

If we first consider the lease, we see that it is in the balance sheet at £8,000 and has been so for at least four years. A short lease depreciates rapidly in value and it would have been usual to see a figure for depreciation. If it has in fact kept its value, then rents must have risen sufficiently to offset depreciation. This can only be determined by getting the opinion of a valuer familiar with the district: valuing a short-term lease is not a job for an amateur. On the face of it, the lease may well be overvalued.

The goodwill is in the balance sheet at £1,700 but we can see that the profits of the company plus directors' fees totalled only £5,500 in Year D. Cannot the customer earn as much as this in wages? If so, he is getting no advantage in making a payment for goodwill. Possibly he can see that turnover and profits will rise in the future, but this will be due to his own hard work. There is little point in paying for goodwill which he will then have to create himself.

On the facts available it certainly looks as if too large a price is being paid and if, after discussing this, the customer still wishes to proceed, he should be advised to consult both a valuer and an accountant before committing himself. If we consider now his future earnings, we see that the directors' fees of £5,500 will be eaten into by the interest that will have to be paid on both the money borrowed from the bank (£11,000) and from his father (£4,000). What a tragedy it would be if the business were purchased without further thought and it was then found that the lease was depreciating rapidly, goodwill was negligible, and that the business was not a success. The wife's father might then find his house in jeopardy.

This customer deserves encouragement and help from the bank, and the best help that can be given is to try and talk him out of going ahead with this purchase unless he can get the price considerably reduced. Otherwise he should look around for a more suitable business to buy.

Conclusion

It will be seen that although new ventures embrace a variety of schemes there are similarities in the way a banker tackles them. Apart from the normal considerations of bank lending the additional items to be considered are:

1. A thorough examination of the proposition at the beginning, and particularly before any money is lent.
2. An assessment of the risk, with risk capital to be provided by the entrepreneur.

3.   If the banker does put up risk capital, it should be secured by readily realisable collateral, and the person depositing the collateral must completely understand that it will be forfeited if the venture does not progress at a rate which is sufficiently satisfactory to provide adequate repayments over a short period of the amount borrowed from the bank.

8. Estate Development

Advances for estate development occur frequently, because considerable finance is necessarily tied up while development work is in progress and before sales can occur. The developer's problem is basically that he produces a relatively small but expensive number of units with slow sales as opposed to, say, a retail shop where prices are low and sales brisk. In a retail shop it does not make much difference to the overall financial position if one line of items fails to sell, but any delay in house sales can have a very large effect on the finances of a developer.

Let us consider the case of a builder who decides to develop a site sufficient for one house. He will need planning permission and must consider whether the site is suitable for building and in the right place to enable a sale of the finished house to be made. He will want the design to appeal to many prospective purchasers unless he is content to have the finished house unsold for a long period, and he will have to be confident that, when he achieves a sale, he will have made a reasonable profit. Additionally he will have to be certain of his labour force and supply of materials if delays are not to occur. Considerable planning is therefore necessary and as delays can occur through many factors like shortage of labour and materials, bad weather, or shortage of buyers, the wise builder will see that he has a reserve of finance available to meet unforeseen events.

If the builder does not provide all the finance himself but asks a bank to help, the bank will similarly wish to know that these points have been considered thoroughly. The bank may well wish a local agent to give his opinion whether a quick sale will be achieved, and it will also have to satisfy itself that the builder has sufficient experience to carry the transaction through in a satisfactory way. Finally, the bank will have to make sure that, should difficulties occur, the builder has a reserve of finance which he can use. This cushion of finance is very important as, unless it is available, the bank many well find itself in the position of accepting the risks of an entrepreneur, and this is not its business.

For example, if a plot of land cost £12,000 and was paid for by the builder, and building costs were estimated at £24,000 towards which the builder had another £4,000, the bank might provide £20,000. The bank might well be happy with this arrangement but, if £20,000 was the top figure to which it wished to go and the builder had no cushion of finance for an emergency, financial trouble could well materialise. This would be evident to the bank because, if all the finance were used before the house was completed, it would be unable to extricate itself without advancing more money to enable it to be finished. To prevent such a situation occurring, the banker must be confident that the builder is experienced and that a cushion of finance is available to meet contingencies: it is simply courting danger to agree to advance a maximum sum on a building project without considering where additional finance will come from in an emergency.

Developments as Security

If no other security is available and the bank is to take as security the house being built, it will be necessary to consider at what stage the building will be worth enough to be considered of some saleable value. The land is worth something just as a plot and lending 50 per cent of its value should see the bank safe in the event of a forced sale and also achieve the object of getting the builder to provide a reasonable stake. Naturally, digging of foundations, laying footings and doing all the preliminary work is of value to the builder, but if it came to a sale at that point (due the the builder's failure or some other cause) little beyond site value would be realised. It is normally advisable to have the roof on if the house is to be completed without difficulty by another builder and, if no other adequate security is available and the builder's finances do not warrant unsecured facilities, this is the point at which a start can be made to value the work for security purposes.

Lending up to two-thirds of the cost of the work done is a reasonable basis, and if one takes into account materials which the builder has provided but not yet used and the delay in certifying the work done, then the finance provided by the builder for the project would probably be near to one-half of the total. At the completion of the building the bank will have provided more finance than the builder, but at that stage, if planning has been good, the house should be under contract for sale and repayment of the advance will be quickly achieved. After the roofing stage, advances can normally be made on completion of plastering, and when the house is finished; this gives a total of three stages. A surveyor could certify the work done at each of them and the bank would then be able to lend two-thirds of the building costs plus two-thirds of the cost of the land. The proportionate increase of one-half to two-thirds of the cost of the land can be taken into account when the property is roofed.

If the builder is experienced, has a good balance sheet, and adequate capital which can be called upon in emergencies, the bank might well agree to advances in four stages — ie, plate (to top of walls), roofed, plastered, finished. In every case, however, both the formula and the stages should be agreed.

Stages of Completion

To take our simple example of one house being built on land costing £12,000 with construction costs of £24,000 for an estimated sale at £48,000, we could come to the following stages for the advance:

Stages	Amount to be advanced
1. **Half cost of land**	£6,000
2. **Plate level**	
Half cost of land (as above) plus two-thirds cost of construction of £4,200	£8,800
3. **Roofing**	
Two-thirds cost of land (two-thirds of £12,000) plus two-thirds of construction costs of £8,400	£13,600
4. **Plastering**	
Two-thirds of cost of land (as above) plus two-thirds of construction costs of £15,600	£18,400
5. **Finished**	
Two-thirds of cost of land (as above) plus two-thirds of cosntruction costs of £24,000	£24,000

At this stage the builder would have provided £12,000 to complete the cost of £36,000 and a sale at £48,000 would realise a profit of £12,000. Alternatively, this could be expressed by saying that, in the house valued at £48,000, the bank's stake is £24,000 and the builder's £24,000, being his costs plus the additional value created.

Large-scale Developments

The principles involved in this simple example apply also to larger developments. Naturally, there are additional complications in dealing with big developments because when a number of houses are being built at once the stage of construction of each house varies. It is cheaper to build a large number of houses simultaneously, as labour can be used to its best advantage without wasted time, and materials can be bought in bulk, but a builder who does not have sufficient capital to build on a vast scale must tailor his development to his resources, getting the bank to agree to the number of houses to be built at one time or when it is reasonable to start another stage of development. If this is not done, and the builder's finances go awry, it may be necessary for the bank to insist that the houses are completed, say, one at a time, in order that sales can take place to bring in more cash. Such disruption of work can easily lead to losses and it is therefore important to see that a proper plan of work is arranged at the outset. A cash projection will enable financial requirements to be seen easily and should always be provided.

In present-day developments, it is often a condition of local authorities that service roads shall be built for estates, and this cost, which is an initial one, must be taken into account. Often a developer asks a bank to advance up to 50 per cent of the cost of service roads and, for an experienced developer, this is reasonable.

Local councils often ask for indemnities concerning the construction of service roads and if a bank is asked to join in an indemnity for a builder it must regard the liability as a real one because local authorities are strict in seeing that their requirements are met. This might mean additional expense to comply with the requirements and the bank may have to advance more money to a builder if the service road is not up to standard. At the outset, therefore, the bank must find out if indemnities are required and consider whether it is able to enter into such liabilities as well as provide the building finance. If the bank feels unable to do so it should advise the builder to approach an insurance company for his indemnity requirements.

Another point which must be taken into account is the amount of retention money and the period for which retained. This is a capital requirement and the builder should have enough resources to provide for all the money he is likely to have tied up in retentions at any given time. A banker should enquire about this when the advance is arranged as he may otherwise find himself lending money in anticipation of repayment of retentions, and if there are defects in the builder's work the retention moneys will not be released until they are rectified.

Repayments

The final point which must be covered in initial discussions with the builder is the eventual repayment of the advance. If his plans are for houses costing £36,000 and selling at £48,000 there should be no difficulty in the advance being repaid if no hitches occur, because it covers only part of the cost and, if all sale proceeds are received into the bank account, it should be repaid before the development is completed. However, difficulties do occur and houses are sometimes sold at a loss. It is therefore essential for the bank to see that at least the amount advanced on each house plus interest is received in reduction of the loan from the sale proceeds of each house.

Trouble most often occurs when other security is deposited with the bank to cover the amount or part of the amount required. To have difficulties then might seem incongruous, because additional security should make the bank advance safer. In fact, it does, providing that the same detailed control is kept over the progress of the building work, which includes seeing that the amount advanced for each house is repaid on sale of that house. However, if the additional security makes the bank feel so safe that it does not keep detailed control, if may well find that the development is proceeding at a loss, or that funds are being used for another purpose. Towards the end of the development, although the bank will no doubt be safe with its outside seccurity, it may well be wondering how repayment is to be effected.

A simple plan of the development will be necessary, or, alternatively, the builder can provide a copy of his own plan for the bank's use. For example, a plan such as the following should suffice:

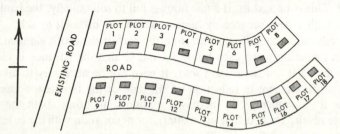

1st Stage — Plots 1 to 6
2nd Stage — Plots 9 to 14   Cost price of land: £216,000 — ie, £12,000 per plot
3rd Stage — Plots 7 and 8, 15 to 18   Cost of services: £54,000

The plan should be marked following regular inspections of the development so that it can easily be seen how it is proceeding. It will also be necessary for a record sheet to be kept in order to calculate the lending figure in accordance with the formula agreed with the customer. Sometimes the individual houses will vary considerably in cost but more usually the range will not be wide and an average cost per house can be applied.

A typical record sheet is shown on the next page.

Loan Account Method

If it had been agreed with the builder that bank finance up to £300,000 would be made available, the best method of control would be to open a separate loan account termed, say, Yew Tree Estate account, and on each valuation date to calculate the lending amount in accordance with the formula (less, of course, deposits, progress payments received, and the agreed sum from the final payment) and to transfer sufficient from the Yew Tree Estate account to the customer's current account to make the debit balance on the Yew Tree Estate account equal to the amount of lending as calculated. All deposits and progress payments should be credited to the Yew Tree Estate account as well as the agreed sum from the final payment.

It will be seen from the record sheet that for plot 1 the total cost was £35,000 and the total sale proceeds amounted to £47,000. The amount advanced by the bank was £23,330 (⅔ of £35,000) and out of the total sale proceeds £31,330 was credited to the Yew Tree Estate account. It will be obvious that at least £23,330 should be used for repayment but, if only an equivalent amount to that advanced is repaid on the sale of each house, the final repayment of the bank advance will not take place until every house is sold. This is unwise as, if a few houses fail to sell quickly, the bank will be left with a debt secured by houses which are difficult to sell.

It is advisable, therefore, to arrange for part of the profit element to be used in reduction when each house is sold so that the advance is cleared before the final few houses are sold. It need not be necessary to take any of the profit element in reduction on the sale of the first few houses but to take it subsequently, in increased amounts, to bring about the same ultimate result. These details are matters for negotiation with the customer.

By using this method, it will be seen that tight control can be exercised over the building finance and that, if bank money is being used for purposes other than the building of the estate or the costing has been wrong, this

Record Sheet

Yew Tree Estate Development of 18 houses
Cost of land: £216,000; £12,000 per plot   Cost of services: £54,000 (being paid by company)

Building cost: £23,000/£25,000 per house
Total cost including plot: £35,000/£37,000 per house
Sale Price: £47,000/£49,000 per house

Lending limit £300,000 subject to formula of ½ cost of undeveloped plots plus ⅔ of development costs in three stages: (1) Roofed (2) Plastered (3) Finished.

Lending formula per house	Cost	Lending value
½ cost of plots	£12,000	£6,000
⅔ of development costs (plus cost of plots)		
(1) roofed	£19,600/£20,320	£13,060/£13,540
(2) plastered	£27,200/£28,640	£18,130/£19,090
(3) finished	£35,000/£37,000	£23,330/24,660

Reduction in limit £8,000 per house sold

No. of Plot	Costs and land (as per agreed scale)					Sales arranged date and amount	Deposit/ payments received	Final payment received	How applied
	10 Apr.	10 May	10 June	12 July	11 Aug.				
1	12,000	19,600	27,200	35,000	—	25.5 £47,000	28.5 £12,000 14.6 £7,600	20.7 £27,400	£11,730 to Yew Tree account £15,670 to current account
2	12,000	19,600	27,200	35,000	—	11.6 £47,000	13.6 £12,000	14.7 £35,000	£19,330 to Yew Tree account £15,670 to current account
3	12,000	19,600	27,200	35,000	35,000	14.7 £47,000	19.7 £24,000		
4	12,000	20,320	28,640	37,000	37,000	13.7 £49,000	18.7 £12,000		
5	12,000	20,320	28,640	37,000	37,000	13.7 £49,000	18.7 £12,000		
6	12,000	12,000	12,000	20,320	20,320				
7/18	144,000	144,000	144,000	144,000	144,000				
Totals									
Undeveloped plots	216,000	168,000	156,000	144,000	144,000				
Developing plots	—	79,120	130,560	190,960	129,320				
Lending value	108,000	136,720	165,020	199,280	158,190				
Less amounts received	—	—	12,000	31,600	48,000*				
Less reduction on houses sold	—	—	—	—	16,000★				
Effective limit	108,000	136,720	153,020	167,680	94,190				

*This figure is the total of payments received on plots 3, 4 and 5

★This is the agreed reduction of £8,000 per house on plots 1 and 2

will be evident when the builder cannot manage to keep his current account in credit.

The reduction terms must be worked out in a practical manner as otherwise the builder's finances will be upset. Although a limit of £300,000 is applicable in this illustration, it is not necessary to make the reductions per house total £300,000 as part of the money received into the loan account will be repayment of the costs advanced for the building work.

For example, if we consider the situation after 14 houses have been sold and imagine that the remaining four houses will all have been completed at a cost of £37,000 each, the position will be:

Totals: 4 x £37,000	£148,000
Lending value: 4 x £24,660	£98,640
Less amounts received: 14 houses at £8,000	£112,000
Effective limit	Nil

Current Account Method

There is another method commonly used for building advances and that is when the borrowing is taken on a current account. In the present instance, with bank lending up to £300,000 being available, the same effective limit would be calculated in accordance with the formula as before and this would be the amount up to which the current account could be overdrawn.

This method works perfectly well with reliable and capable customers but it is easy to see that if the customer has items other than the building finance passing through the account it will not be easy for the bank to keep close control, and indeed the control will have largely passed to the customer. This occurs if a builder is doing jobbing building at the same time as developing an estate or if money is being used for purposes other than the estate development. Any financial difficulties can be masked from the bank for a time and it is therefore deprived of the early warning of danger which is given when the loan account method of advancing is used.

In the same way, when a builder is developing more than one estate it is advisable to open separate loan accounts for each estate. The houses on one estate may sell quickly while those on the other estates may be slow to sell. If the lending is arranged on current account, the unsold houses on one estate will be valued as security and the sales on the quick selling estate will provide the movement in the account, and the overall position will seem satisfactory. The effect will be, however, that the bank advance will be covered by houses which are difficult to sell. Separate loan accounts for each estate and separate arrangements also should make it easy for the bank to see immediately if one estate is selling slowly and call for an early rearrangement of the building programme.

Summary

I have referred up to now to builders as being the developers of sites but this is not always the case, as many estates are planned and brought to fruition by developers who employ builders to erect the houses. The same considerations apply, however, but where a developer is concerned it will also be necessary to make enquiries to establish that the builders to be employed are competent.

If, instead of houses, a block of flats is being built, the proposition will be of a more speculative nature and a lending proportion at one-half of costs instead of two-thirds would be wiser. Sometimes, a bank is asked to finance the purchase of land for future development and it is natural for an active developer to keep a reserve of land available. For good customers, bank finance should be available but as such finance is predominantly short-term, a reserve of one or two years' supply should be all that a bank could help to finance.

A bank, when considering finance for a development, will have to take into account all the usual banking criteria and ask the normal questions which apply to all requests for finance, but, as explained, there are certain specific items which must also be covered and for ease of reference they are listed below:

Has planning permission been obtained?
Is the site suitable?
Are the houses to be of a type which will sell easily?
Are the builders competent?
What is the plan for developing the site?
What will be the amount tied up in retentions?
What will be the arrangements for repayment of the advance?
Is a cushion of finance available?
Has a cash projection been prepared?
Are indemnities required?

CASE 1

One of the bank's customers, an arcitect with a reputation for skill and originality in the design of freehold houses, wanted to reap a direct benefit from his ability. He persuaded members of his family to put money into a specially formed company, Good Build Ltd, and set up as a developer. The company spent £96,000 on a freehold site for six houses which it planned to build at a total cost of £144,000 and sell at £56,000 each.

The bank was asked to lend £144,000, on a formula of one-half cost of land plus two-thirds building costs, and the architect was confident that there would be no difficulty in selling the finished houses. He had some knowledge of the local builders and felt he had chosen the one who was both the most efficient and the strongest financially. Planning permission had been obtained. This, then, was the customer's proposal in outline:

	£	£
Total sales at £56,000 per house		336,000
Less Cost of land	£96,000	
Cost of building	£144,000	240,000
Profit		96,000
		£
Half cost of land		48,000
Two-thirds building costs		96,000
Financial requirement from bank		144,000

The architect's financial requirements matched the lending formula, the bank knew that the builder he had chosen was good, and the local estate agent said that there should be a reasonable demand for the houses. The advance was therefore agreed and the customer was confident of repaying it within 12 months.

The start of the scheme was delayed for three months owing to the illness of the architect and some re-arrangement of the builder's commitments, but satisfactory site inspections were subsequently held at monthly intervals and advances made in accordance with the agreed formula. When the bank advance had reached £128,000, and the six houses, although progressing well, appeared to be still in need of considerable work, a sudden crisis occurred. The architect reported that a rift had developed between him and the builder, who refused to continue on the site without a further payment of £40,000. The builder claimed that the price of building materials had risen sharply during the three month's delay and that the architect had subsequently interfered with the work by altering the plans and specifying more expensive items than originally stipulated. The architect put his own side of the case, but the bank was less interested in deciding where the blame lay than getting out of serious trouble; the architect was planning to switch to another builder and the existing one had instructed his solicitors to take action.

The bank decided to instruct surveyors to examine the site, and their detailed estimate of the cost of completing the scheme came to £72,000. By this time, the architect realised that the builder had purchased special fittings necessary for completion of the houses which, if he did not go on employing him, would have to be made again, with consequent further delay. The bank asked the architect if he could find further finance but was told that he had no funds and neither had Good Build Ltd, the company he was using as a vehicle for the development.

This, then, was the position facing the bank:

1. The debt was £128,000 and the request was for a further £40,000 to get the builder to continue.
2. On top of this another £72,000 was required to complete the scheme.
3. Contracts for sales had not materialised, and the tentative approaches of prospective purchasers had come to nothing, because news of the dispute was common gossip.
4. Lending by the bank, at £240,000, would be greatly in excess of the formula envisaged and, as the customer had no further funds, this placed the bank in the position of risk-taker and organiser. The bank would have to control the work, make necessary payments and, at the same time, endeavour to sell the houses through agents.
5. There would now be no profit for the customer, but at this point he would mainly be anxious to make as little loss as possible on the venture.
6. The bank could well decide to complete one house at a time in order to limit its liability, but this would mean more expense as the labour force would not be able to be used in the most efficient way.
7. Thus additional unremunerative work would be necessary merely to recover the amount of its lending.

This case shows how a building advance can go sour, but an examination of the points which I previously set out as being necessary for consideration when dealing with this type of advance will show why the advance was doomed from the outset unless luck happened to be with the customer.

First, no plan was made to show how the site would be developed and what cash was necessary at each stage. If this had been done, it would have been obvious that the six houses were to be developed simultaneously and sales could not therefore be completed until the whole site was developed. Second, no one asked whether the customer had any funds for an emergency and, in the event, it transired that all his money had been used for the purchase of the land. All subsequent expense therefore fell upon the bank; this lack of a cushion of finance was fundamental.

If a thorough examination of the scheme had been made at the outset, a workable arrangement could still have been made by keeping the expenditure within bounds and arranging for, say, one or two houses to be completed at a time and subsequent houses to be built when sales had been achieved. Into the cash projection would have appeared retentions but, by not overstretching his finances, the customer would have been able to take these into account without worry and could no doubt have completed the scheme over a longer period and at a profit. Had severe difficulties arisen, a cushion of finance would have been available, as spare plots could have been offered for sale.

CASE 2

A wealthy builder of experience asks the bank to help him to develop a building site with planning permission to erect 60 dwelling houses. The builder is known to be proud of his standard of workmanship and very reasonable in his prices, and he expects no difficulty in selling the houses.

Cheap Build Ltd, in which the builder is the major shareholder, will build the houses. The company has £60,000 in cash ready for the development. The land, which was purchased a few years ago at a cost of £240,000, will be charged to the bank as security, and the builder has offered his own guarantee of £120,000, adequately supported by good collateral security. The bank is asked to provide an overdraft of £240,000 to develop the site.

With a good guarantee of £120,000 plus a charge over the land, the bank readily agrees to the advance on the grounds that the customer is a good builder, past experience has been satisfactory, and the amount required is a modest sum in the context of building finance for 60 houses.

The bank might reasonably assume that financial planning could be left to the customer and as it has adequate security for the advance there will be no need to watch the development of the site carefully or arrange for lending to be in accordance with any formula.

Twelve months later, 30 houses have been sold but, when the bank manager is reviewing the loan facilities with the customer, he is asked to renew the limit at an increased figure of £320,000. At this point, the account is overdrawn by approximately £240,000 and the bank holds as security the good guarantee of £120,000 plus land for 30 houses valued, at cost only, at £120,000. The value of the building work already carried out should now have made this remaining land more valuable and the bank will probably have adequate security. Nevertheless, only a poor banker would agree to such a request without further probing. Although adequate security is available for the advance, very little thought is necessary to realise that something is wrong.

The company started 12 months ago with £60,000 cash and land worth £240,000. It now has only half the land left and, despite the fact that it has meanwhile sold 30 houses, it is requesting larger overdraft facilities. The profit on the 30 houses sold should have made sufficient funds available to bring about a good reduction in the overdraft unless these funds had been used for another purpose. The company maintains that no redirection of funds has taken place, so the bank arranges for a statement of the present stage of building to be prepared in order that a full discussion can take place.

When produced, this reveals:

CHEAP BUILD LTD

	With sale contracts	Unsold	Cost £
Houses roofed . . .		1	9,000
plastered . . .	4	13	238,000
finished . . .	3		60,000
Undeveloped plots . . .	1	8	36,000
			343,000

The company's assets in the development at the start of the scheme were £300,000 (£60,000 cash plus £240,000 land) whereas now they total only £103,000 (£343,000 less overdraft £240,000). On the face of it a large loss has been made and this perhaps indicates that the standard of workmanship has not been covered by high enough selling prices. There may, of course, be other reasons, but thorough probing will obviously be needed. It will not only be necessary to find out what has gone wrong but also how the bank lending is to be repaid. Sales of 30 houses have produced nothing towards repayment; what, therefore, will the remaining sales produce, and how much will the bank lending be reduced from each sale?

The lesson to be learnt from this case is that, although security may be adequate, it is still advisable to follow the progress of an estate's development. Although lending to a formula may not be necessary, it is wise to obtain as much information as if it were. If the financial arrangements are not then proceeding satisfactorily, an early warning will be given which may well prevent further losses. It is also advisable to agree, at the outset, a plan for the bank to be repaid out of sale proceeds in order to avoid the situation which occurs in the present example.

CASE 3

A company formed four years ago has already had some assistance from the bank to build a small property costing £24,000 and this transaction was handled satisfactorily. The shareholders' resources as seen from the balance sheet are: capital, £400, plus profit and loss account £36,000, but in addition there are loans from the directors for £67,600 making the resources available to the company approximately £104,000. The equipment owned by the company is worth £20,000 and the remaining £84,000 of assets is in cash or near-cash.

The company's new scheme is to buy a plot of land for £228,000 on which to build 16 houses at a cost of £36,000 each. The development will be phased so that four houses are under construction at a time. The finance required from the bank is £288,000, and the houses are estimated to sell for £72,000 each.

The request is based on the following figures:

	£		£
Cost of land	228,000	Provided by company	84,000
Cost of erection of four houses		Provided by bank	288,000
at £36,000 each	144,000		
	372,000		372,000

Security   £
Four houses worth £72,000 each   288,000
Remaining land (three-quarters of plot)   171,000
                                                                                          459,000

At first sight this might not seem too bad a proposition, apart from the outstanding fact that by far the greater proportion of finance is to be provided by the bank. However, the security of the houses is based upon the estimated selling price and not the cost price, which is a case of counting one's chickens before they are hatched. If a contract of sale is obtained for a completed house, the house might well be valued at the sale price, but up to this time – and especially during the erection of the building – it would be foolhardy to count all or part of the estimated profit in security calculations.

In the present instance, if we take the purchase of the land as being the first problem, the company has £84,000 towards the cost and the bank will have to provide the other £144,000. On the basis of valuing at 50 per cent for bank security, there is insufficient value available. As the company has no other funds, any development of the land will have to be paid for by the bank, which will thereby be taking the risk of the development – acting, in fact, as a developer and not as a bank.

The scheme is really far too ambitious for the company's resources and the directors should be advised to drop it unless they can provide more capital.

CASE 4

Widespread Builders Ltd, who have been customers for 25 years, are reputable builders with wide experience. They build houses at the cheaper range and their sites are normally at some distance from the branch and local valuers are relied upon for reports. A few years ago, the company arranged finance with the bank for the devleopment of three estates which were relatively near to each other. The land involved was sufficient for the building of 200 houses and the limits granted were £280,000 for overdraft and £80,000 to cover indemnities. The company's net worth was £180,000 and, in addition, an associated company had lent it £140,000. The liabilities to the bank were secured by charges over the land and the amount of the overdraft was governed by the formula of half cost of uncovered land plus two-thirds of the cost of developments.

The developments proceeded without undue difficulty and regular valuations showed that, on the combined figures for all three estates, the borrowing was contained within the agreed formula.

One year after the limits had been agreed, a request was made for further finance to develop another site but the bank felt it was committed far enough and was not able to agree to additional facilities.

After a further year, the account was working in excess of the limit, at around £300,000 (although by this time the indemnities had been cancelled), and for a few months the debt had not always been covered by the agreed formula. Moreover, well over half of the 200 houses had been sold. As the developments were in their later stages, it was puzzling to find that the company was still borrowing heavily and that the sales of so many houses had made no difference to its requirements.

The directors were questioned about this state of affairs but their answers were not satisfying. In order to get a clear picture, the bank manager asked the valuers to make their next report in three parts, one for each development, and he visited the sites with the managing director.

He saw that six houses which had been built on unattractive parts of one site were unsold although they had been completed 12 months previously. The money tied up in these houses was a considerable financial burden for the company to carry but, in view of the large number of houses already sold, could not be the full reason for the high level of overdraft at which the banking account had been working.

Funds Diverted

It seemed, therefore, as if considerable money had been taken out of the company, either for dividends, directors' remuneration, or for purposes other than the building of houses on the three estates. In thinking about this, the bank manager remembered the request made 12 months previously for finance to develop another site and ascertained that the development there was going ahead rapidly. It was therefore fairly certain that money which should have been used to repay the advances on the first three developments had been used for the fourth development but the directors of the company, when tackled about it, would not admit that this was what had happened.

The points which now concerned the bank were:

i   how to control the advance;

ii   how to obtain repayment.

The details of the developments at each site were put on the branch record sheet and a summary for each site showed:

	With sale contracts	Unsold	Cost of builder £
Site A			
Houses roofed	3	3	54,000
plastered	1	—	13,500
finished	1	—	18,000
Undeveloped plots.		8	48,000
			133,500

Lending formula ⅔ of £85,500 plus ½ of £48,000 = £81,000

	With sale contracts	Unsold	Cost of builder £
Site B			
Houses roofed	1	—	9,000
plastered		1	13,500
finished		6	108,000
Undeveloped plots. . . .		8	48,000
			178,500

Lending formula ⅔ of £130,500 plus ½ of £48,000 = £111,000

	With sale contracts	Unsold	Cost of builder £
Site C			
Houses roofed	—	1	9,000
plastered	1	1	27,000
finished	1	1	36,000
Undeveloped plots. . . .		12	72,000
			144,000

Lending formula ⅔ of £72,000 plus ½ of £72,000 = £84,000

We can now see that development appears to be progressing satisfactorily on site A, where most of the houses have been sold before completion. On site B six finished houses have not been sold although completed 12 months ago, and site C is making reasonable progress. The company's policy is to obtain deposits of only £100 on houses when agreements to purchase are signed, the remainder being paid on completion. The bank overdraft at this stage is £247,000.

It is obvious that site B is a problem, and the finance tied up in it burdensome. The best plan from the bank's point of view (and probably the customer's also, as it will pinpoint the problems) is to separate the lending into three loan accounts, each applicable to one site, and to establish each loan at the formula figure for each site.

We will then have:

		£
Loan Site A		81,000
Less Deposits, 5 x £100		500
		80,500
Loan Site B		111,000
Less Deposits, 1 x £100		100
		110,900
Loan Site C		84,000
Less Deposits, 2 x £100		200
		83,800

The total of these loans is £275,200, and this sum will be transferred to the current account, thereby eliminating the debit balance of £247,000 and providing a credit balance of £28,200 to cover any outstanding payments and running expenses until the next valuation of the sites. On developments of this size, £28,200 is not very much of a reserve and a thorough probing of the company's commitments will be necessary to see if they will be able to manage. The company may well have to be told to bring in further resources and this is of course the best solution. However, if they cannot do so, the current account will have to be firmly controlled, with the company making payments only after consultation with the bank. It is probable also that more frequent valuations of the sites will be necessary or that work will have to be temporarily curtailed on one or two sites in order to complete houses on the site where there are ready sales. Discussion will also have to take place with the company and with a local estate agent about the six houses which have not been sold on site B with the object either of selling at a lower figure or making some improvements to facilitate sales.

This, then, is the first point — the problem of control. The bank has, of necessity, to become involved in the detailed working of the customer's business and now has to take on onerous tasks which could well have been avoided if separate details of each development had been provided from the start and if the manager had made regular personal inspections of the sites. Difficulties would have come to light much earlier and this would have avoided the additional work and worry now facing the bank.

The second problem is how to obtain repayment. It is obvious that on a sale of each property the sum advanced towards its construction will have to be credited to the appropriate loan account. This, however, would mean that complete clearance would not be obtained until the final house was sold and the bank might well be left with a debt covered by a few houses which could not be sold easily.

Therefore arrangements will have to be made with the customers for additional sums to be credited to the loan accounts from the proceeds of sales in order to clear the advances well before the final houses are sold. This is a matter for negotiation and will have to be considered in conjunction with the company's other financial commitments.

The final point to be arranged is the stage at which unsaleable houses are taken out of the reckoning for calculation of the lending formula. Unsaleable houses are poor security and if, after consultation with the builders and estate agents, it is decided to make some alterations, it may be appropriate to give the company a further three months to arrange sales. Houses not sold by that time should be left out of the calculatoins. To provide for this, the company may have to leave all or most of the profit on other sales with the bank to enable the necessary reduction in the site B loan to be made.

If site B does prove to be a particularly bad one, the company should consider the advisability of selling the undeveloped plots.

CASE 5

It would be as well to look now at a case involving management accounts. No large-scale developer can proceed without making forecasts of the funds that will be required for each development, and such forecasts are very useful to banks for assessment of propositions and for monitoring subsequent progress.

Southside Builders Ltd, are house developers and builders of long standing with a healthy balance sheet showing a net worth of £1m. The company now wishes to develop a site of six acres on which it will build 50 houses. The cost of the land is £720,000 and the company wishes to borrow up to £700,000, being two-thirds of the cost of the land and two-thirds of construction costs in three stages, roofed, plastered and complete. The company estimates that a good profit will be earned and the whole advance will be cleared in 12 months. To substantiate these contentions, three estimates are submitted covering construction costs, viability of the development and cash forecast.

Construction costs
The figures produced are as follows:

SOUTHSIDE BUILDERS LTD

Construction costs	Park Avenue Estate		
House type	*Ayr*	*Falkirk*	*Ness*
Accommodation	3-bed terrace	3-bed. semi	4-bed. detached
Garage	Space	Integral	Detached
Heating	Gas	Gas	Gas
Floor area	770 sq ft	830 sq ft	1,000 sq ft
Expected sale price . . .	£53,000	£66,000	£78,000

Cost	£	£	£
Damp proof course . .	2,840	3,640	4,060
First floor joists . .	2,840	3,640	4,060
Roof completed . . .	5,660	7,060	7,820
First fixing . . .	3,380	4,200	4,840
Plastered	2,180	2,840	3,220
Second fixing . . .	2,950	3,620	3,800
Complete	2,550	3,200	3,600
Turfing	100	100	100
Total cost . . .	£22,500	£28,300	£31,500

Cost of roads and sewers	£
Concrete-mix ducts and kerbs . . .	48,840
Base course	18,700
Wearing course	8,000
Footpaths	10,980
Landscaping	3,508
Sewers	44,640
Culverts	26,540
	161,208

It will be seen that it is proposed to build three different types of houses and the costs have been broken down into eight stages. This is helpful and the bank will be able to make the adjusted calculations necessary to find the cost at the three stages at which it is asked to make advances. There is a large difference between the expected sale prices and the construction costs but the common costs of roads and sewers and the bank interest have to be covered and all other expenses. Additionally, the land cost has not been taken into account.

Viability
This is shown below.

VIABILITY – PARK AVENUE ESTATE

Total of 50 units on 6 acres		£
Sale proceeds 12 (Type *Ayr*) x £53,000 . . .		636,000
24 (Type *Falkirk*) x £66,000 . . .		1,584,000
14 (Type *Ness*) x £78,000 . . .		1,092,000
		3,312,000

Less Construction costs	£	
12 x £22,500 = 270,000		
24 x £28,300 = 679,200		
14 x £31,500 = 441,000		
	1,390,200	

Roads and sewers	161,208	
Land cost	720,000	
Agents, solicitors and VAT . . .	77,014	
National House Builders Council . .	11,950	
Contingencies	92,000	
Bank interest	68,000	2,520,372
Profit . .		£791,628

Average profit per unit: £15,832

It will now be seen that from the total sale proceeds, construction costs and all other expenses have been deducted and a profit of £791,628 is expected which works out at £15,832 per unit. This is a good return but it must be realised that a large amount of money will be involved in the development and considerable risks are involved.

Cash Forecast
this is shown below and is an extension of the viability estimate.

CASH FORECAST

		Borrowing	Drawings	Receipts	Balance
Month	1	480,000	60,000		(540,000)
	2	540,000	60,000		(600,000)
	3	600,000	80,000		(680,000)
	4	680,000	120,000	106,000	(694,000)
	5	694,000	120,000	132,000	(682,000)
	6	682,000	184,000	194,000	(672,000)
	7	672,000	130,000	188,000	(614,000)
	8	614,000	120,000	200,000	(534,000)
	9	534,000	120,000	200,000	(454,000)
	10	454,000	120,000	200,000	(374,000)
	11	374,000	120,000	300,000	(194,000)
	12	194,000	80,000	300,000	(26,000)

It will be seen that the initial borrowing starts at £480,000 being the two-thirds advance for the cost of the land and that no receipts are obtained until month 4. Subsequently, sufficient receipts are estimated to be received to bring down the borrowing rapidly and to clear it entirely by month 12. Month 4 is, therefore, on the figures produced, the critical period and the bank will wish to know the stages estimated to be reached at this time. If it is told that there will be 12 completed houses, four of each type, the construction cost will be 4 x (£22,500 + 28,300 + 31,500) = £329,200.

At that stage, therefore, the lending value of the bank's security on a two-thirds basis will be:

	£
Land	720,000
Construction	329,200
	1,049,200

Two-thirds basis: £699,467   .   Borrowing: £694,000

This leaves little margin. It is necessary, therefore, to decide whether the bank should go ahead and advance the funds but it will not be able to do so without further information.

It is known that the customer has experience of residential developments, has a sound balance sheet and knowledge of management accounts. The bank will, however, wish to know what are the other commitments with which the company is involved as it will wish to assure itself that the company (even though it has a net worth of £1m) is able to provide its own cash injection of one-third of all costs and has a cushion of finance available for emergencies. It will also wish to know that the company's costings are reasonable and that there will be a demand for houses on the site and the types being built are suitable. If favourable reports are obtained the bank will be able to give an unqualified approval to the proposition which, by use of management accounts, has been well presented. Site inspections will subsequently be made and progress both on the building work and on the cash position will be compared with the estimated figures.

9. Produce Loans

It is usual for lending against produce to be concentrated in a few areas, such as ports and the major commercial centres, and relatively few bank staff have therefore much experience of it. Consequently, many people are hesitant about tackling this type of lending.

The theory, however, is not difficult to learn, even though there is more detailed paper work than with other types of lending. The theory is that goods are pledged as security and are then deposited in a warehouse in the name of the bank, and the customer obtains a loan for an agreed amount. Then, in the majority of cases, when the customer has arranged a sale of the goods or part of the goods, he will need to have possession of the goods in order to deliver them to the purchaser. The bank will then appoint the customer as its agent to deal with the sale, and the customer, acting as agent, will complete the sale and deliver to the bank the proceeds in order to repay the loan.

Should bankruptcy, a receivership, liquidation, or a warrant for execution fall upon the customer while he has possession of the goods as agent for the bank, the bank will be able to claim the goods as being pledged to it. Similarly, if the goods have been sold but not paid for, the bank will be able to claim as principal from the person to whom the goods have been sold.

Kinds of Loan

There can be a number of variations on this simple method, as it may happen that only part of the goods warehoused are released at one time or that the goods are not warehoused as they are released on a trust letter to the customer immediately they are pledged. Immediate release of the goods happens when a firm sale has been arranged and delivery can take place straightaway.

Produce loans can be arranged for goods being imported and also for those which have been produced for export or for home sales. When a loan is arranged against imports, it is often the case that a documentary credit precedes the granting of a produce loan. By this means the bank gives instructions for money to be paid to the overseas seller of the goods or a bill of exchange to be accepted against delivery of documents of title to the goods. The bank will then have recourse against the goods and, if the arrangements with the customer are that he need not settle with the bank immediately, a produce loan can be opened and the goods held as security.

If a bill of exchange has been accepted, the customer's account will not be debited until the bill is paid and the produce loan would start from that date. The goods, however, will be in the possession of the bank before the bill is due for payment and they will then be held as security against the liability on the bill of exchange.

Care must be exercised to watch for the arrival of goods, as the bill of lading will have to be sent to the warehousekeeper with instructions to store the goods in the name of the bank.

Naturally the warehousekeeper should be reliable and, when the bank issues delivery or transfer orders, clauses should be included in them stating that delivery is to be made only on payment of the warehouse keeper's charges. Appropriate insurance cover over the goods will at all times be necessary, and special risks such as failure of refrigeration plant for perishable goods should be properly covered. In borderline cases, it may also be considered necessary to hedge in the commodity as protection against a large change in price.

It will be appreciated that it is important for the bank to be able to follow any goods released on trust and to have a valid claim to them. This claim is by virtue of the document of pledge. It is therefore of little use for a customer to say that he has goods which he will be selling and against which he wants an advance, and for the bank to issue him with a trust letter telling him to account to the bank for the proceeds of sale. If the goods have not been pledged to the bank prior to a trust letter being issued, the bank will have no title to the goods. There are some exceptions in law to this, and goods on the sea or in transit from quay to warehouse might be picked up by a trust letter alone, but otherwise the Bills of Sale Acts would apply and the trust letter would have to be registered as a bill of sale if no prior pledge of the goods has been obtained.

Security

The bank's position with a produce advance is therefore that of a lender against stock and when we consider as security the assets in a balance sheet one of the least attractive from a banker's point of view is stock. The test of a security comes at the time when it has to be realised, and, on the break-up of a business, stock is often sold at only a small fraction of its going-concern value. Care must therefore be taken to see that the type of stock pledged as security is one which does not lose its value and is not subject to violent fluctuations in price; it must be easily saleable in a wide market, preferably by description or sample, as costs of sale can mount if this is not so. Some items which fit these requirements are grain, wool, cotton, tea and wine, whereas unsuitable items are mixed retail goods, jewellery, fashionable goods, specialised and luxury articles.

It is as well to keep in mind also that banks rely on documents and, whereas documents may purport to describe the stock they represent, the underlying stock may be of a different quality from that stated in the documents. It is imperative therefore that all parties to the transaction are people of integrity. The customer, naturally, must be a person of honour and must have experience in the trade and be able to buy from well-established and reliable sources. The shipper must be experienced and reliable, as must also be the warehousekeeper.

Produce loans are suitable for financing the quick turnover of commodities in good markets, and in these conditions both the commodities and the money flow quickly. Traders are thus able to sustain a higher level of trading than would otherwise be possible and, if the goods are easily saleable and the market conditions are of a high standard, repayment of loans should be achieved quickly on every occasion.

The bank is of course very much in the hands of the customer, especially when trust facilities are granted, and therefore his integrity, experience and proven ability are of paramount importance. Experience in itself is no justification unless it is allied with ability.

Lending on produce to a person just starting in the trade is therefore hardly justifiable and neither is lending for a speculative purchase of stock. Additionally, if stock pledged as security is not kept separately when released on trust, it will lose its identity and will be merged with other stock with the result that, should financial troubles overcome the customer's business, the stock to which the bank will be looking for security will not be traceable.

Similarly, goods which have to be processed before sale and thereby change their form by having other items added to them or by themselves forming part of larger items are unsuitable as security.

The Amount to Lend

We now have to consider how much of the value of the stock it is prudent for bankers to lend. This will vary and will depend upon the type of stock and whether a stable price for the commodity exists. It will also depend upon whether lending is against goods contracted to be sold or whether the goods are unsold. For example, if there is a steady market, it would be prudent to restrict lending against unsold goods to two-thirds of the forced-sale value. We cannot, however, consider this in isolation because, as has already been said, experience and proven ability of the customer are essential. It would therefore be expected that the balance sheet of the customer would be of sufficient strength to justify some unsecured lending. This may allow a greater amount to be lent against the goods; additional security would have the same effect.

As an illustration, if lending is against grain and the price is stable and it is thought that 75 per cent of the cost price is the forced-sale price, lending could be arranged up to say, 50-60 per cent of the cost price. If the customer wishes to borrow 80 per cent of the cost price, additional security or strength in the balance sheet would have to be looked for to make up the difference.

As a much higher level of trading will be possible where produce loans are arranged, this, in itself, makes care essential as an element of overtrading can be introduced. Additionally, pledged goods are not an ideal security. We must therefore see that proposed advances are suitable for produce lending, that the bank's requirements are invariably kept and that each produce loan is repaid rapidly in accordance with arrangements. If there are any shortcomings in a bank's normal requirements, a banker would be unwise to delude himself by thinking that he will be safe with his security. He will be far better advised either to withdraw the facility or to consider the advance on an unsecured basis.

Legal Aspects

There are a few legal points which we should now consider:

A broker, factor or mercantile agent can borrow on goods even if they are not his own, and lenders get their protection through the Factors Act and Sale of Goods Acts. An agent must, however, be a person, firm or company whose business includes buying and selling goods for other persons and the term cannot be extended to cover a person merely in possession of goods, such as a servant or a caretaker. Therefore, to rely upon protection given by the law, a banker must be satisfied as to agency.

An agent must be in possession of the goods with the consent of the owner before he can pledge them, but a lender is protected by law if he lends in good faith without notice that the agent is restricted by his principal from pledging the goods. Consent is assumed unless there is notice to the contrary. If a principal subsequently withdraws his consent to pledge, the onus is on the principal to give notice to the pledgee. To have a valid pledge from a mercantile agent there must be consideration: a pledge to secure an existing debt would therefore generally be invalid. If substituted security is relied upon, it can only be relied upon up to the value of the goods given up.

The law differentiates between agents, buyers and sellers when considering the pledge of goods for antecedent debts or the substituting of goods or documents and the position is:

Antecedent debts:

Pledge by mercantile agent	This is void except to the extent of any lien the agent has against his principal.
Pledge by seller	This is valid.
Pledge by buyer	This is void except to the extent of any right the buyer has in the goods.

Substituting goods or documents:

Mercantile agents	Valid up to the value of goods or documents withdrawn at time of substitution.
Seller	Valid to the full extent of the advance.
Buyer	As for mercantile agent.

It is easy to imagine how complicated lending would be if, on every occasion, it was necessary to consider whether the pledgor was an agent, a seller, or a buyer.

It is because of these complications as well as the necessity for strict control that lending against produce should be on loan account and not on current account.

The Documents

The documents tendered as security may be in several forms: bill of lading, dock warrant, warehousekeeper's receipt or warrant, or transfer order. A relevant form to pledge the security will have to be used and it will also have to be appropriate to the sale — ie, the sale may be imminent and not warehoused, or the bank might receive a document for goods already warehoused, or a bill of lading could be tendered which the bank would send to a warehousekeeper with any necessary instructions.

If trust facilities are required, an appropriately worded document will have to be used to suit the transaction; and when delivery orders or transfer orders are issued by the bank, it will have to be guided by the requirements of the warehousekeeper. Care must be taken when issuing these orders that the warehousekeeper is directed to collect rent and charges before delivery or transfer of the goods. It is particularly necessary to diarise to watch for the proceeds of sales. The pledgor should advise the bank of the name of the person to whom the goods or each part of them have been sold, and as the bank will then be looking to the proceeds, it will have to consider whether it is necessary to make enquiries as to the standing of the purchasers.

At law, the first party to whom a bill of lading is transferred for value undoubtedly acquires the property, but a shipowner is entitled to deliver the goods to the first person who presents a valid bill of lading (assuming that the shipowner has not had notice of an earlier dealing with another bill of lading). If one bill of lading is negotiated but another one in the set is presented at the quayside first, the shipowner is entitled to deliver to that person even though the property in the goods will belong to the person to whom the first bill in the set was negotiated. A full set of bills of lading is therefore necessary.

Where goods are warehoused it is not sufficient to rely on a warehousekeeper's receipt in the customer's name plus a signed delivery order. The receipt may refer to goods already released against other delivery orders. Before the security can be perfected, the warehousekeeper's receipt will have to be sent to him together with the delivery order and a new receipt issued in favour of the bank.

It is important that the pledgee has possession of the goods. It is not sufficient to have an agreement to pledge without possession of the goods being obtained, as this will only give an equitable charge.

When advancing against goods being exported, it is important that the bank has a good title and that the bills of lading are in the name of the customer and endorsed in blank. The bills of lading must not be in the name of the person to whom the goods are being exported, as the bank will acquire no title.

Similarly, when goods are being imported, the bills of lading must be endorsed in blank in order to give the bank possession of the goods.

CASE 1

A company of produce merchants dealing mainly in tea and coffee has kept satisfactory banking accounts for 10 years. The directors are well known to the branch manager, who considers them to be most reliable, and all arrangements for overdraft facilities have been properly observed. An approach is now made to the bank for additional overdraft facilities on the basis that very good additional contracts have been obtained involving much larger sums than the company has previously dealt in. The directors estimate that there will be numerous occasions when they will need overdrafts but, for the most part, they will be short-lived. The amount they wish to borrow is £160,000.

The directors are willing to provide personal guarantees which will be supported adequately to cover a borrowing of £50,000, and the company's balance sheets for the last three years show that the net worth from profits has risen from £50,000 to £56,000 to £64,000. The net liquid assets were approximately £20,000 less than these figures and the remaining balance sheet figures showed only fixed assets totalling £20,000 in a short leasehold, fixtures and fittings, and motor vehicles.

The first point which should strike the bank manager is that the amount which the company wishes to borrow is much more than the worth of the company and, even if the supporting guarantees of £50,000 are added to the net worth of £64,000, the resultant £114,000 is still consideraly less than the requested overdraft.

If we apply the principles mentioned previously when considering unsecured lending, and say that a reasonable amount to lend unsecured for this company is half the net current assets, or, against a debenture, no more than the equivalent of the net worth, these amounts would be £27,000 and £64,000 respectively and, added to the supported guarantee of £50,000, the total lending amounts would be £77,000 or £114,000.

The proposition is therefore unsuitable for normal overdraft arrangements but it can be examined to see if produce loan facilities can be granted. We know that the customer is reliable, and the integrity of the directors is beyond doubt. The company has many years of experience behind it and is building up its capital regularly out of profits and thereby showing that it has ability as well as experience. The directors have said that overdrafts should be repaid quickly and further questioning may reveal that, for the most part, the expected upsurge in business is based on firm orders, for which payment should be received four weeks after delivery. The company estimates being out of its money for six to eight weeks on each order from the time they pay their suppliers to the time they receive payment from their customers. If it can now be established that the shippers are reliable, and that the company's customers are also reliable and good payers, a favourable situation for produce facilities will have been established.

The company says it is possible that it may buy up to £200,000 of tea and coffee at any one time against firm sale orders. If the bank considers that, in the conditions prevailing, prices are stable and 80 per cent of the invoice value could be considered as the forced sale value, there should be no difficulty in accommodating the company with, say, 70 per cent advances.

We have already said that we would be prepared by lend £77,000 and therefore, to bring our security to the requested £160,000, we must look for further security in goods of £83,000. If we advance up to 70 per cent, the full invoice value of goods to cover £83,000 would be approximately £118,560. It would appear that the company expects to require the full amount of the loan only when it has bought up to £200,000 of goods: adequate margin of security should therefore be available and not just the bare margin.

This, then, is a satisfactory case for produce loan facilities to be agreed.

Before taking this example further, it would be as well to consider the points to keep in mind if a debenture is held as security for produce advances. A debenture naturally strengthens security when lending to a company, as any stock held by the company would be picked up by the floating charge in the debenture. In the case of produce advances, however, the bank is enabling a customer to increase the annual turnover greatly and to deal in a larger volume of stock. The bank would be looking to the stock to provide repayment, and the floating charge of the debenture might not give sufficient comfort to the banker; set-offs between traders, liens, or stoppages *in transitu,* together with warrants for execution, can stand before a floating charge not crystallised. A pledge of goods, however, gives a specific charge over the goods and is thereby stronger than a debenture's floating charge. If the lending arrangements are large in relation to net worth, it is hardly wise to rely only on the floating charge in a debenture.

We can now take our example through to the following year.

After a great deal of activity on produce loans reflecting the increased turnover, the company requests a continuance of the facilities of £160,000 on the same conditions − ie, no change in the security and 70 per cent advances of the invoice value of purchases. A balance sheet is produced showing roughly the same position as in previous years except that the net worth is now £66,000 (up £2,000 on the previous year) and turnover increased by £1m.

The situation on outstanding produce loans is:

No. of loan account	Invoice value £	Amount of advance £	Length outstanding
12	56,000	39,200	six months
16	56,000	39,200	five months
31	24,000	16,800	two months
33	10,000	7,000	three weeks
34	20,000	14,000	two weeks
	166,000	116,200	

This is the time when we must remember that produce advances are not normal bank overdrafts and that the facilities provided are to enable stock to circulate quickly. In the present instance, although the final three loans have been outstanding only a short while, the earlier loans numbers 12 and 16 have been outstanding for several months and this was not envisaged when the original proposition was put to the bank. What has gone wrong? Is the stock bad? Why has it not been moved previously? Has it been released on trust?

Urgent enquiries would seem to be necessary, as the bank's advance of £78,400 on these two loans has in effect provided capital for the company and this amount is also greater than the net worth provided by the proprietors. If the goods have been released on trust, then the position might be even more serious as bad debts might have been incurred or the money used for other purposes contrary to the trust arrangements.

In practice, it is essential to make diary notes for produce loans to be examined regularly to see that they are working strictly in accordance with arrangements; for while a bank can be saved loss on many advances if action is taken at the first hint of trouble, this particularly applies to produce facilities where advances much greater than a customer's net worth are permitted.

In this instance, enquiries should have been made earlier. Why has there been a relatively poor showing in the profit and loss account after turnover has increased by £1m? The balance sheet figure for net worth could of course be completely wrong if there are difficulties on the two early produce loans, and the future conduct of the banking business can only be decided after searching enquiries have been made.

CASE 2

For the next example, we will consider the case of a young man aged 28 who has been employed by commodity merchants for 10 years and now, having inherited £20,000, wishes to start his own business. He says he will be dealing in the grain markets of which he has experience through his employment and he has asked for bank assistance up to £50,000 on produce loans with 80 per cent advances against the value of goods deposited.

The points in favour of the advance are:

1. The customer has had 10 years' experience in the trade.
2. He will be putting in a sizeable stake of £20,000.
3. If he is successful, a very good business could develop.

The points against are:

1. Trade experience as an employee is not the same as experience as a principal, and the same openings for the sale of the grain may not be available to him.
2. There is no record of proven ability and, although experience may have been obtained, the customer may find that as a businessman trading for profits he does not fulfil his expectations. Two men in exactly similar circumstances can make an entirely different showing of their businesses, because trading ability varies greatly. With produce loans, a bank is backing experience and ability and if these are not present the bank which lends money is not only providing capital for a business venture but, if lending more than the proprietor's stake, is becoming the senior partner in the venture.

On balance, it would therefore be unwise to lend on the basis suggested but, naturally, a flat refusal would only antagonise the customer, who could well build up a successful business in the course of time.

A reasonable way to approach this situation would be to explain tactfully the reservations which a bank must have about such a new business and say that it may be possible to help initially on a modest scale when fuller information is available about orders received, providing that firm orders are available from businesses upon whom good reports can be obtained so that loans are cleared quickly on each occasion. The amount to be lent should not exceed the proprietor's stake and an adequate margin in security should be obtained, with an independent valuation if necessary. The valuation will depend to some extent upon the shipper as, if he is a reliable person or company, the invoice valuations could be accepted as a guide.

Constant care will be necessary but, providing the customer is convinced that the banker is helping him to the best of his ability, there should be little difficulty in obtaining regular reports from him about the progress of his business and, if he is successful in his venture, more generous treatment would be justified thereafter.

CASE 3

Let us now consider a grocery wholesaler with a reasonably successful business. He has an overdraft limit of £20,000, which is considered to be about right, although for temporary periods no objection is made to increases of an additional £5,000 or so. He approaches the bank for an addition £15,000 to purchase further stocks of rice on the basis that, in his view, there will be a shortage in six months' time. He realises that he cannot manage this within his overdraft facilities and has asked for produce loan facilities.

There are two points about this proposition which make it basically unsuitable for bank lending. Firstly, the wholesaler is providing no cash stake himself and, secondly, the loan required is for a speculation. It might be possible to rectify the first point, and get the wholesaler to provide a proportion of the money required, but a produce loan is quite unsuitable for a speculative purchase.

We have already considered that produce loans enable a trader to turn over much more stock than he would normally be able to manage. In effect, they provide the capital which a trader would usually have to supply himself, and the only occasion for doing this is when the trader is dealing in goods which are turned over quickly and repayment of the advances follows quickly. They do not serve their proper purpose if used to supplement a trader's capital for any other reason, as bank finance is provided at minimum interest rates whereas the return on capital is the net profit. Capital for speculation, on which a trader hopes to make a good return, should be provided by him or from a source which will either contribute capital or loans on which an appropriately higher interest will no doubt be charged.

It may be possible in this instance for the wholesaler to rearrange his finances in order than he can manage the purchase within his existing overdraft facilities or provide some additional security and arrange a temporarily higher limit. Notwithstanding the speculative nature of the transaction, there may be circumstances in which a banker would wish to help. A suitable proposition could possibly be formulated whereby the stake of the proprietor was at least as much as the overdraft limit and the advance agreed within the normal overdraft terms but, I repeat, the proposition is unsuitable for produce facilities.

CASE 4

The director of a small company of precision engineers asks for help with the finance of a contract for the supply of measuring and testing equipment. Most of the component parts are either manufactured by the company or kept in stock but it will be necessary to order some sets of very small gear wheels, at a cost of £7,000. It is estimated that the assembly of the whole order will take three weeks and that £20,000 will be received on sale. The company suggests that an overdraft would suit it best, as £5,000, at most, will be required and it wishes to keep down interest charges. The company will pledge the gears but they will need to be released straightaway so that the equipment can be assembled.

There are two aspects which should be considered at the start:

1. It has already been mentioned that lending on fluctuating overdrafts is unsuitable for produce advances. It is difficult to keep control of the lending and it may be necessary to take into account and legal aspects concerning antecedent debts and substituted security. A saving of interest is insufficient reason why the bank should not take full precautions.
2. The pledged goods will lose their identity once they are assembled and, should trouble fall upon the company, it would be difficult to recover them and difficult to dispose of them elsewhere.

It may be possible to assist the company with its order, either against security or on an unsecured basis, but produce facilities will achieve nothing in the way of supporting security for the advance.

CASE 5

We will consider now the case of a meat wholesaler who approaches the bank saying that he is dissatisfied with his present banker and wishes to arrange produce loans of up to £200,000 with 75 per cent advances against invoice values and with full trust facilities. He claims to have had considerable experience in the trade both in the United Kingdom and abroad; he started trading on his own account just over 12 months ago, and now produces the following draft accounts for the first year's trading:

	£	
Current liabilities		
Bank	96,000	
Creditors	152,000	Covered by debtors
Taxation	20,000	
Loans	148,000	Relatively large
Total current liabilities	416,000	
Capital	4,000	
Profit and loss balance	26,000	
	446,000	
Current assets		
Debtors	168,000	
Stock	252,000	Sufficient for two months' trading?
Total current assts	420,000	
Plant and machinery	6,000	
Fixtures and fittings	3,000	
Motor vehicles	5,000	
Goodwill	12,000	
	446,000	

	£	
Turnover	1,600,000	Very large in comparison to net worth
Net profit before tax	14,000	
Taxation	4,000	
Net profit after tax	10,000	Small in relation to turnover
Directors' remuneration	12,000	
Net worth	18,000	

The following points should be observed by a banker:

1. We have only the wholesaler's word that he has experience in the meat trade.
2. One year's accounts are insufficient to prove his ability.
3. Nothing is known of his integrity.
4. A very large turnover has been accomplished on a very small net worth which, allied to the small profit, must be regarded as evidence that the business is vulnerable; a small change in the profit percentage could bring about a disastrous loss.
5. Net current assets are only £4,000.
6. The accounts are draft ones only and cannot be considered as satisfactory evidence.
7. The net worth covers the fixed assets and leaves only £4,000 towards the working capital necessary to finance a turnover of £1,600,000.

There are so many reasons why lending on the proposed basis should not be contemplated that a banker could hardly be criticised for giving an outright refusal. Suppose, however, that he started to struggle with the problem and elicited further facts:

1. He was able to confirm that the wholesaler had previous good experience in the trade and that existing bank customers thoroughly versed in it spoke well of him and his ability.
2. The poor showing in the first year's account was due to special factors which had now been overcome and the figures as presented were confirmed as correct by accountants.
3. First-class references were obtained as to the wholesaler's character and reputation.
4. The business was now operating on a better profit ratio which was likely to continue.
5. The reason for leaving the competitor bank was nothing but irritation over mishandling of routine affairs.
6. The loans of £148,000 were loans from close family sources, which were not expected to be repaid other than on a long-term basis and could be postponed to any bank borrowing and thereby be classed to some extent as capital. This would, of course, have the effect of making the net current assets £152,000 and the net worth £166,000.

The proposition now takes on a rather different look but caution is still necessary, as proof of the customer's business ability is lacking and it will be some years before it can be established. It will also be necessary to find out why sufficient stock for two months' trading was held at the balance sheet date. The company cannot afford to keep so much stock on its present capital and family loans. If an adequate explanation is forthcoming, that for example it is intended to turn over stock rapidly against firm orders and not hold meat for future sale, a modest line for produce loans could be contemplated. Until experience has been built up, a figure of £200,000, with the wholesaler given a free hand to make his purchases and sales as he wishes, is too much. If the banker wishes to lend, and lend safely, he will have to take a more than usual interest in the detailed affairs of the business, and the wholesaler will have to provide information on what purchases he wishes to make and what sales will be arranged. The transactions can then be followed through and, if all works well, a more generous attitude can be taken later. Any failure to clear a produce loan quickly will have to be looked upon as a danger signal.

As the business is that of a company, a debenture could be taken, but this would incur the risk, in the case of a recently formed company, of creditor pressure developing after publication of the registration of the debenture. It would seem that the amount in debtors would be sufficient to meet any demands of creditors but this can only be ascertained by detailed enquiry.

CASE 6

A fruit and vegetable wholesaling company which also runs five retail shops has kept a good banking account for many years and has built up an increasing turnover largely as the result of a loan of £80,000 which has now been called in owing to the death of the lender. The bank is asked for overdraft facilities of £80,000 in order that the business can be carried on in the same way in future. It is explained that, apart from a small amount of purchasing, the bulk of the produce received is on consignment from a Spanish company and is normally sold very quickly, partly on wholesale terms and partly through the retail shops. The terms of payment for the consignment are 75 per cent of an estimated value on documentary credits and the balance later when the actual amounts realised are known. The goods are transported by weekly shipments from Spain, and normally take 10 days to arrive. The value of each consignment is between £20,000 and £30,000.

The audited accounts are consistent over the years and have shown increasing turnover and profit. The latest figures are shown below.

Many points are apparent from a study of the balance sheet:

	£	
Current liabilities		
Bank	6,000	
Creditors	36,000	Equal to debtors
Tax	1,000	
Loan	80,000	This is to be repaid
Total current liabilities	123,000	
Capital	9,000	
Profit and loss account	15,000	
	147,000	
Current assets		
Cash	44,000	Will be used to repay part of the loan
Debtors	36,000	
Stock	18,000	Small in relation to turnover
Total current assets	98,000	
Short leaseholds	28,000	Of no security value
Plant and machinery and fixtures and fittings	5,000	
Motor vehicles	8,000	
Goodwill	8,000	
	147,000	
Turnover	1,200,000	Large in relation to net worth
Net profit before tax	45,600	
Tax	28,000	
Net profit after tax	17,600	
Directors' fees	24,000	
Dividends	17,000	Almost full distribution of profits
Net worth	16,000	

1.   The fixed assets plus the goodwill total £49,000 and yet the proprietors' stake is only £24,000. The proprietors have therefore been relying on the loan to make good the shortfall in capital needed to finance the purchase of the fixed assets and to provide some working capital.

2.   A very large turnover has been accomplished on a small net worth, which again suggests the use of the loan as capital.

3.   The stock is less than a week's turnover and in these days of cold stores when fruit can be preserved for long periods this is small for a wholesaler. However, we know that the bulk of the business is received on consignment, and stock so held would not appear in the company's accounts.

4.   The current assets are insufficient to cover current liabilities and repayment of the loan would extinguish all the cash and cause a large overdraft as well.

5.   The business, however, is a profitable one. Although the net profit in relation to turnover is small, in relation to net worth it is large; the directors obviously know their business.

6.   There is nothing which a bank could lend unsecured to the company, and a debenture would pick up very little of realisable worth. The cash will disappear and, as the company deals as an agent, the bulk of the stock does not belong to it. The only way to obtain the stock on consignment as security is to have it pledged to the bank. As explained earlier, an agent has every right in law to pledge goods of his principal unless the principal has given express notice to the proposed pledgee that he is not willing for this to happen.

There are therefore a number of problems for the company to face and the first problem, if the repayment of the loan cannot be delayed, is to introduce more capital to make the net worth at least sufficient to cover the fixed assets and goodwill.

If this can be done, and £25,000 of new capital introduced, a solution to the difficulties might be devised. The amount they require to borrow would be reduced to £55,000 which, plus the overdraft of £6,000 shown in the balance sheet, comes to £61,000.

If produce loans are to be allowed there will be little chance of being able to follow the goods released on trust through to ultimate sale in the five retail shops, where they will be mixed with other stock not pledged as security. It would be far too complicated for them to be stocked and accounted for separately, but goods sold wholesale in bulk would not, of course, cause difficulty.

With the net worth of the company now increased to £41,000, a debenture would be more attractive as security but, as the additional cash is to be used as part-repayment of the loan, there will be nothing extra in the assets for a debenture to pick up. Short leaseholds become valueless in a liquidation, as does goodwill, but, if debtors are spread and normally stand at around £36,000, it might be considered that the profit record of the company justifies an advance up to, say, one-half of the current assets (debtors £36,000; stock £18,000). Overdraft facilities of £28,000 might therefore be agreed with the security of a debenture providing that current asset/liability figures are produced monthly showing a 100 per cent margin of current assets over the bank debt in the company's books.

There is still another £32,000 to be found and, provided that there is satisfactory evidence that the turnover will continue to provide quick cash receipts into the bank, we can look further at produce loans. Although trust facilities for goods sold through the retail shops are unsatisfactory, at any one time there should be two shipments on the sea with a total value of between £40,000 and £60,000. These goods can be pledged, and 50 per cent advances would raise £20,000 to £30,000. The company might find that they can manage on this basis, and that their inflow of cash will enable them to redeem the goods when the ships arrive or shortly afterwards. Trust facilities could only be granted for goods sold wholesale in bulk.

Naturally, this is stretching bank lending facilities considerably and the character of the directors of the company must be considered before agreement. It will also be necessary to stress that these arrangements can only be short-term, as the bank will be looking to the company to build up its resources either from retained profits or by other means.

10. Hire-Purchase and Finance Companies

Before dealing with loans to hire-purchase and finance companies, it would be as well to think once again about some of the points normally applying to bank lending.

One of the sure ways to financial disaster is to borrow short and lend long, and bankers are ever mindful of this. Even a suspicion that a bank might curtail withdrawals of deposits would have very serious consequences, as confidence is paramount to a banker. Normally, therefore, lending by banks is kept to short-term propositions or to the provision of finance for trading purposes on swinging accounts. However, provided deposits are well spread and amount in total to large figures, there can be little danger to confidence if a relatively small proportion of a bank's deposits is lent over a longer term.

Although propositions may start on the basis of short-term lending not all cases work out as envisaged and some of them, unfortunately, develop into long-term lending. These cases, together with those which for policy reasons banks have from time to time granted on a longer-term basis were enough in the past to cover any aspirations of United Kingdom bankers towards long-term loans out of their on-demand and short-term deposits.

Now, however, bankers apart from using part of their funds for house mortgages are also able to arrange medium-term loans through borrowing wholesale funds on the money market but the responsibility of matching lending to borrowing has effectively been put upon the borrowing customer who has to meet the changing interest requirements which may be necessary on roll-over dates (see also Chapter 13).

Bankers have also taken the view that the proprietors of a business should have a larger financial stake in any enterprise than the bank. The proprietor should take the risks and is entitled to the profits and should show his confidence by providing the bulk of the funds. It is easy to be reckless with other people's money.

It is no part of a banker's business to provide risk money at a low rate of interest. Speculative transactions deserve high interest rates to compensate for the risks taken.

For the bulk of transactions, therefore, a bank's stake will be less than the proprietor's, although it will have been seen from an earlier chapter that with produce advances this is not the case, as good market conditions and rapidity of turnover may permit some variation.

It is also common for bankers to lend several times the amount of a proprietor's stake when dealing with hire-purchase and finance companies, and this is somewhat surprising. In produce transactions, loans are quickly repaid and are thereby justifiable as good banking practice, but lending to hire-purchase and finance companies does not satisfy this criterion because it generally becomes solid hard-core. The lending is not subject to quick repayments because of the nature of the business. Instalments from the customers of hire-purchase companies are spread over a period, and although any bank lending would be quickly repaid if the instalments were received without new business being transacted, in practice instalments are needed to transact new business. In consequence, bank lending to hire-purchase companies tends to become hard-core. This is hardly surprising because when banks lend much more than the proprietors' stakes they are, in effect, providing capital.

As this is outside normal bank facilities such lending justifies a higher interest rate.

The reason why banks adopted this generous attitude to hire-purchase companies in the past is not plain to see, but there now appears to be a general movement to reduce the amount of bank lending which is out of proportion to the stake of the borrower. The freeing of the interest rate structure has meant that hard-core borrowing is obtained only at increased interest rates compatible with those applying to the long-term capital market or related to inter-bank rates in the money market.

If we turn now to the practical aspect, we find that there are two formulae which must be kept in mind. The first concerns the overall borrowing of the hire-purchase company in relation to its stake and the second concerns the proportion it is reasonable to lend against the security of hire-purchase or credit-sale documents.

To a well-managed company with a successful record of trading it has been the practice to lend in proportion to the proprietor's stake at the ratio of 4:1 or sometimes as much as 5:1, but, as the standing of the borrower falls, so does the proportion — to 3:1 or 2:1. Any borrowing from other sources or from the public reduces the amount a bank will lend by an equivalent amount, so that the overall borrowing of the company is contained within the agreed ratio.

Let us take a simple example. If a ratio of 4:1 is observed and a company's stake is £260,000, its borrowing will be restricted to four times this amount — ie, £1,040,000. Should goods be financed which are retailed at the wholesale price plus 30 per cent, it would be possible (ignoring interest and charges) to have the following position:

	£
Wholesale price of goods	1,000,000
Add Retailers' mark up of 30 per cent	300,000
Sale price of goods	1,300,000
Finance from proprietors	260,000
Finance borrowed	1,040,000
Total finance	1,300,000

It will be seen that the finance borrowed is more than the wholesale price of the goods and it would be a very fortunate person who, if repossessing the goods, managed to sell them at an amount equivalent to the wholesale price. This situation would not occur in practice as it would not be necessary to repossess all of the goods at once, unless the entire business had foolishly been transacted with one hirer.

So far I have ignored interest and charges on the hire-purchase contracts, and these could well amount to another £200,000 in the example given. No more finance is of course necessary to provide for this, as this is the additional sum which the hirers have to agree to repay over a period. Therefore, as an alternative to the view that the finance provided has supported transactions in goods worth £1,000,000 wholesale or £1,300,000 retail, we can look instead to hirers who have agreed to pay instalments totalling £1,500,000. This puts the situation in a far better light, providing the hirers are well spread. However, we can see that this example illustrates that a ratio of 4:1 is far from ungenerous finance, and a lender's money to a hire-purchase company is only safe if the company is successful in its business and does not incur many bad debts.

Security

This leads us to the point of whether a banker looks to the goods as security for his advance or looks to the debtors under the hire-purchase agreements. In order to appreciate the point fully, it would be as well if we considered the position before the Hire Purchase Act 1965, as well as the current position.

Before 1965 the law gave a hire-purchase company fairly wide powers of repossession if instalments were not paid, and this meant that the hire-purchase company or a receiver or liquidator or mortgagee of hire-purchase agreements could look to the goods as cover for any amounts advanced. It was then policy for a hire-purchase company to see that at the start of each contract the amount owing by the hirer was less than the forced-sale price of the goods, and that the instalments paid were more than sufficient to cover the rate of depreciation of the goods. The amount outstanding on the hire-purchase agreements would then always be less than the price at which repossessed goods could be sold. It followed therefore that the class of goods on which hire-purchase was arranged was important: items such as new motor cars which could easily be sold were thus looked upon as satisfactory for hire-purchase transactions, but small items such as electrical goods and furniture were unsatisfactory as their resale value was so low.

The Hire Purchase Act which came into force on 1 January 1965 changed the situation. It raised the figure for statutory protection from £300 to £2,000. This meant that, except in the case of the hirer being a limited company, where a hire-purchase agreement was for £2,000 or less the goods could not be repossessed without leave of the court if one-third of the purchase price had been paid.

Thus, for the bulk of hire-purchase agreements there were difficulties in trying to repossess the goods. At first sight this seemed to cut away almost completely the security of the goods upon which banks were ultimately looking for cover for their advances to hire-purchase companies.

However, most hire-purchase companies had also been arranging credit sale agreements and they extended this method of finance in preference to hire-purchase contracts after 1 January 1965. Although this meant that the hire-purchase company had no rights in the goods it was financing, the credit-sale agreements were drawn in a way to make the whole of the outstanding balance immediately repayable if the buyer made default on any one instalment. The hire-purchase company could, if necessary, quickly obtain judgement for the amount owing and levy execution against any possessions of the hirer sufficient to enable the outstanding amount to be covered by the sale proceeds.

In a way this strengthened the position of the hire-purchase companies, as they were not restricted for recovery of their money to the specific goods which were being hired, but of course it is no use levying execution against a debtor's goods if his possessions are not worth the trouble of seizing and selling. Care is still necessary to see that credit-sales are made only to suitable people.

The effect as far as banks were concerned was that when debentures or hire-purchase and credit-sale agreements were held as security, instead of looking to the goods covered by hire-purchase contracts which were now of little use, they looked to the hire-purchase companies' debtors instead.

Naturally a spread of debtors provides better cover than fewer debtors for larger figures. Whereas previously small hire-purchase contracts were not attractive as security when looking to the goods as cover, credit-sale agreements for small sums were now satisfactory providing that there was a large spread and the hire-purchase companies took care before arranging transactions.

The necessary care is observed by seeing that the hire-purchase and finance companies are transacting business with people upon whom they can obtain good reports (and there are now fairly extensive credit enquiry bureaux) and by seeing that a reasonable deposit is paid. Obviously, if a person can enter into a credit purchase by putting down a minute deposit, many people will be encouraged to take on transactions which are beyond their means. The collection by a receiver or liquidator of numerous small doubtful debts is an expensive and tedious business.

Bank Lending

Banks therefore should take care when lending to hire-purchase companies to see that their record is good and that they are not losing large amounts by way of bad debts. Enquiries should also be made as to the proportion of hire-purchase transactions to credit-sales and the amounts taken as deposits.

If a bank is lending to a hire-purchase company which is not of sufficient strength to allow unsecured facilities and if outside security is not available, it is normal to obtain a debenture over the assets of the company or a specific charge over the hire-purchase and credit-sale contracts. If a debenture is held and the hire-purchase and credit-sale contracts are deposited with the bank as security, a fixed charge is obtained over these contracts; but if a debenture only is held without the deposit of the contracts, a floating charge only is obtained.

Now we come to the amount which it is reasonable for a bank to lend against debtors which are well spread. Providing the precautions already mentioned have been taken (ie, good reports obtained, reasonable deposits provided and the contracts over not too long a term) a 50 per cent margin is deemed to give satisfactory cover. By this I mean that a bank will lend 66⅔ per cent of outstanding debtors and that one in three of outstanding amounts will have to be bad before the bank lending is in jeopardy. In order to ensure that bad and doubtful debts are not included in the debtor's figure, it is usual to exclude instalments which are in arrears by, say, two or three payments and to obtain from the company (with periodical confirmation by the auditors) a statement of the total debtors outstanding on hire-purchase and credit-sale agreements and a total for instalments in arrears.

In a particular instance a bank might be agreeable to a 3:1 ratio if lending was to be covered by debtors on agreements with a margin of 50 per cent while other security covered borrowing of £40,000 within an agreed limit of £200,000. The composite agreement could be:

1. Limit £200,000.
2. Ratio of all borrowing to capital plus free reserves not to exceed 3:1.
3. Borrowing in excess of £40,000 to be covered with a margin of 50 per cent by the balance of instalments outstanding under aggregate hire-purchase and credit-sale agreements.
4. Instalments three months in arrears and agreements for longer than three years, or where initial payments by hire or credit purchaser do not amount to at least 15 per cent of the purchase price, to be excluded.
5. Certificates to be provided monthly and certified by auditors quarterly.

CASE 1

A company has arranged with its bankers to borrow up to £80,000 on an in-and-out basis for normal trading purposes. The security held by the bank is a debenture plus a guarantee from a director supported by a security which is good for £50,000. The terms incorporated in the debenture are that current assets are to be kept at an amount double that by which the bank debt exceeds £50,000. Certificates of liquid assets and liabilities are to be provided quarterly.

The company has some leasehold shops (held on short leases only) and sells electrical goods.

During the year a new young director is appointed who apparently has go-ahead ideas and whose expressed intention is to put some life into the company and boost turnover. Turnover certainly rises quickly as evidenced by the banking account, on which appears a rapidly increasing debit balance with no swing into credit. Quarterly certificates of liquid assets and liabilities are not produced, but the bank is conscious of the fact that it is holding a director's guarantee which is good for £50,000 and it is not greatly concerned.

Eventually audited accounts are produced and at the same time a request is made for the director's guarantee to be cancelled. This is because the director now wishes to retire from active business and the remaining directors consider that, with the rapid progress made by the company, a debenture alone is sufficient security. The request is also for the limit of £80,000 to continue with a promise of reduction from profits of about £20,000 in the coming year.

The audited accounts produced read as follows:

Current liabilities	£	
Bank	70,000	
Creditors and bills payable . .	270,000	Greatly in excess of debtors
Taxation	9,000	
Total current liabilities . . .	349,000	Equivalent to current assets
Capital	35,000	
Reserves — Profit and loss a/c .	6,000	
Total liabilities	390,000	

Current assets	£	
Debtors.	25,000	
Stock	54,000	
H.P. agreements	270,000	
Total current assets. . . .	349,000	
Leaseholds	20,000	Short leases
Fixtures and fittings . . .	2,000	
Motor cars	19,000	
Total assets	390,000	
Turnover	450,000	Up from £250,000 previous year

Net profit before tax	.	.	.	10,000	
Tax .	.	.	.	4,000	
Net profit after tax .	.	.	6,000	Up from £3,000 previous year
Directors' remuneration .	.	.	35,000	Up from £26,000 previous year
Carried forward	.	.	.	6,000	
Net worth	.	.	.	41,000	

The directors are very pleased with themselves for having pushed up the turnover from £250,000 to £450,000 in the year and for making sufficient to enable them to increase their remuneration from £26,000 to £35,000 and still leave £6,000 profit to be ploughed back into the business. They point to assets totalling £390,000 and consider the borrowing £80,000 from the bank should cause no difficulty with the bank holding a debenture.

Bank Viewpoint

However, let us look at the figures from a banker's point of view. There is no net liquidity, because current assets and liabilities are the same, and the proprietors' funds of £41,000 are just sufficient to cover the fixed assets. The proprietors are therefore providing no working capital for a turnover of £450,000. The leases are all for terms of 10 years or less.

The most remarkable feature of the accounts however is the large amount of creditors at £270,000, which is balanced by hire-purchase agreements of a similar figure. As no working capital was available and the bank borrowing in the accounts is £70,000, there is obviously insufficient money to support a large amount of hire-purchase business. If creditors and bills payable total £270,000 whereas debtors are only £25,000, a liquidity crisis seems imminent. However, further enquiry reveals that there are £70,000 of normal creditors and £200,000 on bills payable to a finance house. The finance house has lent this money against the assignment of hire-purchase agreements with a margin of 33⅓ per cent − ie, the amount advanced to be 75 per cent of the agreements assigned. This means that to cover the advance of £200,000, agreements assigned amounted to £266,000. The total of free agreements remaining was only £4,000 and, with debtors being only £25,000 against normal creditors of £70,000, the company certainly has its liquidity problems. The trouble has been the impossibility of financing hire-purchase contracts or part of the contracts without having the funds to do so.

Let us see what the bank picks up under its debenture. The leases are all short, with, of course, rapid depreciation. It is normal to have clauses in such leases to provide for them to lapse on the appointment of a liquidator or receiver, or the bankruptcy of the lessee. Such leases are not suitable as banking security and could only be looked upon as 'make-weight'. The fixtures and fittings would fetch little in a forced sale but the motor vehicles should be saleable. It is to be hoped that proper depreciation of the vehicles has been provided and the balance sheet figure is accurate.

As for the liquid assets, there are debtors of £25,000 plus free hire-purchase agreements for £4,000 and stock of £54,000. Stock in a break-up fetches only a fraction of its normal saleable value and, as a bank normally looks for a margin of 50 per cent in debtors, the most that could be lent would be say £20,000 against debtors and free agreements and £18,000 against stock plus £3,000/£4,000 against the fixed assets. The finance house is, of course, holding agreements in excess of its advance to the extent of £66,000 and in a break-up the bank would claim these on its floating charge subject to the settlement of the finance house which holds a fixed charge.

Altogether, after ignoring all the adverse factors, there are insufficient assets to cover bank lending of £80,000, and the adverse factor of illiquidity is one which needs immediate attention.

These points were made to the directors and they were strongly advised to put their finances in order. They were also told that the directors' guarantee for £50,000 could not be released. The directors professed not to see the validity of the bank's point of view and said they understood that banks financed hire-purchase companies. This led to a discussion about lending to such companies and the bank pointed out that even for soundly based medium size hire-purchase concerns a ratio of lending of 4:1 was considered not ungenerous, whereas the borrowing of the customers at £70,000 from the bank and £200,000 from a finance house was in excess of six times the capital and profit and loss account of £41,000.

Second Approach

The directors went away to think over the situation but within a fortnight they were back at the bank with interim draft accounts for six months.

The two sets of accounts appeared as follows:

	Previous year £	Subsequent six months £	
Current liabilities			
Bank	70,000	54,000	Down
Creditors and bills payable . . .	270,000	370,000	Large increase
Taxation . . .	9,000	8,000	
Total current liabilities .	349,000	432,000	Now exceeds current assets
Capital	35,000	35,000	
Reserves . . .	—	70,000	New
Profit and loss account. .	6,000	—	
Total liabilities . . .	390,000	537,000	
Current assets			
Debtors . . .	25,000	37,000	Up
Stock	54,000	72,000	Up
Hire purchase agreements .	270,000	305,000	Up
Total current assets . .	349,000	414,000	
Leaseholds . . .	20,000	100,000	Large increase
Fixtures and fittings . .	2,000	5,000	
Motor cars . . .	19,000	18,000	
Total assets . . .	390,000	537,000	

	Previous year £	For six months £	
Turnover	450,000	275,000	Running at increased level
Net profit before tax . .	10,000	(6,000)	Loss caused by bad debts written off
Taxation	4,000	—	
Net profit after tax . .	6,000	(6,000)	Loss
Directors' remuneration .	35,000	20,000	Running at increased level
Carried forward . .	6,000	—	
Net worth	41,000	105,000	Large increase

The directors said that the accounts now produced were a more accurate representation of the business and in view of the better position shown they considered that the bank should now release the guarantor from his liability and rely solely on the debenture for an overdraft limit of £80,000. They said that the amount they were borrowing from the finance house was £210,000 and that, as four times their net worth was £420,000, an advance of £80,000 by the bank would mean that they were well within a 4:1 ratio.

When it was mentioned that their net worth was increased merely by writing up the value of the leaseholds they said that one of their number was an expert on property values and he was confident the leases would sell for this new figure. With debtors up, together with free agreements (£305,000 minus £280,000 − ie, £210,000 plus 33⅓ per cent) plus stock and with the leaseholds in addition, the directors were insistent that their viewpoint was correct. The loss of £6,000 they explained as a misfortune which would not happen again.

True Position

The new set of figures is in fact much worse and the illiquidity problem is now acute. Creditors apart from the finance house are £160,000 and with debtors being only £37,000 a large amount of additional finance is immediately necessary to stave off creditor pressure. Turnover is much increased and the proprietors' stake is now insufficient even to cover the fixed assets and cannot provide any working capital.

The bank's answer now must be, not only a refusal of the request, but an insistence that strict control be taken over the company's finances in order to avoid disaster. The first requirement will be to obtain some additional permanent capital to settle creditors. Meanwhile the company will have to cease hire-purchase trading as it is unable to finance contracts or the margin required by the finance company. A switch to cash trading (and against credit cards) is essential unless the company is able to get a finance or hire-purchase company to take over entirely the hire-purchase business. Contracts would then be drawn direct with the hire-purchase company. A great effort will have to be made to restore liquidity and, apart from cutting out its own hire-purchase finance which the company could not afford, it looks as if it will also have to consolidate its turnover and keep it within the bounds of its own resources.

All too often this type of position occurs when a company with insufficient resources tries to do its own financing of hire-purchase and credit-sales.

CASE 2

Mr Friend, a good customer of long standing and a man of some means, built up a small chain of retail furniture shops which conducted their own hire-purchase finance; six months ago he sold out to a large public company. His experience in this line of business is good and he has been looking around since to find some similar shops to purchase and start again.

He says that he has now found a suitable company whose accounts he has examined with his accountant, and they are confident that Mr Friend can reorganise the company on better lines and thereby make a good purchase. The company is already successful but Mr Friend believes he can make it more so.

The company owns a freehold shop and Mr Friend intends to purchase a further small leasehold shop for £40,000 on which a mortgage of £20,000 has been arranged in principle. The company has been borrowing £30,000 from its bankers unsecured and all its hire-purchase transactions have been financed by a hire-purchase company.

Mr Friend now wishes the company to finance hire-purchase contracts and he has asked the bank to increase the overdraft limit to £120,000, which is to be taken on two separate accounts of £60,000 each as follows:

Account No 1	£	*Account No 2*	£
Existing facilities . . .	30,000	Hire-purchase finance . .	60,000
Part purchase of new shop .	20,000		
Stock for new shop . . .	5,000		
Additional trading finance . .	5,000		
	60,000		60,000

The request is for unsecured facilities and Mr Friend says that the purchase will cost him (and his wife) £194,000, being capital, profit and loss account and reserves of £119,000 and directors' loans of £75,000 to be taken over in addition. The audited accounts for the last three years are produced and, as there has been little change in the fortunes of the company in that period, one set of figures will therefore be sufficient for us to analyse, as follows:

Current liabilities	£	
Bank	30,000	Account swings from Dr £30,000 to Cr £10,000
Creditors	54,000	Less than debtors
Taxation	20,000	
Directors' loans	75,000	
Total current liabilities . . .	179,000	Less than current assets
Mortgage	100,000	
Minority interests . . .	3,000	
	282000	
Capital	9,000	
Reserves	90,000	
Profit and loss account . . .	20,000	
Total liabilities	401,000	

Current assets

Cash	.	.	.	.	.	2,000
Debtors.	.	.	.	.	.	70,000
Stock	.	.	.	.	.	114,000

Total current assetes	.	.	.	186,000	Net current assets only £7,000
Freeholds.	.	.	.	150,000	Subject to mortgage £100,000
					see above

Fixtures and fittings	.	.	.	34,000	
Investments	.	.	.	3,000	
Motor vehicles.	.	.	.	26,000	
				399,000	
Goodwill .	.	.	.	2,000	
Total assets	.	.	.	401,000	
Turnover .	.	.	.	400,000	
Net profit before tax	.	.	.	15,000	
Taxation .	.	.	.	5,000	
Net profit after tax .	.	.	.	10,000	
Carried forward	.	.	.	20,000	
Net worth	.	.	.	117,000	(Proprietor's stake £119,000 includes goodwill £2,000)

Discussing the Loan

The proprietor's stake of £119,000 is shown as the amount to be paid by Mr Friend and his wife, but if we also get Mr Friend to agree that he will not withdraw the directors' loans without the bank's agreement, we could look at the proprietor's stake as being £194,000 and this would also mean that we could look on the net current assets as being £82,000 instead of the £7,000 shown in the accounts. On an unsecured basis, one half of the net current assets would be sufficient for the bank to be lending, especially as stock is a large proportion, and this, of course, is much less than the £120,000 requested. Looking at the remaining assets, we see that a substantial proportion of the freehold valuation has been borrowed on mortgage (66⅔ per cent) and there is therefore very little that the bank could look to as a basis for unsecured lending on the fixed assets.

This is explained to Mr Friend, who then says that he is agreeable to a debenture being given to the bank but he would like an arrangement whereby the hire-purchase transactions are kept separately and financed separately as this will enable him to see more easily if this side of the business helps profitability. Quite sensibly he says that he does not wish to damage the existing business by putting too great a proportion of finance into the hire-purchase side and thereby depriving the normal trading side of adequate funds.

In the discussion that follows concerning the hire-purchase arrangements, Mr Friend says that he intends to run the contracts in the same way as he had done previously, which had proved successful. This entails making enquiries upon the customer and not making a sale if there is any doubt as to the purchaser's trustworthiness or capacity to complete the contract. Normally sales would be made on hire-purchase contracts but occasionally credit-sales agreements would be used.

The general average of prices of the transactions is estimated as follows:

	£
Cost price	300
Add Retailer's margin, say, one-third	100
Retail price	400
Service loading on contracts	80
	480
Initial deposit	80
To be repaid over two years or less	400

It will be seen therefore that for debtors of £400 the company has provided the cost of the goods of £300.

The Manager's Decision

If the bank lent 66 per cent of debtors, the company would be providing only 9 per cent which means that the bank would be providing almost all the finance required for this side of the business. If the proportion to be provided by the bank was dropped to 60 per cent the company would be providing 15 per cent which is a more reasonable proportion and would put the lending on a 4:1 ratio.

However, the company is not providing additional finance by injecting funds into the business to provide for the hire-purchase and credit-sale contracts, and any finance required will have to come out of the liquid assets. If the bank lending on the No. 2 account for this side of the business is to be £60,000, the company will have to find £15,000 which will reduce the current assets for the remainder of the business to £171,000. Borrowing of another £60,000 is required on account No. 1 for the retail trading, and current assets of twice this figure could be kept comfortably.

Would this be satisfactory? Debtors exceed creditors, the length of credit given and received is reasonable. If the business fails and debtors on the retail side do not cover the bank debt the bank should still be safe with whatever can be salvaged from the stock sale and the equity in the freehold and leasehold together with proceeds of sale of other fixed assets. Taking the two accounts together, the overall borrowing would also be less than the proprietors' stake.

Monthly figures should be obtained with quarterly certification by the auditors and care should be exercised to see that stock does not increase unduly at the expense of debtors.

The formula agreed could therefore be:

1. Debenture to be taken as security.
2. The proprietors to agree that directors' loans would not be withdrawn without the consent of the bank.
3. the lending on No. 1 account to be covered by liquid assets with a margin of 100 per cent.
4. The lending on No. 2 account to be no more than 60 per cent of the outstanding amounts due on the hire-purchase and credit-sale agreements deposited with the bank.
5. Monthly certificates of liquid assets and preferential creditors to be provided and also lists of hire-purchase and credit-sales outstanding less instalments which are two months in arrears.
6. Quarterly certificates to be provided by auditors.

11. Importing and Exporting

Although the bulk of the finance for importing and exporting is by means of bank overdrafts in the normal manner, there are several other ways of financing this trade. Some of these apply also to domestic trade, but trade with overseas countries is normally involved.

Exports Credits Guarantee Department

The Export Credits Guarantee Department has had a wide influence on the financing of exports and, as the arrangements made by this government department directly and indirectly affect the facilities which banks can grant, it would be as well to consider briefly some of its activities.

The department's main activity is insurance, with the object of making export trading no more hazardous than soundly conducted home trade. There are many reasons why payment from overseas buyers may not be as easy to obtain as from a buyer in the home market. ECGD insurance is designed to cover non-payment due to exchange blockage or delay, import licensing restrictions, United Kingdom export licensing restrictions, war or civil disturbance in the buyer's country, and insolvency or protracted default of the buyer, as well as some other not so obvious risks.

It is the policy of ECGD that the insurer shall carry part of the risk and, according to the type of policy and the cover required, the range of insurance has been generally between 85 and 95 per cent.

Obviously the holding of ECGD insurance cover is a great comfort to an exporter and likewise to his banker and, as the benefit of any claim can be assigned, it can often strengthen a security position.

However, in the same way in which other insurance may become ineffective, so also may insurance cover with ECGD. Naturally premiums must be paid up and all the stipulations and limits quoted on the policy observed. Prompt and correct declaration of contracts or shipments must be made, and the reason for the exporter not receiving payment must not be a cause within the exporter's control. If an exporter does not comply with a contract and does not deliver the goods on time, or the goods are defective, he cannot expect the prospective buyer to pay for the goods. Likewise he cannot expect ECGD to pay for the loss which had arisen through his own fault.

However, exporters of long experience and undoubted integrity will obtain all the necessary permits and deliver on time to comply with the contracts and, in such cases, their debtors would be insured to at least 85 per cent. If the competence and integrity of the exporter is in doubt it would be unwise for a banker to place much reliance upon the fact that cover with ECGD has been obtained, as a claim could well fail for non-compliance with the policy terms by the exporter.

As the object of ECGD cover is to make overseas trading no more hazardous than home trading, it does no more than this. It does not have the effect of making every overseas debtor good − this is only the case when the terms of the policy have been properly observed, and so often this cannot be known to a banker. If the terms of the policy are correctly observed, the overseas debtors become good to the extent of at least 85 per cent.

It follows that the deposit of the ECGD policy and the assignment of claims to a banker do not constitute a charge over the overseas debts, but valid claims would be paid to the bankers. To establish a charge over debtors a debenture from a company is necessary or alternatively the assignment of specific debts. If debts generally are assigned, the assignment must be registered as a bill of sale. To give himself more protection a banker can (as well as having the ECGD policy deposited and assigned to him) also have an accepted bill of exchange hypothecated to him. There are still risks because the banker cannot be certain that the exporter has observed the terms required by ECGD. The main risks in these circumstances would be because of:

i   non-payment of premium;
ii   exceeding limits of cover arranged;
iii   non-provision of correct declarations of contracts and shipments;
iv   import licensing requirement not observed at the time the contract with the overseas buyer was agreed.

It will be seen that these risks are acceptable ones if the amounts involved are not large in comparison with the resources of the exporter, and providing he is experienced with exports to the particular country involved.

The risks are still there however and each case must be separately assessed by the banker.

Although I have described the ECGD cover as insurance, it is unfortunate that ECGD instead of calling their cover document a 'policy' have called it a 'guarantee', and this leads some exporters to think that the assignment of their cover to a bank is a guarantee which a bank can rely upon. As can be seen, this is far from the case.

For a bank to have complete safety it is necessary for it to have a Bank Guarantee issued by ECGD. These are issued in connection with the larger capital goods schemes where extended periods of credit have to be granted (over two years) in order to meet overseas competition and obtain the business. Bank Guarantees have also been issued in connection with the ECGD shorter term export finance schemes. Details of these schemes follow but it should be noted that the schemes are being phased out and will come to an end in October 1987. They are being replaced by various shorter term schemes promoted by individual banks.

Short-term ECGD Finance — Bills and Notes

In order to obtain export orders in a competitive world market it is often necessary to quote terms for payment which would not be granted to purchasers in the domestic market, and this scheme was devised to help exporters when they had to quote deferred terms for settlement. Naturally, when long credit is given, debtors outstand and are not turned quickly into cash, and if debtors build up in this way the exporter will be deprived of finance which may be necessary for his business.

This scheme was therefore devised to enable the payment by debtors to be anticipated, and application for consideration in the scheme could be made by exporters who had had insurance cover with ECGD for at least 12 months. If approved, a bank guarantee was given by ECGD to protect a banker in making advances under the scheme to the exporter.

The scheme covers those transactions in which credit is given to an overseas buyer for goods sold on terms not exceeding two years.

Applications for bank guarantees were made by the exporters to ECGD through their bankers with the following details:

i   figures showing what export business has been transacted for the past
         three years;
ii   audited accounts for three years;
iii   agreement that information may be given by its bankers to ECGD.

If the application was approved and a bank guarantee issued, the customer
then submitted bills of exchange or promissory notes with shipping
documents or other evidence of export to its bankers for an advance to be
made. The customer also gave in writing a warranty certifying that the
transactions were completely in order in the terms of the ECGD agreement.
At this stage the bank advanced the face value of the bills or promissory
notes and interest was charged at a preferential rate of ⅝ per cent over
base rate. ECGD also charged for giving the guarantee.

In the terms of the ECGD agreement there was recourse by the bank to
the exporter only up to the time when the bill is accepted or the promissory
note signed. The bank is completely covered by the ECGD guarantee and
will therefore incur no risk.

The bank must however keep in mind that the exporter is borrowing in
anticipation of receipt of payment by debtors, and if the bank is lending
in consideration of the customer's net liquid position, it must take into
account that fewer debtors will be available to effect repayment of such
borrowing. This is similar to the position which arises when a company
has factored some of its debtors.

Shorter-term ECGD Finance – Open Account

Although in years past it was normal for most exporters to be paid by way
of bills there has in recent years been a tendency for goods to be sold in
the same way as in the domestic market – that is, by way of credit on open
account. This is more suitable when numerous small transactions are
arranged, where bills might be cumbersome and uneconomic in relation
to the sums collected.

For this reason a further scheme was devised by ECGD to encourage
exporters and allow them to anticipate receipt of debtors on open account.

In the same way as with the bills and notes scheme it was necessary for
the exporter to have had an insurance policy with ECGD for at least 12
months. The bills and notes scheme covers transactions on credit terms of
up to two years but the open account scheme covers sales on open account

on 'cash against documents' terms or for a credit period of up to six months.

Application for ECGD to issue a bank guarantee was made in a similar way as for the bills and notes scheme but after the guarantee had been given the procedure was somewhat different.

When the exporter wished to draw upon the facilities he provided a schedule of exported goods stating when payment was due. This must be supported by copies of invoices and evidence of export and the following are accepted as evidence:

i   shipping bill of lading;
ii   advice of shipment from a forwarding agent or a shipping company;
iii   airway bill;
iv   delivery note (for goods in the exporters' own vehicles for delivery into the Irish Republic);
v   post office certificate of posting.

The exporter also had to complete promissory notes for repayment of the advances requested and the promissory notes have to be dated for the last day of the month during which the debtors are due to make payment.

The bank then advanced up to 100 per cent of the net invoice values. The interest rate is the same as for the bills and notes scheme, as also is the ECGD fee. There was also a small bank charge for each batch of documents covered by each promissory note.

In the terms of the ECGD agreement there was recourse to the exporter throughout but the bank will be covered by the ECGD guarantee and will therefore incur no risk. As for the bills and notes scheme the bank will have to keep in mind, if there is other lending by the bank to the exporter, that receipt of payment by debtors is being anticipated.

Smaller Exports Schemes

Individual banks and their subsidiary companies have devised schemes to help the smaller exporter and have themselves arranged ECGD cover. This makes documentation much simpler for exporters and these schemes are supplanting the ECGD shorter term schemes. The detail arrangements made by each bank vary but the overall arrangements are for the exporter to be able to have immediate advances up to around 85% on all acceptable overseas invoices and for the balance to be paid either on a stated date or on settlement. The overseas debts are insured by ECGD up to 95%.

Discounting and Negotiating Bills of Exchange

There are differences between discounting and negotiating but a lending banker need not concern himself greatly with the differences providing he understands the liabilities which are incurred. If a bill of exchange in sterling is discounted the resultant amount is also in sterling. If a bill of exchange in German marks is converted to sterling and then the sterling is discounted the resultant amount will also be in sterling. However, an additional transaction has taken place − ie, the conversion into a different currency.

We can look upon both transactions in a similar light, except that in the second instance if the bill of exchange is dishonoured (and recourse to a customer is invariably obtained by a banker), the banker will charge his customer with the sterling equivalent of the bill of exchange at the rate of exchange then ruling and not the rate ruling at the time the bill was negotiated. Except under the ECGD shorter-term scheme for bills and notes bankers do not normally discount or negotiate bills of exchange of longer than six months' tenor, and an additional customer liability in such circumstances would only be applicable when dealing in a volatile currency.

A bill of exchange can be discounted or negotiated whether or not it has been accepted. All parties to a bill of exchange become liable on it and, although the proposed acceptor of a bill of exchange cannot be liable on it until he has accepted it, the drawer of the bill of exchange is liable from the time he discounts or negotiates it. A banker can therefore discount or negotiate an unaccepted bill of exchange with recourse to the drawer. Once the bill of exchange has been accepted by a third party, a banker would have a claim on both the drawer and the acceptor. This could give the bill more substance but a banker would prefer to rely upon his own customer of whom he has knowledge than upon a third party of whom he may have no knowledge. If the acceptor was a bank or a large and prosperous commercial concern the situation would of course be different.

Bills of exchange can be drawn to be payable at sight or at usance (a number of days after sight or date). This gives a large variety to the types of bills of exchange which can be encountered but it must always be kept in mind that bankers take the precaution of retaining recourse against their customers. This is the starting point when considering the liabilities which may have to be faced by a customer. The bill of exchange may gain added strength through having attached a complete set of documents giving title to the goods underlying the transaction, so long as the goods are easily saleable. Also acceptance by a bank or reputable commercial concern would likewise enhance the value of a bill of exchange.

Exporting with Settlement by Bills of Exchange

An exporter can transact his business in several ways and obtain settlement by bills of exchange:

1. He can export the goods and send all documents to the importer together with a bill of exchange. The importer then accepts the bill of exchange and returns it to the exporter, who may then ask his bankers to collect the proceeds, or to discount or negotiate the bill of exchange. A banker when discounting or negotiating will firstly consider whether his customer will be good for the liability if the bill of exchange is dishonoured.

2. He can export the goods but send all documents to his banker with instructions for the documents to be released against payment, or to be released against acceptance of a bill of exchange payable after a certain term. If a banker is asked to discount or negotiate the bill of exchange before acceptance he will again consider whether his customer is good for the liability if the importer refuses to accept the bill of exchange or if it is dishonoured when presented for payment. If the documents are complete and give a good title, the goods would provide additional security so long as the documents are only to be released against payment. Naturally, if the documents are released against acceptance of a bill of exchange, the goods will then be obtained by the importer. Whether or not a banker will rely upon the added security of documents to goods will depend on the circumstances. He should certainly take into account that, if he is relying upon the goods as security, he may be faced with paying storage charges for the goods in a warehouse abroad pending an alternative sale or auction. It might also be necessary for the goods to be re-shipped with all the attendant expense.

3. He can ask the importer to arrange for a letter of credit to be established in this country whereby he can obtain payment or have a bill of exchange accepted by a banker upon presentation of stated documents. A bill of exchange accepted by a banker in this way can be discounted at fine rates and, although an exporter's banker when asked to discount such a bill would still retain recourse to his customer, he could naturally look first to the good name of the acceptor.

Sometimes exporters consider that there is no risk to a banker in discounting bills of exchange if the exporter holds an ECGD policy which is assigned to the bank. This can certainly strengthen the position if the exporter is reliable and experienced but if any of the conditions of the ECGD policy have not been observed there will be no valid claim. This type of security falls far short of an ECGD Bank Guarantee, under which borrowing can be obtained at a preferential rate of interest.

Advances against Bills of Exchange

An exporter with a bill of exchange, instead of asking his banker to discount or negotiate it, can ask for an advance to be made, prior to maturity, of less than the face value of the bill. The bill of exchange can be accepted or unaccepted, have documents attached or be clean, and similar considerations will apply as for discounting or negotiating. In the case of an advance, however, the liability of the customer on recourse would be less than when the full value is discounted or negotiated.

Theoretically an advance is repayable on demand, and repayment can be demanded before maturity, but in the case of discounting or negotiating a banker may consider that he must present the bill at maturity and have it dishonoured before he can demand settlement from his customer. This difference should concern the practical banker only when he has knowledge that the finances of the drawer or acceptor are precarious. It would then be better for any facilities to be by way of advances against bills of exchange in preference to discounting or negotiating. Alternatively it may be preferable to decline facilities entirely.

Documentary Credits

An importer can arrange for his banker to establish with a bank abroad a credit in favour of a third party upon which payment is to be made when certain specified documents are presented. If a complete set of documents is insisted upon (possibly an endorsed bill of lading, endorsed insurance policy and invoice) a good title to the goods can be obtained and the bank will therefore have the goods as security. The documents can then be handed to the importer against his payment, and the importer will be able to collect the goods.

If an importer is unable to get goods shipped to him on open account he may have to establish documentary credits, and these involve him in a liability to his banker. The importer has some protection, as the money is not paid away until documents showing shipment are produced, but it must be kept in mind that money is paid away against documents which purport to represent certain goods, and the goods have not been examined. An importer will, for his own protection, have to assure himself of the integrity of the exporter abroad and likewise, if a banker is relying upon the goods in any way as security, he will have to satisfy himself that the importer has ability and experience of the trade. If the goods are suitable as security for a produce loan (ie, easily saleable in a wide market preferably by description or sample) they could, of course, be suitable as security for a documentary credit as, should payment from the importer not be immediately forthcoming, the goods could be warehoused and a produce advance created. If other security is not available a banker would have to decide to what extent he would rely upon the goods and ask for any shortfall to be deposited in cash on a margin account before the documentary credit is opened.

Acceptances

Just as an importer can arrange for his bank to tell a correspondent bank abroad to pay an overseas exporter against the production of specified documents, so too can arrangements be made for a bill of exchange to be accepted when specified documents are produced. Overseas exporters require cash but, if instead of cash they have bills of exchange accepted by bankers, they can readily discount the bills if necessary. They may well make a difference in their pricing to cover the cost of discounting but importers may consider this worthwhile in order to get a period of credit. The goods may be sold during this period and the resultant cash used to meet the liability on the bill of exchange on the due date.

As far as the importer's banker is concerned, he would be in the same position as with a documentary credit up to the time he released the goods to the importer. At that time, however, he would have given up the security of the goods but would still be liable to the bank abroad on the bill of exchange which would be presented for payment at the end of its tenor.

If other security was not available and a banker wished to retain the security in the goods he could either:

i   warehouse the goods after having them pledged to him and release them against payment (or part of the goods against part payment), or

ii in suitable cases, after the goods had been pledged to him, release them to the importer on a trust facility. The importer would then have to keep the goods separately, and account to the bank for all sales made. The proceeds of the sales would be credited to a separate banking account to meet the liability on the bill of exchange at maturity.

In order to judge whether or not there is a suitable case for releasing the goods on a trust facility, the same considerations would apply as for a produce loan — ie, the importer would have to be experienced in his trade and a person of undoubted untegrity, and the goods would have to be of a type easily sold in a wide market and identifiable by simple description or sample.

This type of facility should not be confused with the acceptance credits which are provided for exporters by merchant bankers. The exporter draws a bill of exchange on the merchant banker and produces the export documents. The merchant banker accepts the bill of exchange, which can be discounted immediately, and then collects payment against delivery of the documents. It is more usual for a clearing banker to make an advance to the exporter or to discount or negotiate bills of exchange drawn by the exporter on the importer abroad.

Indemnities and Guarantees

Although indemnities and guarantees occur in domestic banking, they are also often encountered in importing and exporting. In order to assess the liability involved, every indemnity or guarantee has to be carefully examined not only for amount, and the circumstances under which payment has to be made, but also for the time involved. Where importing is concerned, bankers are often asked to give indemnities because of missing bills of lading. When a vessel arrives at a port and goods are unloaded, an importer will wish to pick them up as soon as possible. If the shipping documents have somehow been delayed, the shipping company will wish to have a banker's indemnity covering the missing bills of lading before releasing the goods.

A banker's liability will be the amount of the value of the goods, as they could of course have been pledged or previously sold to a third party. Also, the banker will have difficulty in establishing the value of the goods, as the shipping documents will be missing and he can only accept the importer's word. Copies of orders for the goods or correspondence relating to the shipment can often be produced but even so the banker can only rely upon the importer's integrity.

It is necessary therefore for the importer to have built up confidence with his banker and to have audited accounts sufficient to justify the banker accepting these liabilities on his behalf.

If a banker is asked to give a guarantee or indemnity for an amount established in foreign currency he will have to take into account that the rate of exchange may have altered by the time he could be called upon to settle any liabilities.

Forward Exchange

Importers and exporters are concerned with trade, and price their goods accordingly. A fluctuation in an exchange rate could turn a profit into a loss, and traders normally wish their bankers to take the exchange risks from them and allow them to concentrate on their normal business. Therefore, when it is known that foreign currency will be received or will be required at a future time, a purchase or sale of the foreign currency can be made in the forward exchange market.

When a banker arranges for a customer a future purchase or sale he will have to complete the deal whether or not the customer eventually honours the contract. The liability is generally relatively small because if the currency which has been purchased is not required it can be resold and vice versa.

Forward contracts are generally for short periods of time, say two to three months, and in the more stable currencies any movement in the exchange rates would not be large and a margin of 10 to 15 per cent might be considered adequate to cover the liability involved. The longer the period and the more volatile the currency the greater the exchange risk will be. In these circumstances a banker will have to consult his forward exchange dealers before assessing the risk.

CASE 1

Metal Objects Ltd is owned by two working directors and it makes door knobs and handles, coat hooks and other small household items. The company has been selling to hardware stores in the United Kingdom and its results have been reasonably consistent for several years. Only one year's balance sheet figures are therefore necessary to obtain an idea of the company's business and these are as shown below.

		£	
Current liabilities			
Bank .		8,000	
Creditors .		20,000	£4,300 more than debtors
Directors' loans .		10,000	Postponed to the bank
Future corporation tax		1,000	
Total current liabilities .		39,000	Almost equal to current assets
Deferred tax .		1,000	
		40,000	
Capital .		5,000	
Profit and loss account .		3,000	
Reserves		6,000	
		54,000	
Current assets			
Cash .		300	
Debtors .		15,700	
Stock .		25,000	
Total current assets		41,000	
Leasehold		1,000	Short lease only
Plant and machinery		11,000	
Fixtures .		1,000	
		54,000	
Trading turnover .		85,000	
Net profit after tax		500	
Directors' fees		19,000	
Net worth .		14,000	

The present limit for overdraft is £10,000 with the security of the directors' joint and several guarantee supported by good-class stocks and shares of £8,000. If we assume that we can lend, say, £6,000 upon the security of the stocks and shares, we should be looking to the balance sheet to be good enough to justify the remaining £4,000. There is a net current liquidity of only £2,000 but as the directors have agreed not to withdraw their loans without the consent of the bank this effectively increases the net current assets to £12,000. The company is making small profits and the turnover should produce sufficient monthly income which, allied to the total of debtors, should avoid any creditor pressure and produce a reasonable swing in the banking account. The situation from the bank's point of view is satisfactory and a further lending of say £2,000 would not cause difficulty.

Export Proposition

Six months ago the company decided to go into the export market and the initial response has been so good that the directors expect a doubling of turnover. They have examined their financial requirements and have asked the bank to increase their facility to £30,000, to cover an overdraft of £25,000 and forward exchange of £5,000. As additional security they have produced an ECGD policy covering their overseas debtors, which they anticipate will amount to £15,000 and have offered to assign it to the bank.

The directors state that in their opinion the company's banking account is perfectly satisfactory, that the balance sheet is good enough to support borrowing of £15,000, and the remaining £15,000 will be risk-free for the bank, as the ECGD policy will make the debtors good.

In these circumstances a banker must examine each part of the proposal to assess the risk. We have already said that an additional £2,000 of lending would be acceptable to the bank. Liability on the £5,000 for forward exchange would be only small (say 10 per cent equal to £500) and could also be accepted.

However, a banker would still be about £13,000 short of security for the total requirements, and an assignment of the ECGD policy could be ineffective as security.

The effect of an ECGD policy is to make overseas trade no more of a risk than internal trade, and an assignment of a policy does not constitute a charge over the debtors. There are risks if the policy-holder has not observed the terms of the policy and, in particular, has exceeded the cover limits agreed; has not paid the premium, has not made correct declarations of contracts and shipments, and has not observed any import licensing requirements.

If the customers are adamant that a debenture will not be given to the bank (which would of course give a charge over the debtors) and will not provide additional security to cover an increased guarantee, a banker would probably still wish to help because the customer has kept a good account and because after the ECGD policy has been held for a year, application can be made to the department for a bank guarantee.

It would be good banking, therefore, to nurse the account for six months and to try to minimise the possible risk meanwhile.

As the customers are new to exporting, care would have to be exercised to see that they understand all the requirements of the ECGD policy and also the import licence requirements of the countries to which they are exporting. An attempt should be made to see if letters of credit can be established in the customer's favour but, if this fails, arrangements could be made for documents to be forwarded via the bank either against payment or against acceptance of bills. If the terms of the ECGD policy have been observed, debtors will then be covered up to, say, 95 per cent and, as the bank will be controlling the delivery of the documents and the subsequent collection of the bills, advances up to 90 per cent could be made. As a further protection, it would be preferable for the debtors to be spread and for status enquiries to be made about them.

On a short-term basis, therefore, it would be reasonable to ask the directors to increase their joint and several guarantee to £30,000 (still supported by stocks and shares of £8,000) and for the bank to agree a continuance of the overdraft limit of £10,000, a new forward exchange limit of £5,000, and a new advance bill limit of £15,000 with 90 per cent advances, with documents routed through the bank and the ECGD policy assigned.

An alternative would be to examine the terms of the bank's Exports Scheme to see if it offered any advantages.

CASE 2

Importers and Exporters Ltd are an expanding company under good management, with directors of integrity and experience. The company has had overdraft facilities of £50,000 with small credit lines to cover documentary credits and forward exchange. Some good new contracts have been obtained and the directors have re-assessed their requirements and have asked the bank to provide facilities to cover liabilities of £250,000. The bank already holds a debenture and the company insures with ECGD.

Progress has been made annually and the latest balance sheet is as shown.

£

Current liabilities

Bank	20,000	Fluctuates between nil and debit of £50,000

Creditors.	.	.	.	40,000	
Bills payable .	.	.	.	15,000	
Corporation tax	.	.	.	3,000	
Total current liabilities		.	.	*78,000*	
Future Corporation tax		.	.	*6,000*	
				84,000	
Capital	.	.	.	.	*80,000*
Profit and loss account		.	.	*22,000*	
				186,000	

Current assets

Cash	.	.	.	.	500	
Debtors	.	.	.	.	48,500	Exceeds creditors and bills payable
Bills receivable		.	.	.	12,000	
Stocks	.	.	.	.	80,000	
Total current assets	.		.	.	141,000	Well exceeds current liabilities
Freehold warehouse	.		.	.	30,000	Worth £100,000
Plant and machinery	.		.	.	9,000	
Fixtures and fittings	.		.	.	6,000	
					186,000	
Trading turnover	.		.	.	600,000	Expanding
Net profit after tax	.		.	.	12,000	
Directors' fees	.		.	.	30,000	
Net worth .	.		.	.	102,000	Or £172,000 if equity in freeholds is added

The balance sheet is a satisfactory one, and progress has been good, but liabilities to the bank of £250,000 seem to be too great for the company. If we rely upon the debenture, a risk-free facility would appear to be about £100,000. Half of the current assets would be £70,000, and although stocks are the largest item the debtors and bills receivable amount to £60,500, and we know that the company's record is good. There would therefore be an acceptable risk in lending £70,000 plus say half the value of the freehold warehouse (£50,000) − in round figures, £125,000.

Detailed Consideration

There is still, therefore, a large gap between what is acceptable to a bank and what the customer requires. However in order to assess properly the liabilities with which a bank will be faced, it is necessary to split the requirement into its constituent parts and these are as follows:

		£
Overdraft	. . . .	60,000
Documentary credits	. . . . .	50,000
Bank acceptances	. . . .	10,000
Forward exchange	. . . . . .	50,000
Negotiations	. . . . . .	70,000
Indemnities	. . . .	10,000
		250,000

Let us now examine the individual items. As the liabilities on ancillary lines are sometimes not as large as they appear at first sight we will examine them in reverse order.

The directors say that much of the trade will be with European countries and it is their experience that when a short sea route is involved the ship often arrives before the bills of lading. They consider that £10,000 would cover any liabilities they would wish the bank to accept for such indemnities and they expect that most missing bills of lading will turn up a few days later. This liability, as far as the bank is concerned, is £10,000 but it is known from experience that the company is well-managed and the directors are people of integrity. The balance sheet indicates that the company is successful and as £10,000 is very small in relation to the turnover, a banker could, in this instance, accept this liability without specific cover and without qualms.

The company will require the bank to negotiate its bills up to £70,000 but enquiry indicates that letters of credit are sometimes established in the company's favour and £20,000 of the bills will be accepted by banks. Of the remaining £50,000 bills of tenor of approximately nine months will account for £30,000, and those of tenor of up to 30 days will be about £15,000 for good-class commercial concerns and £5,000 for smaller businesses.

There will be no risk in negotiating the bank paper, and an assignment of the ECGD policy would give added protection. However let us assume that the bank's Smaller Exports Scheme is suitable, in this case, for advances up to £50,000.

We now have to consider whether the borrowing arranged with the bank's Smaller Exports Scheme makes any difference to the resultant credit which the company can raise from the bank.

In our assessment of the company's assets we have already looked at the liquid situation but this will now be altered as borrowing of £50,000 is to be arranged on the security of debtors of a similar amount. The current liabilities will therefore be increased by the borrowing of £50,000 and the cash in the current assets will be similarly increased. However one asset (ie, debtors) cannot be used to support borrowing in two different directions. Out of the debtors and bills receivable we shall have to deduct £50,000 when considering the normal bank lending which will be covered by the debenture. The remaining current assets will now look as follows:

	£
Cash	50,500
Debtors and bills receivable	10,500
Stocks	80,000
	141,000

The cash will be used to reduce bank borrowing and we will therefore have to look to the other two items. We previously said that we would be looking to the current assets to cover £70,000 of borrowing but on the face of it this amount would look distinctly over-generous, as half of the debtors would be approximately £5,000, and we could hardly lend £65,000 against stocks of £80,000 over which the bank with its debenture holds only a floating charge.

It would be necessary to find out the composition of the stocks and, for the purpose of this illustration, we will assume that the bulk consists of easily saleable grain. If the grain was pledged under a produce facility a lending agreement of up to 80 per cent of the forced-sale value could be established but, on the basis of a floating charge only, half the debtors and bills receivable plus half the stock (£45,000 in all) would be enough. This, too, could only be agreed because of the experience of the customers, and if their bad debt record was practically negligible.

Additionally, we have said that we will look to the freehold warehouse to support borrowing of £50,000 and the total we are therefore prepared to allow on the security of the debenture has been reduced from £125,000 to £95,000.

Some people consider that a release of cash by factoring of debtors immediately enables a company to increase its turnover and produce more debtors to replace those factored, the result being that the bank can still look to the same amount of debtors as security for its borrowing.

How simple life would be for bankers if this was the case! Whenever difficulties occurred with an account the remedy would be to lend more money in order to increase turnover, debtors and profits.

Unfortunately, business is not as simple as this. Finance is only one of the ingredients needed by successful companies. Stocks of raw materials cannot always be increased at a moment's notice; factory space cannot quickly be enlarged or new machinery purchased and the sales force cannot, at will, increase its sales just because the products are available. A successful businessman takes into account all the factors relating to purchasing, stocks, labour force, production, advertising, marketing, finance etc, and the adjustment of one of the factors does not immediately alter all the others.

I do not say that it is impossible to increase turnover, debtors and profits by an injection of cash; I am just saying that it does not necessarily follow, and a bank would be wise in not assuming that debtors which are factored will be quickly replaced by additional debtors of the same amount.

The next item to be considered is the forward exchange one of £50,000. If the currencies are stable, a liability of 10 per cent of the full amount should be enough for short periods. For the less stable currencies or for long periods, it would be necessary to consider each transaction separately in conjunction with the bank's forward exchange dealers.

Next we come to bank acceptances and documentary credits. The liability on these lines will be the full amount, although the bank would have the goods as security up to the time it released the documents to the customer. Where documentary credits are concerned, the customer's account can be debited at the time the documents are released, but on a bank acceptance the customer's account will not be debited until the bill is due for payment.

We can now look at the limits requested in a fresh light. Amount of liabilities acceptable on the evidence of the balance sheet: £95,000.

Facility	Limit £	Probable liability £	
Overdraft . . .	60,000	60,000	
Documentary credits . .	50,000	50,000	
Bank acceptances . . .	10,000	10,000	
Forward exchange . .	50,000	5,000	
Negotiations . . .	50,000		To be covered by the bank's Exports Scheme
	20,000	Nil	(accepted by banks)
Indemnities	10,000	Nil	
	250,000	125,000	

The bank is still being asked to accept larger liabilities than can be justified, and discussions will have to take place with the customers to consider one or more of the following points:

i   Can additional security be provided?
ii   Can any of the facilities be reduced?
iii Are the goods which are being purchased by documentary credits suitable for security? If grain is involved, then the documentary credit line might be properly secured by having the grain pledged to the bank on a produce facility with say 70−80 per cent advances. The total facilities requested could then be agreed, with the customer depositing 20−30 per cent of each documentary credit on a margin account. Trust facilities might also be agreed for reliable customers.
iv   Can the bank acceptances be dealt with in the same way?
v   Can a cash margin of 10 per cent be deposited on a margin account for forward exchange transactions?

If it is possible to make some rearrangement covering some of these points, it should also be possible for facilities acceptable to both customer and banker to be agreed.

Note. I have explained the principles in dealing with propositions involving ECGD but as the requirements of the Export Credits Guarantee Department change from time to time it is necessary to obtain up to date information before dealing with propositions in practice.

12. Farming

All bank managers should try to acquire knowledge of the trades and industries with which they deal, but they should always remember that as bank managers they are concerned with the finances of a business and not the actual detail of running it.

If too much attention is paid to the mechanics of a business, there can be a danger of looking at it from a proprietor's point of view and thinking that, if some particular course of action is taken to cater for a specific demand, then a certain amount of profit will be made. A banker wishes to know that a proprietor is thinking along these lines and also has a good idea as to the possible success, but he must still view the transaction from a banker's point of view (ie, reasonable amount to lend, short-term, swinging account, security if necessary) and not from a proprietor's point of view (ie, reasonable risk for capital in the hope of good profits).

There are of course very many different varieties of trades and industries, and it is not therefore possible for bank managers to get as close to all the different types as to be able to have an intimate knowledge of them all, but this does not apply in the same way to farming.

Many of the branches of banks in the United Kingdom are in country districts, and lending to farmers naturally forms a large part of their business. Country bank managers, in consequence, gain considerable knowledge of farming. Therein lies the danger of looking at farming problems from the wrong point of view. The country bank manager will know that certain ways of farming are successful in his district and, if he does not resist the temptation, he can soon find himself getting so involved with the industry that he will be providing in effect the risk and long-term capital needed by the farmer. It is therefore important for bankers to keep in mind that they should concern themselves with the finances of farming in the same way as they concern themselves with the finances of any other business to which they lend.

The Natural Cycle

To the city and town bankers, farm lending can be something of a mystery, but the financial knowledge necessary is not difficult to acquire and can soon be learned by reading a simple book on farming and a study of the agricultural press. It is also necessary to keep one's knowledge up to date and particularly now that we are members of the E.E.C. as quotas and subsidies make considerable differences to income and to the methods of farming employed.

In some areas of business, in retail shops for instance, we find that some lines are quickly turned into cash while others are slower, and a change in site can mean a variation in the time taken to turn a certain quantity of goods into cash. Farming is different, in that nature does not take kindly to attempts to hurry the normal cycle, and a banker has to know the length of the cycle for the different types of farming and be patient until the moment of fruition comes. For example, eggs are laid daily and can be turned quickly into cash; receipts from milk sales are received monthly; pigs can be turned into cash after 12 weeks or less; corn is gathered annually in the autumn and can be sold then or stored for future sales; wool is sheared annually; lambs are produced annually; and cattle raised for beef are normally over two years old before being sold.

Therefore a banker dealing with a borrowing farmer primarily interested in milk production would generally expect a good swing in the account monthly, whereas with an arable farmer he would expect an increasing overdraft during the summer months followed by a substantial reduction when corn is sold.

Stock

There are some essential differences between the normal commercial and industrial business and a farm business, and to a large extent these lie in the values of stock. Normal commercial practice is to value stock at the lower of cost or market price, and a certain consistency is generally evident or the percentage of gross profit to sales will have wide fluctuations which could well cause queries from inspectors of taxes. Stock, of course, is a liquid asset and is either held for sale or is sold after being processed in some way. Plant and machinery which is used to turn raw materials into finished stock is a fixed asset because it is not the normal function of the business to sell such plant and machinery.

A farmer's stock of animals can, however, be both a liquid and a fixed asset at the same time. There are regular cattle markets throughout the country and a farmer's stock can therefore easily be turned into cash. This illustrates the liquidity of the stock. On the other hand it is the product of the animals (ie, milk, wool, additional growth of meat) for which many animals are kept and then they act as fixed assets. There are very few businesses outside farming which have such a ready sale for their fixed assets.

Farmers are constantly changing their cattle as older ones are replaced by younger ones, and the value naturally varies with such changes. A further variation in value takes place as the stock can grow into more valuable assets. This does not happen in, say, a retail shoe shop, as the shoes do not grow and become more valuable, whereas a young steer grows daily.

It can be appreciated that it is not easy for consistency to be expected in a gross profit percentage for farmers when the stock is constantly changing in value. This can lead to abuses and avoidance of tax. All farming branch managers will know of farmers making very little profit according to their balance sheets and living on apparently an insignificant amount of drawings. There is little doubt that a farmer can live more cheaply than a town-dweller, as many of the essentials of life for which a town-dweller has to pay are at hand on the farm. Even so the cash drawings on which some farmers live, and out of which they save, take some believing.

There are different ways in which a farmer's stock can be valued for balance sheet purposes but as the values are generally below market price the figures quoted in balance sheets are for the most part below the actual values. As cattle can quickly be turned into cash, and bankers are interested in the liquid assets, the market value should be obtained.

Confidential Statement

The way in which a banker obtains a more accurate value of stock is by asking a farmer to complete a confidential statement. This statement is alternatively called a farmer's balance sheet or a stock and crops form, and an example follows:

FARMER'S CONFIDENTIAL STATEMENT

Date: March 19..

Name: F. Giles. Address: Old Farm, Brookside.
Area: 200 acres (150 acres grass, 50 acres arable). Rental: £3,000 pa.

	Value each £	Total £		Value each £	Total £
Assets			*Brought forward*		55,130
Cattle					
50 dairy cows	500	25,000	*Growing crops*		
10 heifers	250	2,500	40 acres barley	40	1,600
7 calves	90	630	10 acres wheat	40	400
12 steers (18 months)	300	3,600			
10 steers (12 months)	200	2,000	*Debtors*		
30 pigs (various)	50	1,500	Milk Marketing Board	2,300	
500 poultry	2	1,000	Subsidies	500	
		36,230	Eggs	150	
			Sundry	450	3,400
Produce to sell			Life policy (surrender value)		700
Barley		Nil			
Wheat		Nil	*Stock and shares*		
			National Savings Certificates		500
Implements and machinery					
3 Tractors		5,000	*Any other assets*		
1 Trailer		400	Private car		3,400
1 Baler		1,600	Total assets		65,130
1 Combine		5,000			
1 Set of haymaking			*Liabilities*		
machinery		2,000	Bank		9,300
Milking machine		1,400	Creditors		2,000
Land Rover		3,500	18,900	Rent		Nil
			Relations		2,000
Carried forward		55,130	Total liabilities		13,300
			Balance being capital		51,830
			Total liabilities and capital		65,130

In practice these confidential statements are very often filled in by a bank manager from information given to him by his farming customer either in the branch or at the farm. There is no need to visit the farm on every occasion that a confidential statement is completed. If the farmer is doing well and this is reflected in the banking account, a visit is unnecessary although pleasurable. If there is doubt about the farmer's ability and progress then a visit should be arranged. In such cases it is a good plan to complete the confidential statement before walking around the farm and agreeing on an overdraft limit. The confidential statement will give the bank manager a good idea of the extent of the farm and whether it is fully stocked, and in the subsequent look at the farm the figures for numbers of stock can be checked without difficulty. It is much harder to try and keep a mental note of numbers of animals in categories of type and ages and check this against the farmer's figures at the end of the tour of the farm.

A bank manager will also wish to keep himself abreast of market prices and he can check these from agricultural journals. He can then compare the market prices against the figures quoted to him by the farmer and, as is natural, will find that in many cases the farmer's figures are optimistic. A certain scaling down will then be necessary before a view on lending can be taken.

The branch manager should also compare the figures with those on the confidential statements in previous years in order to watch the trend, and he should also examine the banking account.

Comparison with Banking Account and Balance Sheet

It might be thought that to reach agreement on overdraft limits after perusing rough figures is a most inaccurate way of banking; but a bank manager is in a position to verify whether the figures can be relied upon, because he is able to examine the banking account. For example, if the confidential statements show capital increasing annually, whereas stock is approximately the same year by year, then a reduction should be seen in the overdraft level. If at the same time the overdraft is tending to increase and harden, it is obvious that further enquiries must be made and an explanation sought.

The bank manager should know from the agricultural journals and his talks with other farmers and farming auctioneers what income should be received from the various types of farming activity. A check can then be made to see if the appropriate income has been received into the banking account. An alert bank manager has sufficient information available to be able to make a reasonable assessment of a farmer's financial position. There is no reason why he should be misled by being shown cattle which do not belong to the farmer, though claimed by him, as the comparison of the banking account with conclusions which can be reached by studying the confidential statement will reveal a discrepancy.

A third comparison can also be made, and that is between the confidential statement and the balance sheet when it is subsequently received. It is very easy to think that as the balance sheet is 12 months or so out of date it need only be filed because the review of the overdraft limit has already taken place in the light of the figures shown on the confidential statement. It is, however, important that the figures should be compared and, if there are inconsistencies, enquiries should be made.

Naturally, confidential statements are taken at all times in the year and a comparison with a balance sheet taken at a different time will not be completely straightforward. For example, a balance sheet for an arable farm will probably show a large amount of grain in stock ready for sale if the balance sheet date is at the end of September. A confidential statement taken in March would show little grain still left and possibly only seed for the new season's sowing. Nevertheless, a bank manager should be able to make allowances and compare both sets of figures for large discrepancies.

It has already been mentioned that there will probably be a difference in the cattle valuations, and another figure which will differ in the two sets is that for creditors. Perhaps it is natural for one to underestimate the amount that one owes: it certainly seems to be true, in practice, for most farmers to consider that they owe very little but for their balance sheets to show that they owe much more. The time of the year must, of course, be taken into account as arable farmers often build up creditors before harvest and settle large amounts to their merchants out of their harvest proceeds. After a possible adjustment in the creditor figure for such a reason, it would be more prudent for a banker to rely upon the higher creditor figure shown in the balance sheet than on the farmer's estimate. Coversely, for the reasons already given, the valuation for cattle (after deductions for any over-optimism) can be taken from the confidential statement rather than from the balance sheet.

Let us look again at the farmer's confidential statement.

We see that it was taken in the spring and that the farmer has 200 acres for which he is paying rent of £15 per acre. On his grassland of 150 acres, he is keeping a dairy herd of 50 cows with 17 followers and is also fattening 22 steers, making a total of 89 cattle of various ages. It depends upon the type of land and situation as to the number of cattle which can be kept to the acre, but the local bank manager should know this. There is also a small pig unit and some poultry.

As the statement is taken in the spring there is no produce to sell. A look at the implements shows that there is haymaking machinery for such grass as will be made into hay, a combine harvester for the arable crop, and a baler for hay and straw, with tractors and trailers and a Land Rover. The items under growing crops show that the 50 acres of arable land have been sown (the amount per acre being the cost of ploughing, fertilising and seeding).

There is a milk cheque due from the Milk Marketing Board plus a few other debtors, and the farmer also owns a life policy with a surrender value of £700, National Savings Certificates worth £500 and a private car.

At this stage, we should be able to work out the income which we would expect to see in the banking account, and a farming branch manager will be able to make his calculations from information in the farming press. For the sake of this example, we will work on the following average figures:

> A cow produces £650 of milk per annum.
> Steers at 30 months sell for £500.
> Pigs are sold at 16 weeks for £60.
> Hens will lay 240 eggs per annum at 50p per dozen.
> Wheat and barley yield £200 per acre.

The amount of money received from the Milk Marketing Board should be about £32,500 and, although there will be variations, a monthly credit averaging £2,700 should be seen in the banking account. In approximately a year's time 12 steers will be sold to produce about £6,000 and, six months later, a further 10 will sell for £5,000. Pigs should be going for sale shortly and, dependent upon the ages, it looks as if regular cheques should be received with a total throughout the year of £5,400 (30 pigs at £60 each turned over every four months). From the poultry regular cheques should be received amounting in a full year to about £5,000. If we turn now to the arable crops, the 50 acres should produce £10,000, but this will not be until after harvest and the time of receipt will depend upon whether the farmer stores his grain in the hope of better prices and whether he keeps some of it for feeding his own cattle.

In the figures for liabilities, we see the bank as £9,300, and this figure should be the same as that shown in the farmer's cash book. There may be a difference between the cash book figure and the figure in the bank ledger because of unpresented cheques, but to expect such perfection from the majority of farmers who dislike book work is expecting too much. At the time of completing the statement a bank manager will have to ask whether cheques have been issued recently, and adjust accordingly. The figure for creditors, as already mentioned, will be low, and enquiry will have to be made about the loan from relations and when it is repayable. Let us suppose that the loan is long-term, and that several past balance sheets prepared at the same time of the year show creditors at about £4,000.

We now have a very good picture of the farm finances.

The Amount to Lend

From the trend of past confidential statements and balance sheets it will be known whether the farmer is operating profitably or not, and if overdraft facilities are required a banker will wish to have a proposition put to him. If we now assume that the proposition is satisfactory and that the repayment terms suggested seem capable of achievement, we now have to consider how much it is reasonable to lend as bankers.

In a previous chapter, I said it was reasonable for a banker to lend unsecured to a successful business up to one-half of the net liquid assets of the business. This was on the basis that the underlying propostion was satisfactory and that the composition of the net liquidity was not such as would cause concern. For example, too much stock in relation to turnover might indicate some unsaleable stock; or perhaps the proposition might involve a purchase of fixed assets and a depletion of the net liquidity. I stressed that although a formula was being used as a starting point, when considering lending, it did not absolve a banker from asking questions and using his experience and enquiring mind to judge the position.

A banker is not in day to day control of his customer's businesses, and naturally he does not know as quickly as they do if their businesses have changed from being profitable to being loss-making. A margin is therefore necessary to a banker and, if he lends up to one-half of the net liquidity of a business, he would still be covered by the net current assets until half the net liquidity was lost. An overriding proviso is that the proprietor should have more capital behind the business than the lending of the banker.

The usual danger signs of pressure on the limit, lack of swing in the banking account, cheques for round amounts, should alert a banker to action, and, if necessary, he can ask for monthly or quarterly statements of current assets and current liabilities. The same considerations can apply to farm lending but the assessment of the liquid position should be taken from the confidential statement and after considering past balance sheets.

Past balance sheets show the normal amount of creditors as being £4,000 and it would therefore be less than prudent to work on the figure of £2,000 shown in the confidential statement. If by a check of the agricultural press and his own knowledge a branch manager considers that the cattle have been overvalued by £3,000, a calculation of the net liquidity would be as follows:

	£	£
Current assets		
Stock (£36,230 less £3,000)		33,230
Produce to sell		Nil
Debtors		3,400
Cash		Nil
Total		36,630
Less current liabilities		
Bank	9,300	
Creditors	4,000	
Relations (long-term)	Nil	13,300
Net current assets		23,330

One-half of the net current assets is approximately £11,500 and this is not an unreasonable amount to lend on these figures. If the life policy and the National Savings Certificates are held as security, a banker could feel able to increase his lending to £12,700.

Examination of Balance Sheet and Confidential Statement

The next stage is for the banker to examine the balance sheet, when it is eventually received, with the confidential statement.

The balance sheet reads as follows:

F. GILES
Balance sheet as at March

Capital Reserves and Liabilities	£	£	*Assets*		£
Capital at start of year .	26,000		Implements and machinery .		12,200
Add Profit . . .	5,000		Valuation		26,000
	31,000		Debtors		3,800
Less Drawings . .	3,200	27,800			
Sub total		27,800	Sub total		42,000

Brought forward	27,800		42,000
Bank overdraft . .	8,200		
Creditors. . . .	4,000		
Relations. . . .	2,000		
	42,000		42,000

The first point that will strike us is that the farmer's capital is only £27,800 according to the balance sheet, whereas we have been working on the basis that in his confidential statement it worked out at £51,830. It is necessary, therefore, to compare the individual items if we are to satisfy ourselves that the unsecured lending is still sound.

	Balance sheet	Confidential statement	Comments
Assets	£	£	
Implements and machinery .	12,200	18,900	Depreciation allowance could account for this and an optimistic view of the value of second hand machinery
Valuation . . .	26,000	36,230 ⎫	Already considered and £3,000
Growing crops . .		2,000 ⎬	deducted from farmer's figures
Debtors. . . .	3,800	3,400 ⎭	Small variation
Life policy . . .		700 ⎫	Not included in balance sheet
National Savings Certs. .		500 ⎬	
Private car . . .		3,400 ⎭	
Total assets . . .	42,000	65,130	
Liabilities	£	£	
Bank	8,200	9,300 ⎫	Taken together, difference is £900
Creditors . . .	4,000	2,000 ⎬	and we have adjusted adequately by £2,000 in our calculations
Relations . . .	2,000	2,000	
	14,200	13,300	
Balance being capital . .	27,800	51,830	See below
	42,000	65,130	

Reconciliation of Capital		£
As per balance sheet		27,800
Add Implements and machinery . .		6,700
Valuation and growing crops .		12,230
Life Policy		700
National Savings Certs.. . .		500
Private car		3,400
		51,330
Less Debtors		400
		50,930
Add Bank and creditors. . . .		900
As per confidential statement . .		51,830

There are large differences in the valuation and in the bank and creditors, and we have already considered these items and have made satisfactory adjustments; the life policy and the National Savings Certificates are additional to the balance sheet figures. As for the implements and machinery and the private car, these items are not liquid ones and have not entered into our calculations previously.

Therefore, although at first sight there appears to be a large difference when looking at the balance sheet figures, analysis has shown that satisfactory adjustments in our calculations have already been made for the material items of liquid assets and quick liabilities. If such were not the case, careful enquiry might be necessary.

Other Methods

Over the years many other methods have been used for assessing farm lending, and providing these methods are supported by sound analysis there is no reason why they should not be used.

One system, which some farmers think satisfactory, is for bank lending to be covered by stock. the argument is that stock is easily sold and therefore the bank is safe. Only a little thought is necessary to realise how unwise this can be as the full situation is not apparent — particularly the liquid situation. The following will illustrate:

Capital and Liabilities		£	Assets		£
Capital		1,000	Stock		9,000
Bank		8,000	Implements		3,000
Creditors		5,000	Debtors.		2,000
		14,000			14,000

Although the bank overdraft is covered by stock, there is a net deficiency in liquidity as the bank and creditors total £13,000, whereas stock and debtors only account for £11,000. The proprietor's stake, too, is totally inadequate: the bank and the creditors are taking practically all the risk in running the business.

Use of Gross Margins

Another method is by the use of management accounts and cash projections as in other industries. Management accounting and comparing gross margins is recommended by the Agricultural Development and Advisory Service (ADAS) and is used by the larger farmers. Unfortunately, the majority of farmers prefer working in the open air and only tackle books as a hated necessity. Nevertheless, the use of management accounts is becoming more prevalent and will surely grow as the advantages become more apparent.

Farming is a business which can be subdivided into specific activities and obviously a considerable amount of valuable information can be made available if the income and expenses relating to each activity can be extracted from the books. This will enable a farmer to see what return he is achieving on each activity and what the return is on the capital invested in each. ADAS and the farm economic departments of universities collect statistics from farmers and they publish lists showing average figures for differing sizes of farms. Farmers are therefore able to compare their own results with these averages.

There are numerous ways of farming and there is no simple system which should be applied in all circumstances. Much depends on the soil and weather conditions and on the size of the farm. If a farm is small there is little alternative but to farm the land intensively in order to make sufficient income but if a large farm is involved there is scope for considerable variety.

Farmers are able to call upon ADAS to help them to decide on the methods suitable for their farms and to set up management control systems. First of all, a decision must be made on the activities to be carried out on the farm and a projection can then be made of the likely gross margins. This could appear as follows:

COMPARISON OF GROSS MARGINS

Long Meadow, Lea Bank and Warren Field. Total 40 acres

	Plan A (all barley)	Plan B (all cows)	Plan C (all sheep)
	£	£	£
Income	4,800	14,000	6,200
Less allocated costs . .	1,300	9,600	3,800
Gross margin . . .	3,500	4,400	2,400

This example is shown in a very simple form; in practice many detailed aspects will have to be considered before the figures can be produced. Gross margins will vary according to the actual farm analysed.

The income shown is the total income expected and the allocated costs are those costs which can be specifically related to the individual plans. For plan A these will cover such items as seeds, fertilisers, casual labour, contract services, sprays and machinery expenses. For plan B, veterinary fees and regular labour will have to be included as well as machinery repairs and milking parlour expenses. Likewise, plan C will have allocated to it only the expenses specifically related to the activity.

This, then, will have dealt with 40 acres of the farm and alternative plans can be made for the remainder of the farm.

All the plans can then be brought together in various combinations and the total gross margins compared. In order to obtain a profit figure there will have to be deducted from the gross margins all the farm expenses which have not been allocated to specific activities.

An example is as follows:

COMPARISON OF ALTERNATIVE FARM PLANS

Gross margins	£	£	£
Plan A	3,500		
B		4,400	
C			2,400
D	3,000	3,000	3,000
E	2,800		2,800
F		3,200	
Total gross margins .	9,300	10,600	8,200
Less unallocated expenses .	3,300	3,300	3,300
Anticipated net profit . .	6,000	7,300	4,900

The unallocated costs will be such items as secretarial expenses, rent, rates, depreciation, insurances, telephone, professional and financial charges and the labour of the farmer and his wife.

Obviously, such plans cannot be drawn up without considering the kind of farm involved, its location and its buildings. It will, however, be seen that a reasonably simple method is available for farmers to be able to devise plans to bring in the best returns. Whether or not they follow systems which will bring in the best returns will depend upon the individual preferences of the farmers concerned.

It is only a small step to using such estimates for the preparation of cash projections. Monitoring actual results against the anticipated ones can then follow.

From a banker's point of view, management accounts of this nature, when allied to traditional methods of assessment, will help the banker to make decisions on new propositions and will assist in subsequent control.

13. Medium-Term Lending

Most of this book has dealt with lending by means of overdrafts because this is what customers have preferred. It is the cheapest way of borrowing money, as interest is charged on only the actual amount borrowed each day. Overdrafts are suitable for the finance required for normal trading where current assets and current liabilities vary and the overdraft limit at the bank is available to provide the balancing factor. However, overdrafts are not suitable for long-term projects, for purchases of fixed assets over an extended period, or for projects which require finance for a period of longer than a year. For example, if finance is required for a three-year period before any repayment can be envisaged, then the correct finance to balance the requirements would be a loan for the three-year period and then an arrangement whereby this loan would reduce in line with the cash projection. There are obviously a variety of projects which require finance for different lengths of time. The finance should be suitable to the project with repayment geared to it. An overdraft which is repayable on demand is, in these circumstances, not a suitable form of finance.

Before 1970, banks generally worked on the basis that as the money deposited with them could be withdrawn quickly, the money they lent should be repayable on demand. However, certain overdrafts inevitably did not plan out as arranged and hard-core borrowing developed. This borrowing, obviously, could not then be repaid on demand and it took on a medium-term character. Additionally, since vast sums in total were deposited with the banks a certain amount of medium-term lending was not an embarrassment for the banks and some "one-off" style loans were devised for different sectors of the borrowing public in order to try and get more business from these sectors. However, these loans were not referred to as medium-term loans and it was only at the beginning of the 1970s that a concerted effort was made by the banks to try and supply medium-term finance appropriate to the needs of customers.

In order to overcome the objections of using short-term deposits for long-term loans, the banks endeavoured to match the customers' requirements by obtaining funds from the money market. Naturally it was not always possible to match requirements as far as the length of the term was concerned. However, the banks felt able to undertake to provide the money for the terms required on the basis that the customers were responsible for meeting changes in the rates of interest. For example, if a five-year term was envisaged and the banks could only raise money for a six-months' period, the loan would be rolled over every six months and the customer would pay the agreed margin over the rate actually paid by the bank. The interest rate margin is generally expressed as being a certain number of percentage points over LIBOR (London Inter-Bank Offered Rate) and the interest rates charged for such loans are generally higher than overdraft rates. A longer term should naturally attract a higher rate because the risk is increased. Sometimes, the quoted rate to the customer is related to base rate instead of LIBOR. In these circumstances, the banks take into account the volatility of LIBOR in fixing the margin.

Additionally, the banks are obliged to keep a percentage of their resources in reserve assets or deposits with the Bank of England on which the interest obtainable is relatively low. If funds are obtained from the money market, these count as deposits and the appropriate reserve assets and special deposits will have to be held. The extra cost to the bank, which fluctuates around ¼ / ½ per cent, must also be considered when arriving at the rate to be quoted to the customer.

From the customer's point of view a medium-term loan is a more sensible way of financing projects for which repayments cannot be provided within a 12-month period. It also provides protection for a customer against a future credit squeeze as he has the certainty of having the finance for an agreed period. There is a flexibility available which does not occur if additional equity or loan stock finance is sought. Companies can, therefore, plan ahead with more confidence. Of recent years more companies have used planning and management techniques in the normal course of their businesses and it has become obvious that different types of finance are required for a company's needs. The correct fit of term finance to needs is valuable. Medium-term loans, therefore, are very suitable alternatives to overdrafts. They can also on occasions be preferable to long-term mortgages, sale and lease-back arrangements or debenture borrowing.

Types of Medium-Term Finance

Medium-term finance can be made available for numerous purposes but this form of finance must not be looked upon as being merely another source of funds. It should be made available for the purposes for which it is most suitable — ie, for a period in excess of 12 months and where repayment can be envisaged over a period of up to five to seven years. Any finance for longer periods than this should be regarded as long-term finance for which there are different considerations. Medium-term finance is provided for purchases of plant and machinery, re-equipping, and for new projects. If the return on such expenditure does not enable the borrowed money to be repaid within a period of five to seven years, questions should be asked as to whether the return on the capital involved is large enough.

Let us consider finance for the following and whether medium-term facilities are suitable.

New Plant and Machinery

Quite often a hire-purchase or a leasing transaction would be suitable. However, if the plant and machinery are to be installed over a period, followed by a running-in time with full production and profitability to be achieved later, then a medium-term facility could well be tailored to meet these requirements.

Extension to Factory

This could well be similar to plant and machinery, where some time is being taken for the factory to be built and to be put into full use.

Refinancing

This is probably not suitable for medium-term facilities but any proposition will have to be looked at carefully. If refinance is necessary it would appear that the repayment originally envisaged has not been forthcoming. There can, however, be special circumstances.

To Supplement Lack of Capital

This could well be a suitable purpose if the period over which repayment is envisaged is not too long. It could well be that certain projects have not yet come to fruition and in the following few years sufficient cash flow will be generated to repay the borrowing. The lack of capital would be, therefore, only a temporary deficiency.

Normal Trading

Medium-term finance is not suitable for this purpose although this finance would be the opposite of borrowing short and lending long. Normal trading finance is required for balancing the current assets and current liabilities as they circulate around and overdrafts provide the appropriate means. Medium-term finance is, therefore, unnecessary for this purpose and is also more expensive. Of course, if a company is making poor progress hard-core borrowing will develop and in certain circumstances this hard core could be put on to a medium-term basis. However, there is little point in doing this if repayment will still be difficult to achieve.

New Products

This is suitable for medium-term finance as new products can take some while to get established before the cash flow is sufficient to provide repayment. However, new products and new enterprises entail considerable risk. Repayment proposals for medium-term lending must be achievable and too much reliance must not be placed on the successful outcome of the particular new product or enterprise. An alternative source of repayment should be available if the new enterprise is unsuccessful.

Acquisition of Another Company

This, too, is suitable for medium-term finance and it should be possible from the record of the company being acquired to see whether the cash flow will be strong enough to produce the necessary repayment.

It will be appreciated that with all the proposals for which medium-term finance is suitable, it is necessary to examine the future cash flows; management accounting is therefore important. It is necessary for the company's accountancy staff to prepare forward plans and budgets, and the use of discounted cash flow techniques are vital to obtain accurate appraisals of the returns expected on capital commitments. The establishment of future profitability and adequate cash generation is necessary in order to show that the proposal has a good chance of a successful conclusion.

Assessment of Risk

Sometimes, sales of fixed assets at a future time or raising of additional loans or capital can be used for repayment but if repayment is to come from cash generated within the business a banker will wish to examine the company's budgets and cash flows projected over several years. This can give a general picture but it would be foolish for a banker to expect, in times of rapid inflation and widespread change, that a cash projection for some years ahead can be relied upon. Therefore, although the cash projection overall should make sense when viewed from the present time, it must be examined in detail for the preliminary 12 months. Subsequently, future cash projections will also have to be examined with the same object in mind — ie, looking in detail at the figures for the coming 12 months with a general commonsense look at the future projected figures.

When a loan is being made for several years, it is insufficient to look merely at how the current assets will appreciate, as so much can go wrong over this period. It is, therefore, very important to look also at the fixed assets and liabilities for the general substance of the company to which the loan is made. There must be a record of competence in the management of the company, and it is as well for a banker to look back at the record of the company for the same length of time as the period for which he is asked to lend forward. The statements of source and application of funds should be examined to see what cash generation has been produced in the past and how such cash has been used — ie, whether it has been used for the purchase of fixed assets or whether it has assisted with the growth of working capital. It is necessary to look at overall worth in relation to borrowings. If a company is too highly geared, a bank would be taking a risk in putting forward a medium-term facility. Naturally, the worth of a company will change over a period of years and so, too, will its borrowing. Therefore, a banker will wish to see that these items in relation to one another do not get out of hand.

When assessing the risk on projects, the customer, if he is capable, will have made a study of his market, the growth of it and its limitations, the impact of competition, the method of promotion he proposes to use and his potential orders. Also, he will be aware that even the most carefully drawn plans can go awry and alternative strategies should be considered. Plans and budgets must be prepared and the various methods for control by management information laid down. All this would be done before the finance is requested and a banker should encourage his customer to produce these feasibility studies for him to examine. The relationship of a customer and his banker should be close if they are both going into a project which has some risk attached to it, and it is of mutual help if all the facts are made available at the outset. However, many people think that bankers are being too inquisitive when they enquire about such matters and there is often a reluctance to divulge essential information. This is something the banker must try to overcome as tactfully as possible.

There is obviously more risk in advancing medium-term money for new businesses or new products as no assured market has been built up over a period of time. There is, therefore, less risk for an established business which can show a record of profitability over a number of years with its existing products. All industries are different and it is as well to know whether the business concerned has cyclical booms and slumps. Sometimes, it is necessary to have a report on the industry concerned and this can often be obtained from the Department of Trade or from the banks' own economic units. These will incorporate views on the general prospects for the particular industry. Often interfirm comparisons are available within the industry, and if these figures can be seen a banker will know how his customer ranks in efficiency in comparison with his competitors.

Control

When dealing with medium-term lending at the time of the initial assessment there will also have to be consideration of the factors necessary for control of the advance. A medium-term loan is evidenced by documentation because the loan is not repayable on demand. There must, therefore, be set out the terms under which the loan is granted. Obviously, this will include the amount of the loan, the interest rate, the repayment terms, and the security. In addition to this, however, the bank will wish to have other clauses incorporated which lay down certain minimum criteria which must be observed. For example, a bank would not wish to stand idly by if it could see that its customer was quickly approaching insolvency and it would therefore wish to have clauses included which would enable it to take action in these circumstances. Therefore, the bank will carefully examine past balance sheets and accounts and work out the worst position it would wish to see developing in the company before it took action to recover its debt. A margin should be allowed on these figures to provide for the fact that it generally happens that deterioration occurs before the bank has notification of it. The required ratios and covenants can then be stipulated.

Obviously, a bank will not wish its borrowing customer to arrange to borrow vast sums elsewhere and get himself too highly geared, as this could endanger the safety of the medium-term loan. It is quite usual, therefore, for a gearing ratio to be specified or for any other outside borrowing to be obtained only with prior permission of the bank. The proportion of debt to equity is therefore often specified, as also is the debt to net assets. Working capital and current ratios can be specified and negative pledges are common. By this, assurances are given that assets will not be given as security for other borrowings without prior permission of the bank. The documentation can also cover covenants concerning the sale of assets, the amount of dividends which can be declared, repayments of other loans, future capital expenditure, and provide, if necessary, for the loan to be repaid if there is a change in control of the company to which the lending is made. Naturally, if such ratios are not kept or covenants are broken there must be provision for repayment of the debt and the default clauses must be specifically drawn to cover all eventualities.

It is, of course, of no use to make the clauses so restrictive that the borrower will be able to comply only with great difficulty, as the object of the documentation is to provide for those extreme circumstances when action is necessary to obtain repayment prior to the original envisaged repayment date. The repayment specified must, therefore, be related to the earning capacity of the business and must allow the business to have sufficient liquidity for its normal trading. If this is denuded, trading prospects suffer and the repayment of the loan is thereby made much more difficult. The drawing up of the documentation is a matter for specialists but the terms to be incorporated in the documentation must be decided by the lending banker.

CASE 1

The Benson Rivet Co Ltd has kept its account with the bank for many years and there has been a happy relationship. The chief accountant is particularly co-operative and produces forward projections for profits and cash annually and these projections turn out to be as accurate as can be expected. The bank provides an overdraft limit of £1m and the banking account swings well between the limit and just into credit during the course of the year. The overdraft is unsecured.

The company has raised a long-term loan of £3,700,000 which is not due for repayment for a further 12 years, and it has given security of freehold and leasehold deeds which you understand are of just sufficient value to satisfy the requirements of the lender.

Balance sheets are regularly produced, and those for the last five years show the following figures:

BENSON RIVET CO LTD

Years	A	B	C	D	E
Current liabilities			(£000s)		
Creditors	2,180	1,750	1,800	1,700	1,900
Bank	800	800	700	900	1,000
Taxation	500	400	300	400	600
Dividends	200	200	200	250	300
	3,680	3,150	3,000	3,250	3,800
Long-term liabilities					
Loans (secured)	3,700	3,700	3,700	3,700	3,700
	3,700	3,700	3,700	3,700	3,700
Proprietors' funds					
Capital	9,300	9,300	9,300	9,300	9,300
Reserves and profit and loss account	2,890	3,210	3,650	4,270	5,020
	12,190	12,510	12,950	13,570	14,320
Total liabilities	19,570	19,360	19,650	20,520	21,820
Current assets					
Stocks and work in progress	2,720	2,430	2,310	2,650	3,000
Debtors	2,150	1,970	2,090	2,100	2,400
	4,870	4,400	4,400	4,750	5,400
Fixed assets					
Freeholds	5,000	5,000	5,000	6,000	7,100
Long leaseholds	2,900	2,700	2,500	2,400	2,200
Short leaseholds	600	450	400	300	200
Plant and equipment	5,700	6,380	6,930	6,450	6,300
Motor vehicles	400	350	340	550	560
Office equipment	100	80	80	70	60
	14,700	14,960	15,250	15,770	16,420
Total assets	19,570	19,360	19,650	20,520	21,820

Turnover .	.	.	.	.	.	9,100	9,300	9,500	10,000	11,000
Net profit before tax	.	.	.			1,000	1,100	1,100	1,350	1,650
Tax .	.	.	.	.	.	550	480	360	380	500
Net profit after tax .	.	.	.			450	620	740	970	1,150
Dividends	.	.	.	.		300	300	300	350	400
Net current assets	.	.	.			1,190	1,250	1,400	1,500	1,600
Net worth	.	.	.	.		12,190	12,510	12,950	13,570	14,320

An examination of these figures shows that creditors have been reduced over the period and in year E stand at an amount equivalent to approximately two months' turnover. This indicates that payments are made promptly by the company. Debtors have risen only slowly over the year and are now equivalent to just over 2.5 months' turnover. Control is therefore satisfactory. The average stock held is about four months' turnover (and, of course, more than this proportion of cost of sales).

The net current assets are reasonable at £1.6m but have been somewhat static for the last three years; the liquidity is sufficient for the business of the company. Turnover has only increased relatively slowly.

The plough-back of profits is satisfactory and the net worth has been increasing. From the bank's point of view the account is a good one and there are no worries.

However, looked upon from a shareholder's point of view the situation is not so good. The net profit before tax as a proportion of turnover is 15 per cent, but as a proportion of proprietors' funds it is only 11.7 per cent, and the dividend as a proportion of proprietors' funds is a low one at 2.8 per cent.

It is therefore not surprising to hear from the chief accountant that there has been some agitation for more growth in the company's activities. Apparently, there is plenty of business available but to be able to capture this it will be necessary to re-equip very substantially. The directors have decided to do this and spend about £5m on new equipment. Some of the old equipment will be sold but the prices which can be obtained are expected to be relatively small.

The company has asked to borrow its requirements from the bank and this will mean much heavier borrowing for five years.

A cash projection for the future five years has been produced and is as follows:

CASH PROJECTION FOR FUTURE FIVE YEARS

(£000s)

Years	F	G	H	I	J
Trading receipts	11,500	13,000	14,500	15,000	15,000
Less Payments	10,000	10,750	11,750	12,000	12,000
	1,500	2,250	2,750	3,000	3,000
Add Equipment sales . . .	500	400	100	200	200
	2,000	2,650	2,850	3,200	3,200
Less Equipment purchases . .	3,500	1,000	800	200	200
	(1,500)	1,650	2,050	3,000	3,000
Less Taxation	550	650	750	850	950
Dividends	450	500	750	1,250	1,250
	(2,500)	500	550	900	800
Bank borrowing at start of year .	(1,000)	(3,500)	(3,000)	(2,450)	(1,550)
Bank borrowing at end of year .	(3,500)	(3,000)	(2,450)	(1,550)	(750)

It will be seen that the trading items and the extensive reorganisation of the equipment are included in the cash projection, but this tends to confuse the issue. The company normally has an overdraft limit of £1m which it wishes to continue and if this is deducted from its other requirements the company will require £3m for equipment in the first year and will reduce rapidly in the second year and more slowly in the following three years. It is explained that the normal retention of profits in excess of distributions will enable £1m to be repaid in year G. No repayments are offered in year F as delivery of part of the equipment scheduled for year G could be brought forward. In the three subsequent years amounts of £500,000, £500,000 and £1m should be repaid.

It will be much easier if the true requirements of the company are examined by separating the equipment purchases and sales. These are:

CASH PROJECTION FOR EQUIPMENT REQUIREMENTS

Years	F	G	H	I	J
Sales	500	400	100	200	200
Less Purchases . . .	3,500	1,000	800	200	200
	(3,000)	(600)	(700)	—	—

Let us therefore look at the overdraft requirements on the basis that a term loan of £3m will also be necessary with repayments of £1m in year G and the remainder spread over the following three years. This will be as follows:

REQUIREMENT FOR OVERDRAFT FOR FUTURE FIVE YEARS

(£000s)

Years	F	G	H	I	J
Trading receipts	11,500	13,000	14,500	15,000	15,000
Less Payments	10,000	10,750	11,750	12,000	12,000
	1,500	2,250	2,750	3,000	3,000
Less Tax	550	650	750	850	950
Dividends	450	500	750	1,250	1,250
	500	1,100	1,250	900	800
Less Requirements for equipment in years G and H . . .		600	700		
Repayment of term loan . .		1,000	500	500	1,000
	500	(500)	50	400	(200)
Overdraft at start of year . .	(1,000)	(500)	(1,000)	(950)	(550)
Overdraft at end of year . . .	(500)	(1,000)	(950)	(550)	(750)

After this analysis the proposition becomes easier to understand. The company requires to continue with an overdraft limit of £1m and this can be reviewed annually in the light of actual results. It also requires £3m for equipment with repayment from equipment sales and profits over a period of five years.

The record of the company with the bank is good and help is justified. However, the company has not been dynamic and the change-over from being a staid and steady company to a thrusting one may not go smoothly. The bank will, therefore, need some protection both in having sufficient security and being able to take some action if the company is unsuccessful in its new role.

It will be necessary now to talk to the directors to find out what security is available. Let us assume that freehold and long leasehold deeds are available with a present value of £5m and the company is opposed to giving a debenture. With security of £5m and net current assets of £1.6m the bank should feel satisfied.

However, we now have to examine the position of the term lending as this will not be repayable unless conditions are breached. Conditions will have to be inserted into the documentation to turn the term loan into an on-demand loan if circumstances arise which make the bank anxious about its lending.

The conditions can cover the level of net assets, net worth, debtors to creditors, amount of stock retained, amount of dividends and other matters, but the more conditions that are imposed the more likely they are to be breached. If it is thought necessary to impose a vast number of conditions, it indicates that the bank cannot be very happy about the advance and it might be better not to lend. The minimum of conditions should be sought consistent with safety.

In the present instance, we are looking for the bulk of the repayment to come from future profits. Profits are reflected in increases in net current assets provided that fixed assets are not purchased out of the increase and/or dividends are not distributed to excess. It would, therefore, be possible to devise a formula to cover the amount of the net current assets, to specify the proportion which must not be exceeded by investment in fixed assets and also to quote a limit to dividend payments.

However, this can be considered to be too complicated, as if a condition is applied to the net current assets alone the company will have to decide its policy on fixed assets and dividends in the light of this condition. One condition will therefore be sufficient.

How should this be applied? We know the bank is to have security of deeds worth £5m but this is somewhat thin for a lending of £4m but sufficient with net current assets of £1.6m. If the net current assets are not allowed to drop below £1.6m without triggering the clause to convert the term lending into on-demand lending, the bank would probably feel safe, but this is impracticable. During the change-over the net current assets could well drop but the bank should be concerned only to fix the lowest level to which it is prepared to see them drop before taking action. We have said that the security on its own is thin and therefore if the bank feels that it has to rely on its security alone the time will have come to exercise more control. Therefore, the trigger clause on net current assets could allow them to drop to unity (current liabilities equivalent to current assets) but no more.

This will have the effect of restraining the company from investing too much in fixed assets and/or distributing too much to shareholders and if neither of these courses is followed and the net current assets still drop to unity it will show the bank that substantial losses will have been made and the time will certainly be right to take action. In practice, regular figures will be supplied and any deterioration will be observed over a period. Advice to the customer will undoubtedly be given by the bank well before the trigger point is reached.

The quality of the net current assets will also have to be considered as it will obviously be unsatisfactory to have the bulk of the current assets in stocks and work in progress with a corresponding increase in creditors. A look at past balance sheets shows stocks and work in progress at higher figures than debtors, but not greatly so. A stipulation could, therefore, be made that stocks and work in progress should be no more than 150 per cent of debtors. This should provide protection for the bank and at the same time not unduly restrict the company.

The company is embarking on a big change in its mode of operations and the bank will, therefore, wish to have full knowledge of its progress. It will not wish the company to decide on yet further changes without its knowledge and concurrence, and in order to guard itself against this the bank will want regular figures supplied, balance sheets submitted by certain times, and an undertaking from the company that it will not pledge its further assets or take on other borrowings without first obtaining the consent of the bank.

Obviously, each term lending proposition must be considered in the light of the company's own figures and projections, and the conditions imposed must be agreed by negotiation. They must be sufficient to protect the bank and at the same time leave sufficient room for the company to conduct its trading activities without undue burden.

The final agreement in this particular case will depend upon negotiations with the company but from the bank's point of view a satisfactory agreement would be:

1.   Overdraft limit of £1m subject to annual review and supported by an annual cash forecast and submission of actual figures on a quarterly basis.
2.   Audited accounts to be submitted promptly.
3.   Term loan of £3m repayable by £1m in year G and £500,000 per year in years H and J with final repayment in year I.
4.   Security to be deeds value £5m.
5.   Net current assets not to fall below unity.

6.   Stocks and work in progress not to exceed 150 per cent of debtors.
7.   Negative pledge re other assets of the company.
8.   No further borrowing without prior permission of the bank.

CASE 2

Keith Adams Foods Ltd has a bank overdraft limit of £45,000. The company has developed rapidly over the past few years. It has a factory in which foods are prepared for use in a retail chain of shops specialising in take-away meals. The account has been troublesome as the company has extended itself fully on its financial resources and at times it has been difficult to keep the company within its overdraft limit. As security for the overdraft the bank holds the deeds of its factory valued at £90,000.

Figures from the balance sheets of the company for the past three years are set out below, although the one for year C is in draft form only.

KEITH ADAMS FOODS LTD

Year	A	B	C	
Current liabilities				
Hire-purchase . .	6,400	14,400	18,000	Increasing
Creditors . . .	107,000	105,600	94,000	Reducing, but large
Bank overdraft . .	24,800	41,000	48,000	
	138,200	161,000	160,000	
10 per cent				
unsecured loan . .	20,000	29,000	27,300	
Capital	20,000	20,000	20,000	
Reserves . . .	(62,000)	(55,000)	(6,000)	
	(42,000)	(35,000)	14,000	Improving
	116,200	155,000	201,300	
Current assets				
Stock . . .	38,000	40,000	56,100	One month's supply
Debtors . . .	2,800	3,000	4,300	Small
Cash	1,400	1,000	6,800	
	42,200	44,000	67,200	
Fixed assets				
Freeholds . . .	22,200	22,200	12,200	Property sold in year C for £40,000
Plant	33,300	48,600	58,900	Increasing
Motors . . .	8,000	8,700	26,000	Increasing
	63,500	79,500	97,100	

Intangibles

Goodwill . . .	7,000	25,000	28,000	Annual increases
Premium on leases .	3,500	6,500	9,000	Annual increases
	10,500	31,500	37,000	
	116,200	155,000	201,300	
Turnover . . .	280,000	480,000	640,000	Rapid increases
Net profit before tax .	(16,400)	7,000	19,000	Considerably improving
Capital profit . .			30,000	Resale of property
Directors' fees . .	18,000	22,000	26,000	
Net current assets .	(96,000)	(117,000)	(92,800)	Heavy deficit
Net worth . . .	(52,500)	(66,500)	(23,000)	Rapid improvement

It will be seen that the hire-purchase liability has been increasing and presumably this is related to the increasing amount in plant or motors. The creditors have been reducing, whereas turnover has been increasing rapidly. There has either been some creditor pressure or the company has exercised more control in bringing down the amount of this liability. The amount of creditors indicates that about two months are outstanding and the amount greatly exceeds the relatively small figures for debtors. The low debtor figure reflects the cash retail element of the bulk of sales. An unsecured loan is outstanding and enquiry reveals that no repayment is due for a further 10 years.

The combined capital and reserves have made remarkable progress and a look at the profit figures at the foot of the tables shows that £7,000 was made in year B and as much as £19,000 in year C. The reserves also improved by a capital profit of £30,000 in year C on a sale of property.

About one month's supply is held in stock and the remaining property (which on enquiry is that held by the bank as security) is in the balance sheet in year C at only £12,200.

Goodwill and premiums on leases have increased each year showing the development of the company in acquiring new retail outlets on short leases. Care will have to be exercised to see that the goodwill is being written off over its economic life and that the leases are adequately depreciated annually. The net worth, which is the capital and reserves less the goodwill and premium on leases, has improved annually although it is still in deficit. However, if the additional value of the freeholds (£90,000 less £12,200 is £77,800) is taken into account the net worth will be a surplus of £54,800 (£77,800 less £23,000). From this will have to be deducted a sum for tax in year C. No tax was payable in years A and B because of the large loss in year A, but the accounts for year C are in draft form and the tax liability has yet to be calculated. Apart from possible tax on trading profit there will be tax to pay on the capital gain on the sale of property.

There is a large deficit on net current assets and the amount of the profit before tax is very small in relation to the turnover. The turnover, however, which exceeds £50,000 per month should have created a good swing in the banking account. Let us assume that the swing is £35,000.

We now have a picture of the company. It has a true net worth of £54,800 subject to a deduction for tax. It also has a number of leasehold outlets which might have some current value. Apart from borrowing £45,000 from the bank (£10,000 of which is solid borrowing) it has also borrowed £27,300 on long-term and £18,000 on hire-purchase. It has, therefore, considerable gearing. To be able to keep its borrowers content the company has had to make a profit by rapidly extending its turnover. This, allied to a deficit on net current assets must cause considerable difficulties over financial control.

Let us consider that the company now asks the bank to lend it a further £50,000 for new plant and equipment and to add to this the £10,000 solid section of the overdraft with repayment spread over eight years. As security a debenture is offered.

The bank already holds a charge over the deeds and the debenture will pick up a sizeable asset in stock but the plant and motors are likely to be sold for only a fraction of book value on a forced sale. The hire purchase liability will also have to be settled out of any proceeds. There is not, therefore, sufficient additional security for the extra borrowing requested.

Would it be possible to devise a suitable formula to trigger an on-demand clause if the company's trading results turned sour? Yes, but the turnover has to be kept at a very high level to generate profits and any slippage could result in the trigger clause being operated almost immediately. This is not suitable for term lending.

When lending is on a longer term than for overdrafts, there is more risk and only a sound company can qualify for consideration. In the present instance the company, although now successful, is still living dangerously and the risk is great.

What is needed is more equity stake.

CASE 3

Rogers Clark Ltd is an old-established engineering company under sound financial control and run by a board of directors known to be careful and shrewd though perhaps conservative in outlook.

Their latest balance sheet is typical of those produced for many years showing strength in assets with a good profit plough-back. It is as follows:

ROGERS CLARK LTD
Balance Sheet as at 30 September

	(£000s)	
Current liabilities		
Creditors	10,000	Only one-half of debtors
Current tax	6,000	
Bank	3,000	Unsecured (limit £5m)
	19,000	
Unsecured loan stock	3,000	Repayment due
Future tax	5,000	
	8,000	
Capital	20,000	
Reserves	40,000	
Profit and loss account.	26,000	
	86,000	Strong base
	113,000	
Current assets		
Stock	20,000	Reasonable in relation to turnover
Debtors	20,000	Reasonable in relation to turnover
Cash	1,000	
	41,000	
Fixed assets		
Freeholds	35,000	
Long leaseholds	4,000	
Plant and equipment	32,300	
Motor vehicles	700	
	72,000	Well covered by net worth
	113,000	

Turnover .	.	.	.	.	100,000
Profit before tax	.	.	.	.	15,000
Tax .	.	.	.	.	7,000
Profit after tax .	.	.	.		8,000
Dividends	.	.	.	.	5,000
Net current assets	.	.	.	.	22,000
Net worth .	.	.	.	.	86,000

This shows that the proprietors' funds cover all the fixed assets, and the current assets are double the current liabilities. Stock and debtors are not too high and creditors are only one-half of debtors. The unsecured bank account has a limit of £5m on it and with a turnover of £100m there must be a very good swing into credit at various times in the year. Repayment is due on the £3m of unsecured loan stock.

The directors have decided to build a new production line in specially built premises. The cost of the premises plus the plant and equipment will be £3m. Projections have been made showing that the building work will take 18 months with a further six months before full production is achieved. Thereafter, the plant should be running profitably. To cover the cost the board has decided to ask the bank for a term loan of £3m to be taken at £1m every six months, and it also wishes to borrow from the bank the £3m for repayment of the unsecured loan stock. Repayment is proposed of £1m per annum starting in the second year. Additionally, the company requires its £5m overdraft facility to continue.

The directors have also said that they consider the company to be strong enough to be able to have these facilities from the bank without the provision of security and they point out that they have not had to give security for any borrowing for the past 10 years.

Peak total requirements of the company are therefore £11m (£5m on overdraft and £6m on term loan). The term loan will be repaid at £1m per annum starting in the second year and will, therefore, cover seven years.

The company is very strong, has a good record, and is under sound financial control. With net current assets of £22m and a net worth of £86m the total requirements of £11m should cause no difficulty. In fact, if the company required to borrow £11m on overdraft, the net current assets and the swing on the account would well justify an unsecured facility.

However, a term loan is a different matter. Once it is granted it cannot be called in unless the terms on which it was granted have been breached.

Although the company is strong, unexpected events can occur over a period of seven years and the bank would not wish to stand idly by and see the company get into difficulties and be powerless to intervene to protect the loan.

Security is not offered and as the bank would not seek it in the face of the directors' opposition if an overdraft facility had been requested, all that is necessary is to insert some conditions which will have the effect of turning the term loan into an on-demand loan if a catastrophe should occur.

A drop in the net current assets could be a signal that perhaps all is not well but this could be rectified by long-term borrowing against fixed assets and a suitable trigger clause related to net current assets only would not be appropriate.

There will have to be very large losses if the loan is to be endangered and as the company has been making profits regularly it may well accept that the loan can be turned into an on-demand one if cumulative losses of £20m/£30m are incurred.

A negative pledge would hardly be acceptable to the company as the borrowing proposed is so small in relation to its size. However, it might be prepared to agree that it will not pledge certain of its freehold assets without the prior approval of the bank.

Similarly, a prohibition on further borrowing would hardly be acceptable to the company but it might accept that its total borrowings should not exceed twice the borrowing from the bank at its peak − ie, a total borrowing of £22m.

One of the above alternatives is all that would be necessary in the present instance; which one to incorporate in the documents would depend upon which is acceptable to the company.

14. The Effect of Inflation

So far, we have considered lending propositions in relation to historic cost accounts. Such accounts are prepared with the pretence that the value of money is constant whereas in inflationary periods this is patently not the case.

Banks appear to have managed fairly well in dealing with propositions with only historic cost accounts to guide them and it would be as well to examine therefore, what faults there are in such accounts.

Historic Cost Accounts (HCA)

First of all, let us think about the items in a profit and loss account. The figure for sales is the actual amount for which the goods or services were sold in the accounting period. During inflationary times, prices could well have risen over the accounting period and stock purchased at the beginning of the period could well have been sold for much higher prices than originally anticipated. This, therefore, means that part of the profit made was a trading profit but the remaining part was attributable to the rise in prices caused by inflation. The value of stock also affects the profit figure and if prices have been rising throughout the period it would be usual to find the monetary value of the stock in hand at the end of the period to be greater than the stock at the start of the period. This, of course, is on the supposition that the company keeps approximately the same volume of stock throughout the period. This extra monetary value has to be paid for and the company therefore needs additional profits merely to be able to finance the same volume of stock. However, as we have seen when considering the figure for sales, additional profits should be made in inflationary periods and there can, therefore, be some set-off against the increased cost of stock. After the gross profit has been struck, expenses and depreciation are deducted before the net profit is shown but depreciation is calculated with reference to the historical cost of the items depreciated. such items are generally depreciated over a period of several years. At the end of the depreciation period, when the asset stands in the books at nil, if calculations have been correct, the time for replacement is due. However, the replacement cost will, in times of inflation, be much greater than the original cost of the item which has been depreciated. In order to provide for this, a company should really make additional provisions in its accounts annually. A simple example of a profit and loss account showing the points to be considered is shown below.

XYZ COMPANY LIMITED
Profit & Loss Account

	£	£	Points to Consider
Sales		110,000	Were prices raised in line with inflation?
Stock in Hand		15,000	What volume of stock is involved?
		125,000	
Less Purchases	69,000		Were costs rising during the period?
Stock at start of period	18,000	87,000	Was this volume of stock normal for the business?
Gross profit		38,000	How much would have been made if inflationary gains were eliminated?
Less Expenses	27,000		
Depreciation	5,000	32,000	Will total amount of depreciation cover the replacement of assets?
Net profit		6,000	How much profit is attributable to
Taxation		3,000	trading and how much to inflation?
Net Profit after Tax		3,000	

It will be seen in this example that there is a net profit after tax of £3,000 and it may well be that, after getting the answers to the questions posed, it appears that the trading profit is really only £1,000 and the profit from inflation factors is £2,000. No extra provision has, however been made for the anticipated extra cost of replacement equipment.

Let us now consider the items in a balance sheet.

Freehold and leasehold properties are normally put in at cost less depreciation but there are so many different values that can be put upon properties. A property can be in a poorly sited locality and therefore be worth relatively little but its insurance value could be much greater as this would have to cover the cost of replacement of the building. A banker, when looking at property, generally looks at the forced sale value, whereas directors of companies often look at what the sale price will be on the basis of a willing buyer. There can, therefore, be a great deal of difference between the figures appearing in balance sheets and the values which various people will put upon properties.

As for plant and machinery and fixtures and fittings, we have already considered this to a certain extent when dealing with the profit and loss account. The cost of replacement of such items in inflationary periods is generally much greater than when previously purchased.

Stock, too, we have considered. In a balance sheet prepared on historical cost lines this is put in at the lower of cost or market value and there can well be some additional value in the amount of stock held if it is valued at the actual cost of purchasing similar stock at the end of the accounting period.

The amounts of debtors and cash are, of course, figures determined by fact but in inflationary periods such items are reducing in value and this particularly applies to debtors if they are not collected regularly. As for cash, if it is left unused it will, of course, depreciate but normally only enough cash needed for immediate purposes is held in a business.

Where creditors and bank loans are concerned, different considerations apply. Creditors will be reducing in value if left unpaid but this, of course, cannot be done to any great extent without some harm being caused to the company's credit. Any solid borrowing in a bank account or any long-term loan is of benefit to the company as repayment is eventually made in depreciated money. A simple example of a balance sheet and the points to be considered is shown below.

XYZ COMPANY LIMITED
Balance Sheet

	£	Points to Consider
Freeholds	100,000	Is this the current value?
Plant & Machinery	40,000	ditto
Fixtures & Fittings	5,000	ditto
Stock	15,000	What volume of stock is involved?
Debtors	15,000	
Cash	1,000	
	176,000	

Capital	60,000 ⎫	How will this be altered by
Reserves	30,000 ⎬	current values of assets?
Profit & Loss Account . .	7,000 ⎭	
Taxation	3,000	
Long-term Loan	50,000	Benefit to the company as it will be
		repaid in depreciated money
Bank overdraft.	8,000	Ditto − if any solid portion
Creditors	18,000	
	176,000	

If sufficient information could be obtained it would be possible to re-write the balance sheet with current values instead of the historical cost values. Let us suppose that the current value of replacing the freeholds is £130,000 and that suitable plant and machinery and fixtures and fittings could be purchased for £50,000 and £6,000 respectively. Also, let us suppose that the present stock of £15,000 could only be repurchased at current prices for £18,000. If we also take into account the net profit in the profit and loss account of £3,000, included £2,000 which was due to inflation and should be eliminated from trading results, we could redraw the balance sheet. It would then appear as follows:

XYZ COMPANY LIMITED
Comparative Balance Sheets with Current Values

	Historical Cost	Current Values	
	£	£	
Freeholds	100,000	130,000	
Plant & Machinery . .	40,000	50,000	Replacement value
Fixtures & Fittings . .	5,000	6,000	ditto
Stock	15,000	18,000	at current prices
Debtors	15,000	15,000	
Cash	1,000	1,000	
	176,000	220,000	
	£	£	
Capital	60,000	60,000	
Reserves	30,000	30,000	
Profit & Loss Account . .	7,000	5,000	Inflationary amount of £2,000 deducted

Taxation	.	.	.	.	3,000	3,000	
Long-term Loan.	.	.	.	50,000	50,000	
Bank Overdraft .	.	.	.	8,000	8,000	
Creditors	.	.	.	.	18,000	18,000	
Balancing Item .	.	.			46,000	Increased value of assets plus inflationary profit
					176,000	220,000	

It will be seen that there is a balancing item of £46,000 and this consists of the increased value of the assets by £44,000 and the £2,000 inflationary profit from the profit and loss account. The balance sheet under current values certainly appears much stronger than under historical cost values, but how will a banker view the difference? As far as the freeholds are concerned, the banker will still be concerned with the forced sale value and any other values would, to a large extent, be immaterial for his purpose. As for plant and machinery and fixtures and fittings, it might well be comforting to the company to know that they have the items undervalued in their balance sheet but, on a forced sale, which is really the only time when a banker is interested in such items, they will not fetch high prices. The point the banker is more likely to keep in mind is that, when these items have to be replaced, the cost is going to be much greater than anticipated and he will wish to see that sufficient provision has been made for such replacement. It is comforting also to know that there is a hidden reserve in the stock which, when sold, should produce extra profit. The balancing item of £46,000 is a large one in relation to the overall assets of the business but this is only a book entry and although it increases the intrinsic value of the proprietor's stake in the business it does nothing more than this.

Overall, a banker, while paying attention to balance sheet values, should see that sufficient profit is being made and retained to cover the extra burdens which inflation will impose on businesses. This, of course, is particularly valid in times of high inflation.

Current Cost Accounts (CCA)

The accounting profession has been trying for a very long time to bring into operation accounting systems which will reflect the effects of inflation on business enterprises.

Discussion has been generated by Exposure Drafts, Guidelines, and Accounting Standards but all, it seems, to no avail. The last Statement of Standard Accounting Practice on this subject (S.S.A.P. 16) which was effective from 1st January 1980 was withdrawn towards the end of 1985 when it was announced that only 15% of companies were complying with the standard. The Accounting Standards Committee announced that it had exhausted its powers of persuasion and said that it considered that it would be necessary to have legislation if the government wished companies to produce inflation adjusted accounts.

Thus, for only a brief period have inflation accounts been produced and the demand for such accounts has fallen as the rate of inflation has fallen. However should inflation rise rapidly again there will probably be renewed demand for such accounts. It would be as well, therefore, to look briefly at the stipulations set out in S.S.A.P.16 and to consider the principles involved. This will enable bankers to appreciate more fully the points which they have to take into account when examining profit and loss accounts and balance sheets.

It is not within the compass of this book to deal with details of accountancy practice and for the full understanding of current cost accounting a study should be made of the Statement of Standard Accounting Practice No. 16 (SSAP16) together with the guidance notes which were issued as a separate booklet. However, before we can decide upon the usefulness to bankers of the resultant figures produced by CCA we must understand the concepts which were used. CCA was not a complete method of accounting for inflation; accounts had still to be prepared using units of currency which depreciate in value during inflationary times. However, the object of CCA as stated in SSAP16 was to provide more useful information than historic cost accounts (HCA) on the following matters:

i   The financial viability of the business
ii   Return on investment
iii   Pricing policy, cost control and distribution decisions
iv   Gearing.

This was achieved through adjustments to both the trading figures and balance sheets.

Adjustment to Trading Figures

In the trading figures adjustments were made to arrive at a current cost accounting profit and there were four adjustments.

1. *Depreciation Adjustment*

The charge of depreciation in HCA is for the part of the fixed assets consumed in the period but in CCA the replacement cost was taken into account and depreciation was calculated on the replacement cost with the object of retaining in the business sufficient to cover the cost of replacement at the time the asset required renewal. As replacement costs in times of inflation are much greater than original costs, a much larger charge was made against profits which were thereby reduced. Apart from making the annual charge and relating it to replacement cost, it was also necessary to make an additional charge (back-log depreciation) to bring up to date the depreciation charged in the accounts for previous years.

2. *Cost of Sales Adjustment* (COSA)

This allowed for the impact of price changes when determining the charge against revenue for the stock consumed. In effect, it segregated the profits made from rises in prices due to inflation.

3. *Monetary Working Capital Adjustment* (MWCA)

As COSA dealt with one aspect of working capital, i.e. stock, so MWCA dealt with the remainder, i.e. debtors, creditors and cash or overdraft if significant. This adjustment represented the additional (or reduced) finance required for monetary working capital as a result of changes in the prices of goods and services financed by the business. COSA and MWCA complemented each other and together they allowed for the impact of price changes on the total amount of working capital. In times of rising prices additional finance is necessary.

Use of indices was suggested for calculating the adjustments for COSA and MWCA.

4. *Gearing Adjustment*

It will be appreciated that the three adjustments already mentioned would normally cause reductions to profit figures calculated on HCA lines. However, the net operating assets (i.e. fixed assets plus working capital) are generally financed by a combination of shareholders' funds plus borrowing. Repayment rights on borrowings are normally fixed in monetary amounts; it was not therefore necessary when borrowing was involved to reduce the HCA profit by the full adjustments for depreciation, COSA and MWCA. A proportion of the adjustments only were necessary, i.e. that proportion applicable to shareholders' funds. This was the gearing adjustment. It was achieved in the accounts by a deduction calculated on the total of the other three adjustments and related to the proportion applicable to the borrowed moneys. Borrowed money, when repaid is repaid in depreciated currency and there is therefore a benefit to the borrower. This can easily be seen if, instead of deducting the gearing adjustment from the other three adjustments, the interest on the borrowed funds is deducted from the gearing adjustment. The following example should make this clear.

		£(000's)
Profit before interest		2,000
as in (HC accounts)		
Less current cost adjustments:		
Additional depreciation	350	
Cost of sales	480	
Monetary working capital	170	1,000
Current cost operating profit		1,000
Gearing adjustment	380	
Less interest payable	150	230
Current cost profit		1,230

A company's profit is subject to taxation and this is calculated according to the terms of Finance Acts. The resulting profit after taxation is available for distribution to shareholders and/or retained in the business. Directors should therefore not be misled into thinking that they can distribute the whole of the historical cost profit less interest and taxation. This adjustment was to assist in maintaining in the company the value of the shareholders proportion of the assets of the company.

Adjustments to Balance Sheets

In balance sheets the objectives of CCA were met by including the assets at their value to the business at current price levels. The value of assets to the business is generally the net current replacement costs unless a permanent diminution to below net current replacement cost has been recognised. The current cost balance sheet included a reserve in addition to those seen in HCA and was known as 'the current cost reserve'. To it were transferred the revaluation surpluses on fixed assets, stock and investments, and the amounts for the adjustments made to the trading figures for depreciation, COSA, MWCA and the gearing adjustment.

Additionally, earnings per share calculated on a CCA basis were also stated for information and companies had to give adequate explanations in the notes to the accounts to enable readers to understand how CCA had been implemented.

Positive Aspects and Failings of CCA

The favourable aspects to managements and readers of accounts were:

1. There would have been a better appreciation of:
    i   the amount of the actual profit of the business;
    ii   the amount of funds required to be retained in a business to replace depreciating assets;
    iii the amount which was required to maintain the value of shareholders' funds;
    iv   the net worth of the company;
    v   the amount which could be distributed as dividend.

2. Ratios would have been more realistic and this would have applied to such ratios as:
    i   profit to net assets employed;
    ii   return on capital employed;
    iii gearing;
    iv   asset cover;
    v   dividend cover.

3. A fairer picture would have been provided for outside observers.

The failings of CCA which must be recognised were:

1. It was not a complete system for accounting for inflation.
2. Several years of debate had been necessary before the present standard for CCA had been produced. It was therefore a compromise.
3. Companies vary. There are different lengths of production cycle, different levels of amount of stock and work in progress and CCA did not suit all companies.

4. It was difficult to implement for management accounts which have to be related to management requirements and the organisation of the company. Divisions, departments or sections would not be able to encompass easily the MWCA and gearing adjustments. Management accounts indicate performance against targets and are not so concerned with how the business is financed.

5. Not all companies replace assets when fully depreciated. Some concentrate on renovation and repair and cannot afford to buy new expensive equipment when the market for their products is falling. The depreciation adjustment would, in these cases, be over-cautious.

6. The price of replacement equipment is not easily determined as the introduction of the micro-chip and other technological inventions make for rapid changes in improved equipment.

7. The indices used might not have been fully appropriate to the circumstances.

8. A degree of subjectivity was introduced, particularly with MWCA.

Usefulness to Bankers

All additional information provided with CCA accounts would have been a help to lending bankers and would have enabled them to have a better appreciation of the businesses they are examining. Naturally, the notes to accounts would have had to be read thoroughly. The favourable aspects mentioned above would have been appreciated and, in particular, the more realistic view of profits. It would also have had to be kept in mind that:

1. The net worth of the business may have been increased by the current cost reserve but this would have been only a book entry as far as the revaluation of the assets was concerned. The on-going nature of the business would not have been changed by revaluing the assets. A banker would still have wished to look at the forced sale values if he required to rely upon security.

2. Liquidity would not have been improved if the additional funds retained had been sunk into more fixed assets. This would have been particularly apparent when machinery was old and well depreciated and replacement was due.

3. If the gearing adjustment had not been sufficient to cover the interest cost of the borrowed money, perhaps the borrowed money had not been used to proper advantage.

4.   It would have been a help that companies would have been better placed to appreciate the amount of the necessary funds that would have had to be ploughed back to maintain the business entity and to support increasing turnover and capital expenditure.

In essence, a banker would have continued to employ the usual tools of his trade in assessing propositions but the additional information provided by CCA would have undoubtedly assisted him in his appreciation.

15. Other Sources of Finance

Bank managers naturally try to help their customers with the finance they require, but it is not always possible for banks to provide all the resources needed. During times for credit squeeze banks cannot give as much assistance as perhaps they might be able to provide at other times, and often customers' requirements are for longer terms than banks wish to supply. For the most part, clearing banks' lending resources come from their customers' deposits, all repayable on demand or at short notice, and a bank must necessarily keep the bulk of its lending short also. Borrowing short and lending long is a quick way to financial failure.

Although much bank lending is for trading purposes and provides the liquid resources for trade and commerce, there is also a considerable amount of money lent for capital expenditure. This is acceptable to bankers when profits ploughed back into the businesses will provide reductions and repayment over a short number of years. Naturally there will be other instances where the requirements for capital expenditure cannot be serviced over a few years, and longer-term borrowing is necessary if proprietors' capital is not available. The banks are suppliers of funds in certain circumstances over the longer term but, naturally are not willing to go down the longer term route as normal policy for the lending of a large proportion of its funds. Customers often have to look elsewhere for such finance.

The provision of alternative sources of finance for quoted public companies is not too difficult. The Stock Exchange provides an excellent market, and successful companies can raise capital or loans. If the time is not right from the company's point of view to approach the market, it is still possible to find funds even outside the clearing bank system, as such funds can be provided on a short-term basis in the knowledge that an approach can be made to the market later. The unlisted securities market also provides a means of raising finance for those companies quoted in this market.

However, for the other unlisted and private companies the situation is much more difficult. There are many organisations, companies and associations which provide finance and a very long list can be made.

The provision of venture capital has been a growth industry for some years now with many companies being formed to provide funds. In December 1986 a report was published by Peat Marwick, the accountants in conjunction with the U.K. Venture Capital Journal showing at least 147 institutions offering venture capital in the U.K. The type of finance offered varied considerably, some organisations offering 3 to 5 years finance, others up to 7 years, others up to 10 years and others being flexibile or offering medium and long term finance. Funds are provided as loans or equity and sometimes a seat on the board is required.

Even so, one of the most difficult tasks for bank managers is to try and help a good customer to find financial resources on acceptable terms.

The plain fact is that a joint stock bank in the United Kingdom can provide short-term funds with the minimum of formality and at a comparatively cheap rate, and it is only when funds are sought outside the clearing bank system that this fact becomes very apparent. There is more risk in tying up funds for a long period and, without a capital market to dispose of such an investment, the number of people willing to supply such funds will naturally be limited. During times of inflation it is a brave person who is prepared to lend for a long period. The interest rate must be high, as the capital lent continually dwindles in value.

Sometimes medium- and long-term finance is offered only if participation in the share capital of the enterprise is permitted. This too provides an obstacle to many entrepreneurs. When a man has worked hard and built up a successful business, he is often very reluctant to sell a share in the equity. He can perhaps see that the efforts he has put in will from then on bring him a justified reward if only the bank will put up the funds he requires. He feels frustrated if his bank will not provide the funds. Goodwill may be damaged if the bank introduces a possible long-term lender who also wishes to obtain a share in the equity capital of the company.

The fact that the provision of larger sums may enable a company to progress much faster is generally not considered sufficient compensation by many people. Bank managers often come across the situation where a businessman prefers to keep his independence regardless of the financial difficulties he encounters through lack of finance. This is, therefore, a somewhat gloomy picture. This lack of a market for medium- and long-term funds for the smaller companies was pointed out by the Radcliffe Committee years ago. Several attempts have been made since to rectify this state of affairs, but the provision of such funds can, at times, still be difficult and a major obstacle in the development of many businesses.

The Clearing Banks have responded in several ways in providing medium-term loans and, on occasions, longer term funds and help with venture capital. These services are in addition to those provided by the subsidiaries in hire purchase, factoring and leasing. Naturally, a bank manager will approach the appropriate subsidiary when faced with suitable propositions which may justify assistance within his own bank's organisations.

However, not all enquiries will fit the criteria expected within the Clearing Bank subsidiaries and other lines of enquiry may have to be pursued. I am therefore giving some brief information on other sources which may be explored.

Hire-purchase Companies

The large clearing banks all have subsidiary or associated companies dealing in hire-purchase business, and it is often possible for finance to be made available from a hire-purchase company for customers of the banks. Primarily the hire-purchase companies are interested in dealing with hire-purchase finance or finance for credit-sales or invoice discounting, and use of these facilities can often provide much needed funds for a customer. Working capital need not therefore be tied up in providing financial help to customers when this type of finance can be off-loaded on to a hire-purchase company. Additionally, when a good continuous supply of business is put in the way of hire-purchase companies, they are prepared to provide some fixed loans for, perhaps, showroom extensions or additional buildings. Such loans are often provided at very favourable rates. Also when a customer has to provide stock to show in order to make sales, the hire-purchase companies can provide stocking loans to cover the capital outlay.

Factoring Companies

The business of these companies is to take over the accountancy side of sales ledgers. They send out statements of amounts owing, collect the funds and pass them over to their clients, and among the services they offer are advances against the debtors being collected. Naturally, as they are dealing with the sales ledger and have made their enquiries about the debtors, they are well able to tell whether such debtors are good and, consequently, are in an excellent position to judge that any loan made in anticipation of receipt of debtors will be good. They are therefore able to lend a far greater proportion of debtors than a banker. Much needed working capital can be turned more quickly from debtors into cash by using a factoring company, or sampling of the market by a controlling body. The market is volatile and of course the rates vary from currency to currency. It is generally preferable to borrow the same currency as will be generated to provide repayment; otherwise an exchange risk will also have to be borne.

Insurance Companies

These companies have large continuous incomes accruing to them and therefore always have in hand funds to be invested. Most is invested in large sums but funds are often made available in smaller amounts on long-term mortgages. It is generally a question of searching around to find out which insurance company has funds available for such purposes at any particular time. The insurance companies will really only be interested in those cases where the insurance business which can be placed with them is substantial.

Pension Funds

Numerous companies now run their own pension funds and, although many of them are restricted as to the investments they may purchase, there are some pension funds whose trustees have very wide powers. Government securities have proved very poor investments for trustee funds in the past and many pension funds now have the authority to make wider investments. Loans on long-term mortgages are sometimes made available and some pension funds have even taken equity stakes in unquoted companies.

Merchant Banks

The largest merchant banks are also members of the Accepting Houses Committee and naturally a large proportion of their business is acceptance business. This provides the means of financing a large volume of international trade. However, merchant banks are also interested in all methods of financing trade both overseas and at home. They will grant overdraft and loan facilities in the same way as the joint stock banks, but they are not competitive where small accounts are concerned because they do not have the wide branch coverage. The branch coverage of the joint stock banks also enables them to gather in deposits, an advantage which the merchant banks lack.

The merchant banks therefore concentrate on the large companies and specialist financing. Most of the facilities they provide are also provided by joint stock banks, and the branch manager will not have need to get in touch with a merchant banker for facilities which he himself will be able to provide. The joint stock banks, however, are not specifically interested in providing long-term finance and this is where the merchant banker may help. Merchant bankers are quite willing to consider lending substantial sums on a medium or long term but, as they do not readily have the deposits available, they will probably have to arrange for such financing to be taken by borrowing in the money market. Longer-term financing is not attractive and the merchant banker will therefore be looking for some benefit in the way of profit sharing or equity participation. Some inducement must generally be offered when long-term finance is sought, but the comfort of having a merchant bank interested in a company and providing finance for it more than outweighs the disadvantage of giving up part of the profits of an enterprise. A merchant bank is really interested in providing facilities for enterprising and fast growing small companies which, after a few years, can be brought to the London stock market and have its shares issued.

There are numerous small merchant banks, finance houses and financial trusts, all of which will, under certain circumstances, help with finance. If equity stakes are not required, a much higher interest rate is expected.

Investors in Industry

This group is carrying on the functions of the financial institutions (Industrial and Commercial Finance Corporation (I.C.F.C.) and Finance Corporation for Industry (F.C.I.)) which were formed under the lead of the Bank of England to try and provide facilities for small and medium sized companies. The capital of I.C.F.C. was originally provided by the Bank of England and the Clearing Banks and that for F.C.I. by the Bank of England, insurance companies and investment trusts. Investors in Industry now provides a range of services and makes loans in both large and small amounts and is the leader is providing venture capital.

Agricultural Credit Corporation (ACC)

Farmers looking for increased bank overdrafts are sometimes faced with the fact that no more can be provided for them without additional security. The ACC is prepared in acceptable cases to guarantee the bank overdrafts of farmers, and it normally guarantees the whole of the bank overdraft and gets the farmer's agreement that the securities held by the bank are thereafter held for the benefit of ACC should it have to pay up under its guarantee.

Lands Improvement Company (LIC)

This is a very useful company, although comparatively little used. It provides long-term loans for capital improvements to farms. The improvements must be approved by the Ministry of Agriculture, and the repayment of the loans can be spread over a period of up to 40 years. The land on which the improvement is made can in fact be mortgaged elsewhere, as the title deeds are not required by LIC. The rate of interest on the loan remains the same throughout the whole term and the capital cannot be called in.

Leasing Companies

Of recent years, the leasing business had been a fast growing one and it had developed mainly because of the tax allowance on capital investment. When a company made a capital purchase of, say, a machine, it was entitled to write off a large amount of the capial cost against its taxable profits. If the company was making little in the way of profits or was not liable for UK taxation, then the advantage of this tax allowance was lost. The company, therefore, benefited by keeping its capital intact and leasing the machine. All the expenses of leasing were written off in its accounts. Another company with tax liabilities welcomed the chance of purchasing the machine and gaining the full benefit of the tax allowance and at the same time getting the income from leasing the machine to the company which used it. Between the two companies, there was obviously a useful advantage and this was split to give a favourable leasing contract to the user of the machine.

This capital tax allowance has now been phased out and leasing, in consequence, is not so popular. There are occasions, however, when it will suit a company to lease equipment rather than buy it.

Venture Capital Companies

As already mentioned there are many companies which have been set up

Estate Duties Investment Trust Limited (EDIT)

This company is run by Investors in Industry and its object is to help companies where difficulties have arisen or may arise through the death of one large shareholder. The company is prepared to buy shareholdings in private companies or in small public companies where the market is restricted, and this often allows such companies to continue in existence in the same form and not be swallowed up by larger companies. In some instances where a controlling shareholder has a very large interest, the company could even cease to exist because of capital transfer tax problems. EDIT is able to step in such circumstances and purchase shares to release money to pay the capital transfer tax.

Technical Development Capital Limited (TDC)

This company is also administered by Investors in Industry. The funds were originally provided by a number of insurance companies, merchant banks and financial institutions, and the object of the company is to help to develop worthwhile innovations. TDC does not wish to lock its capital up indefinitely, as the object is to bring worthwhile projects to the market. Therefore TDC will sometimes wish to realise its investment at an appropriate stage in order to use the finance to support other inventions.

Agricultural Mortgage Corporation (AMC)

In my opinion, this is one of the most successful of the producers of long-term finance. Although a bank manager, when looking for long-term finance for an industrial customer, might try several sources without success, he will feel on much firmer ground when dealing with the long-term financial requirements of farm customers. The AMC generally provides the funds for farmers if they can show a modicum of success and have the security of the freehold agricultural land to mortgage. Loans can be taken for periods not exceeding 60 years but normally they are not granted for periods longer than 40 years. The capital of the AMC was subscribed by the Bank of England and other banks but most of its funds have been derived from public issues from time to time. If only there was a source of funds for industrial companies comparable to the AMC for farmers, industrialists would have little cause to grumble about not being able to raise long-term funds to further the interests of their companies.

to provide venture capital but the enthusiasm of venture capitalists depends very much upon the encouragement of the government in promoting schemes giving incentives, generally by tax advantages, to the risk-taking companies.

Financial Companies

There are a number of financial companies which will also provide long-term loans and take equity stakes. However, a large amount of money is necessary to provide a continuity of business and in consequence the number of companies which can be financed by any one corporation is relatively small. One of the most active finance companies providing this type of finance is Charterhouse Development Ltd.

There is also Commonwealth Development Finance Co. Ltd., which is financed in the main by Commonwealth banks. This company specialises in providing finance where there is a strong overseas involvement.

Regional Agencies

Some specialised agencies have been formed to help industrial companies and service industries in particular geographical areas. The most important of these are the Highlands and Islands Development Board, the Scottish Development Agency and the Welsh Development Agency.

Council for Small Industries in Rural Areas (CoSIRA)

This is a government financed organisation which provides loans for the smaller industries (say, employing up to about 20 people) in rural communities.

Equity Capital for Industry Ltd.

This company was set up after pressure from a Labour government following the views of itself and the TUC that the City had failed to find much needed finance for manufacturing industry. The backers are mainly insurance companies, and finance is available for medium- and long-term investments. There has not been a great demand for the company's services as it was subsequently confirmed that there was, at the time of setting up the company, adequate finance available for industry, which had not availed itself of the finance as it had little confidence in future prospects.

National Enterprise Board

This is a public corporation financed by the government. It has had very large funds available to it and has supported large companies which were in financial difficulties and has also provided funds for developing companies and to help with mergers and amalgamations. Its influence under the Conservative administration in the 1980s has diminished.

Sale and Lease-back

A company which owns its freehold property or has a long leasehold can raise money on it by mortgaging the property or by selling it at market price. A mortgage can only be obtained for a proportion of the market price but a sale of the property means that there will be a new owner. However, a company which wishes to raise as much money as it can against its property can in fact raise more money than the market price by an arrangement called sale and lease-back. The sale is arranged concurrently with a lease so that the existing owners continue in occupation. The rental charged is based on the sale price, and it is therefore possible to raise more than the market price on the sale of the property provided that the occupants are prepared to pay a relatively high rental subsequently. Sale and leaseback arrangements are generally made with insurance companies, but some financial trusts, property investment companies and pension funds are prepared to tie up money in this way.

Solicitors

In the past solicitors quite often had clients' funds at their disposal. These funds were left with them for investment, and the solicitors in certain circumstances were prepared to recommend to their clients the investment of these funds in property mortgages. However, with the general spread of financial knowledge, there is not now such a demand for solicitors to look after clients' funds. Nonetheless, in many towns there will still be found solicitors who have funds available or who have small investment companies which provide mortgage facilities. Knowledge about these companies will only be available in the localities in which they operate.

The Government

In the 1980s the government has been anxious to promote small and medium-sized businesses and there are schemes operated through the banks which help entrepreneurs who have little capital. It enables them to have the opportunity of making more rapid progress than would otherwise be the case. Obviously, there are advantages to the entrepreneurs in these schemes but, unfortunately, such schemes suffer from the drawback that more unjustifiable risks are taken when one's own money is not at stake.

There are many government schemes for giving financial assistance, both by grants and by loans, for development industry in specific areas of the country where unemployment problems exist. Naturally these alter from time to time but up to date information can be obtained from the Regional Development Boards or from the appropriate ministries, or from the National Enterprise Board.

European Investment Bank (EIB)

This is an institution set up by the European Economic Community and its object is to further the balanced development of the Community by making or guaranteeing long-term loans. It is therefore of interest to companies operating in the less prosperous regions of the country. Normally loans are made for periods of between seven and 20 years for amounts of £½m to £15m, and security is required unless the liability can be covered by a guarantee from a member country. To help with smaller transactions the EIB is empowered to make lump sums available to credit institutions to be disbursed by them. In the United Kingdom, for example, a loan has been granted to ICFC, to whom application for the smaller sums can be made.

Notes. Only very brief notes on the various lending sources have been given and in practice it will be necessary to check with the particular source concerned to find out its present policy.

16. Conclusion

Review

In the preceding chapters, I have covered the main types of lending problems encountered by clearing bankers. There are, of course, numerous variations and, although it would be possible to cite many more examples, I think little would be gained by doing so. It is better now that we take stock and review the methods, the proportions, and the margins which I have mentioned. It is appropriate to do so in the light of changing economic circumstances. In recent years, British banks have gone through a difficult period. In the early 1970s there was a period of very free lending followed by tight monetary conditions, and the sudden change inevitably threw up some unsatisfactory situations. Inflation has since been high and subsequently dropped and industry has in some sectors been struggling to lift itself from somewhat depressed conditions.

Warning of the change from free lending came in 1973 when the housing boom levelled out and was followed by a drop in house prices. The unsettled stock market and the dramatic fall in share prices left previously secured loans with uncovered positions. We then had the motor industry and garages facing problems as a result of the rise in oil prices and the difficulties of the second-hand car market. Industrial unrest and the firm control by the authorities over credit supply completed the picture, and clearing bankers found themselves very quickly faced with a situation not envisaged a few months earlier. Since then unsettled conditions in the oil markets have caused other problems. Economists have, of course, known of the cyclical booms and slumps which occur in business life, and bankers with a well documented history of banking to draw upon should, of course, be aware that booms do not go on for ever and that slumps gather strength very quickly.

It is appropriate then to see whether one's own lending methods have stood up in periods of both optimism and pessimism. I said in my first chapter that I had no quarrel with anyone who had a method of lending different from mine, providing he had a reason for employing such a method. For those young bankers who have the capacity for self-examination, I suggest they might like to review examples of their own lending in new ventures, estate development, produce, etc; and consider whether the methods they used were good or could be improved. It is, of course, not easy in a free lending period to keep to traditional methods because there will generally be freer lenders who are willing to take extra risks. In a time of boom, the risks can often be worthwhile, but the reverse is true once confidence ebbs. A lending banker who eagerly allows advances at one time, and then just as eagerly retrenches at another, will end up with few friends. To be able to get the best of all worlds is not possible, but a banker conscientious about his own business and conscientious about community life, will probably sway a little one way and then the other in the wind of economic change.

Margins on Property Advances

I will not deal with all the changes that have occurred in the various types of lending but, as an example, I will mention property finance. Before the boom of 1972-73, bankers normally looked to providing no more than two-thirds of the finance for erecting dwelling houses and not more than 50 per cent for the building of flats. I have dealt with the reasons for this in the chapter on estate development and will not repeat the reasons again. During the boom in property development many fringe financial houses and some clearing bankers were prepared on some occasions to lend 80 or 100 per cent on flat developments. Bankers who were exposed to this position were later very concerned by having little or no margin with which to protect their lending. A cushion of finance is essential when lending to property developers, as otherwise the bank can quickly become a property developer itself without the equity stake.

Confidence

A further trouble which came upon the financial scene was the uncertainty which descended upon fringe banks. Lack of confidence by depositors in one concern produced a parallel lack of confidence elsewhere, and very quickly a drain on the resources of fringe banks was evident. Confidence is a very frail quality which can fade rapidly. A good reputation takes a long while to build but not to lose. A bank is not in business for a short period of years but intends to go on for generation after generation. Sound financing, a wide spread of lending, and adequate reserves to enable it to keep going must not be lightly thrown away. Regardless of opportunities lost, is is far more important for a bank to see that its depositors have no fears about the safety of their funds. Nevertheless, a bank cannot afford to stand still and keep looking to the past for its inspiration. It must adapt and go forward but must be wary about departing from proven methods.

Unsecured Lending

I have dealt with unsecured lending in relation of businesses, but not in relation to private individuals. There is no rule of thumb to be adopted in such circumstances, such as lending one, two or three months' salary, and each proposition must be dealt with on its merits. The points to be considered are the assets and liabilities of the customer, together with income and expenditure and evidence of ability to save. For example, if a man aged 55 has no assets and his financial liabilities consist of supporting a wife and three children, he will have shown no ability to save, and repayment of a loan will obviously be difficult for him. It does not matter, therefore, whether his income is £100 per week or £500; unsecured lending would be unsafe.

As another example, let us consider a man aged 35 with two children who has been able to meet instalments of a building society mortgage regularly and has an equity of £6,000 in his house. If he approaches his banker and says he wishes to buy a car costing £3,000 and he has saved £1,000 towards it, the banker should feel reasonably safe in lending £2,000 unsecured. In the present instance, the customer has been able to prove that his income is sufficient for his normal expenditure and he has been able to save. He is therefore worthy of support.

This type of lending is therefore merely a question of thought and of trying to put oneself in the shoes of the customer. The banker should try and see how the customer will be able to manage to keep to his present standard of living and also service the borrowing. If the banker is in any doubt, he should have no qualms about refusing the loan. He will be doing the customer no service by lending and subsequently causing hardship in trying to get repayment.

An Enquiring Mind

This brings me to the point that I have mentioned before — that all bankers must have enquiring minds. However, there are very few people who will admit to not having enquiring minds and we should perhaps examine this aspect a little further.

An enquiring mind is not always a natural attribute, and generally willpower and extra effort are necessary to acquire it. A lending banker must probe deeply for the right answers and examine in detail propositions which are put to him. He should search, and search again, for the right answers and not easily be put off by inconclusive replies. A slightly cynical and disbelieving attitude is not a bad start when a banker looks at a new proposition, but at the same time he should be willing to be convinced of the viability of any scheme. There are some people who seem to have a natural instinct in summing up a proposition. In my opinion, however, this decision-making does not come through instinct but rather through experience. A lending banker can look at the records of a customer's account and tell what income he receives, and by examining the cheques can see how this is spent. A good knowledge of the customer can therefore be obtained before even meeting him. A bank manager with long experience will also quickly size up a customer by drawing on his experience of meeting hundreds of people. With the background knowledge of the branch records to help, his conscious or subconscious mind will quickly note when shaking hands whether the customer does manual work. The way in which he dresses, the manner of his speech, the look on his face all combine in helping the branch manager to assess the customer before he has even stated his business. The probing of the proposition can then begin but, of course, the branch manager must have a pleasant personality and a friendly manner or the probing will seem to the customer like an inquisition before he is finally put to death.

Knowledge of Accountancy

It might perhaps be thought to be commonsense to say a banker should have a knowledge of accountancy but, nevertheless, I think it worth while emphasising that a banker should keep up to date with modern accounting practice and understand how the Finance Acts affect taxation in company accounts. Also, of course, it is particularly important for bankers to differentiate between circulating and fixed assets. The circulating asset of stock, which is turned into debtors and then turned back into cash in order to buy new stock, can increase in amount as profits are made. If circulating assets decrease, then losses are being suffered or money is being withdrawn from the circulating assets for the purchase of capital equipment or for some other purpose.

It is necessary also to keep in mind that, if a proposition is put forward for the purchase of a fixed asset, this will have an effect on the circulating assets even if no money is provided from the circulating assets towards the cost of the capital equipment. This is because part of the circulating assets must be used to service the repayment terms of the advance. It is also important to realise that, however strong the finances of a company are, it is not always wise to try and satisfy its borrowing requirement by taking all of this on overdraft from a clearing bank. A clearing bank is interested in relatively quick repayment of advances and, if the amount borrowed cannot be repaid quickly without strain, it is far better to arrange for some of the advance to be taken by means of a longer-term loan. Proper financing of a business is important, and a package deal covering both long- and short-term borrowing is very often necessary for many businesses.

Control

A study of the initial proposition is perhaps more interesting than the subsequent control of the advance, but very often the control is the more important aspect. Unless adequate control is established from the outset, many advances will take on an aspect not envisaged when the initial proposition was considered. Bankers faced with situations such as this soon find that much time-consuming work could have been avoided by asking questions earlier. Naturally, some advances control themselves and cause no trouble, but marginal propositions inevitably take up more time and perhaps give more satisfaction to a banker who is able to nurse an ailing advance into better health.

Over the years, inflation has caused considerable increases in prices and has protected many inefficient businesses from trouble. Bankers too have benefited from the large increases in property prices and have been able to rescue some less secure advances by realising security at enhanced prices. Lessons should be learnt from these situations in order to prepare for a possible era of static prices or government-induced deflation.

GENERAL INDEX

Acceptances . . . . 169 – 70
Accountancy, Knowledge of . . . . 237 – 38
Accounts, Appreciation of . . . . 2 – 3
Accounts for Tax Purposes . . . . 19 *et seq.*
    Balance Sheet Items 24
    Depreciation 23
    Profit and Loss Account Entries 23
    Purchases 22
    Repairs and Renewals 23
    Sales 21
    Stock 22
Accounts, Management . . . . 52 *et seq.*
Accounts, Solid and Swinging – see Solid and Swinging Accounts
Adjustment to Trading Figures – see Effect of Inflation
Agricultural Credit Corporation (ACC) 229
Agricultural Mortgage Corporation (AMC) . . . . . 230 – 31
Appreciation of Accounts . . . . 2 – 3

Balance Sheet, Lending against a . . . . 8 – 10
Balance Sheets, Adjustments to – see Effect of Inflation
Banker, Proprietor and . . . . 12 – 18
Bank Lending – General Considerations . . . . . . 1 *et seq.*
Bank's Stake, The . . . . 10 – 11
Bills of Exchange
    Advances against 168
    Discounting and Negotiating . . . . 166 – 67
    Exporting with Settlement by . . . . 167 – 68

Confidence . . . . 235 – 36
Comparisons of Accounts . . . . 5 – 7
Conclusion – Review of Bank Lending . . . . 234 *et seq.*
Control of Advance 238
Cost of Sales (COSA) 219
Council for Small Industries in Rural Areas (CoSIRA) 231
Current Cost Accounts (CCA) . . . . 217 – 18, 221 – 24

Debenture as Security 11
Depreciation 219
Detailed Considerations – see Importing and Exporting
Development, Estate – see Estate Development
Discounting Bills of Exchange . . . . 166 – 67
Documentary Credits . . . . 168 – 69

Effect of Inflation . . . . 213 *et seq.*
Adjustment to Balance Sheets . . . . 220 – 21
Adjustment to Trading Figures . . . . 218 – 20
   Cost of Sales 219
   Depreciation 219
   Gearing . . . . 219 – 20
   Monetary Working Capital 219
   Current Cost Accounts (CCA) . . . . 217 – 18
   Historic Cost Accounts (HCA) . . . . 213 – 17
   Positive Aspects and Failings of CCA . . . . . 221 – 24
   Usefulness to Bankers . . . . 224 – 25
Enquiring Mind – in Examining Lending Propositions 237
Equity Capital for Industry Ltd 231
Estate Development . . . . 105 *et seq.*
   Current Account Method . . . . 112 – 13
   Developments as Security . . . . 106 – 07
   Funds Diverted . . . . 120 – 23
   Large Scale Developments . . . . 108 – 09
   Loan Account Method 110
   Record Sheet 111
   Repayments . . . . 109 – 10
   Stages of Completion 107
   Summary 113
Estate Duties Investment Trust (EDIT) 230
European Investment Bank 233
Export Credits Guarantee Department . . . . 161 – 65
Exporting – see Importing and Exporting
Export Proposition . . . . 173 – 74

Factoring Companies . . . . 224 – 27
Farming . . . . 180 *et seq.*
   Amount to Lend . . . . 187 – 90
   Confidential Statement . . . . 182 – 84
   Comparison with Banking Account and Balance Sheet . . . 184 – 87
   Natural Cycle 181
   Other Methods of Assessment . . . . 190 – 91
   Stock . . . . 181 – 82
   Use of Gross Margins . . . . 191 – 92
   Financial Companies 231
   Finance Companies – see Hire Purchase and Finance Companies
   Finance for Farmers – see Farming
   Finance – see Other Sources of Finance
   Forward Exchange 171

Gearing . . . . 219 – 20
Government, Assistance from . . . . 232 – 33

Hire Purchase and Finance Companies . . . . 146 *et seq.*
   Bank Lending . . . . 150 – 51
   Bank's Viewpoint . . . . 153 – 54
   Discussing the Loan . . . . 158 – 59
   Manager's Decision . . . . 159 – 60
   Second Approach . . . . 154 – 56
   Security . . . . 149 – 50
Hire Purchase Companies – as Source of Finance 226
Historic Cost Accounts (HCA) . . . . 213 – 17

Importing and Exporting . . . . 161 *et seq.*
   Acceptances . . . . 169 – 70
   Advances against Bills of Exchange 168
   Detailed Consideration . . . . 175 – 77
   Discounting Bills of Exchange . . . . 166 – 67
   Documentary Credits . . . . 168 – 69
   Export Credits Guarantee Department . . . . . . 161 – 63
   Export Proposition . . . . 173 – 74
   Exporting with Settlement by Bills of Exchange . . . . 167 – 68
   Forward Exchange 171
   Indemnities and Guarantees . . . . 170 – 71
   Short-Term ECGD Finance . . . . 163 – 65
   Smaller Export Schemes 165
Indemnities and Guarantees . . . . 170 – 71
Inflation – see Effect of Inflation
Insurance Companies 227
Investors in Industry 228

Knowledge of Accountancy . . . . 237 – 38

Land Improvement Company (LIC) 229
Lease-Back, Sale and 232
Leasing Companies 229
Loans, Produce – see Produce Loans
Management Accounts . . . . 52 *et seq.*
Margins on Property Advances 235
Medium-Term Finance – see Medium-Term Lending
Lending
   Against a Balance Sheet . . . . 8 – 10
   Bank – General Considerations 1
   Medium-Term . . . . 194 *et seq.*
   Supervision of 43
   Unsecured 236

Medium-Term Lending . . . . 194 *et seq.*
    Assessment of Risk . . . . 198 – 99
    Control . . . . 199 – 212
    Types of Medium-Term Finance 196
    Acquisition of Another Company 197
    Extension to Factory 196
    New Plant and Machinery 196
    New Products 197
    Normal Trading 197
    Refinancing 196
    To Supplement Lack of Capital 196
Merchant Banks 227
Monetary Working Capital 219

National Enterprise Board 232
Net Profits . . . . 3 – 4
New Ventures . . . . 87 *et seq.*
    The Customer's Interest . . . . 101 – 12
    What kind of Bargain . . . . 102 – 13

Other Sources of Finance . . . . 224 *et seq.*
    Agricultural Credit Corporation (ACC) 229
    Agricultural Mortgage Corporation (AMC) . . . . 230 – 31
    Council for Small Industries in Rural Areas (CoSIRA) 231
    Equity Capital for Industry Ltd 231
    Estate Duties Investment Trust Ltd (EDIT) 230
    European Investment Bank 233
    Factoring Companies . . . . 224 – 7
    Financial Companies 231
    The Government . . . . 232 – 33
    Hire Purchase Companies 226
    Insurance Companies 227
    Investors in Industry 228
    Land Improvement Company (LIC) 229
    Leasing Companies 229
    Merchant Banks 227
    National Enterprise Board 232
    Pension Funds 227
    Regional Agencies 231
    Sale and Lease-back 232
    Solicitors 232
    Technical Development Capital Ltd (TDC) 230
    Venture Capital Companies 229
Overtrading . . . . 25 *et seq.*

Pension Funds 227
Produce Loans . . . . 128 *et seq.*
    Amount to Lend 131
    Documents . . . . 132 – 33
    Kinds of Loan . . . . 128 – 29
    Legal Aspects . . . . 131 – 32
    Security . . . . 129 – 30
Property Advances, Margins on 235
Proprietor and Banker . . . . 12 – 18

Regional Agencies 231

Sale and Lease-Back 232
Smaller Export Schemes 165
Solicitors – as Source of Finance 232
Solid and Swinging Accounts . . . . 35 *et seq.*
    An Alternative Approach . . . . 41 – 42
    Normal Trading Finance . . . . 35 – 36
    Remoulding a Proposition . . . . 38 – 40
    Solid Borrowing . . . . 36 – 37
    Term Lending . . . . 37 – 38
Sources of Finance – see Other Sources of Finance
Stake, The Bank's . . . . 10 – 11
Supervision of Lending . . . . 43 *et seq.*
    Analysing the Figures . . . . 50 – 51
    Current Assets and Liabilities . . . . 43 – 46
    Need for Enquiry . . . . 48 – 50
    Variations . . . . 46 – 47
Types of Medium-Term Finances – see Medium Term Lending

Tax – see Accounts for Tax Purposes
Technical Development Capital Ltd 230
Trading Figures, Adjustment to – see Effect of Inflation

Unsecured Lending 236

Venture Capital Companies 229

Working Capital, Monetary 219